Reel Love

A CELEBRITY, HIDDEN IDENTITY, SWEET
ROMCOM

SAVANNAH SCOTT

Connect with Savannah Scott

You can connect with Savannah at her website
www.SavannahScottBooks.com

You can also follow Savannah on Amazon.

For free books and first notice of new releases, sign up for
Savannah's Romcom Readers email at https://www.
subscribepage.com/savannahscottromcom/

For Jon
You were my friend first.
And then we fell in love.
And we keep falling–again and again,
but more softly these days.
And I believe my heart
would have found you any other way.
Because our hearts belong together.

～

To those who have wondered
if someone could ever love them
Truly, really love them just as they are
The answer is a resounding YES.

🤍

～

Who you are matters
more than anything else about you.
To someone you may be a symbol of the unattainable.
To another you are a means to an end.
But to those who matter most,
You are simply YOU
And they are recipients
of the best gift you can give them.
Yourself.

～

ONE

Alana

Fame is a lot of pressure ...
~ Nick Carter

"It's not ideal," my mother aptly assesses from her end of the phone call.

With her next breath, she tells her massage therapist, "A little to the left, Jobert. And deeper into the tissue. Ahhhhh. Ungh. Yessss." She draws out Jobert's name so it sounds like zshow-bear, only the *bear* part takes her a count of three. Always a flair for the dramatic—that's my mother—even off screen.

I stare out the window of my home, out through the copse of trees that keeps me happily secluded from the property to the east of me, past the rooftops of the house and cottage on my neighbor's estate, to the vast expanse of ocean in the distance. I should feel separated from my Hollywood life here—protected from any demands and intrusions. But one minute on the phone with my mother catapults me across the twenty-five miles separating my island home from the mainland. I may as well be sitting in a chair across a desk from a producer in a Burbank high rise right now.

My mother returns her attention to me, "Alana, sweetheart, you have a legacy to uphold here, not to mention the importance of your influence for generations of female actresses who will come after you. You simply cannot take this role. It's beneath you. It's a typecast. It's soooo Alana Graves twenty-seventeen. You've evolved since your *Are You Kidding?* days. You've made such headway, redefining yourself, claiming the relevance worthy of your namesake. This role would be a setback. An attractive nanny, flirting with the single dad she's hired to work for? Talk about cliché. I ... I highly advise ... ahhhhh. Yes, Jobert, that's the spot ... You are the best."

A groan takes the place of whatever my mother was about to say, followed by a long sigh. She seems to momentarily forget she's on a call with me, leaving me to briefly reminisce about my time as a television nanny on the hit show *Are You Kidding?* I do miss the camaraderie of being in a TV series. That cast became like a second family to me—one I never see anymore.

"Anyway, what was I saying?" My mother's voice somehow manages to convey both relaxed and uptight tones. "Oh, yes. I remember now. It's a no on the role, Alana darling. Just talk to Mitchell and explain your reasoning. I'll handle the fallout with Starshine Productions." Then she adds, "I don't know why you won't consider the script I had sent over last week."

"The one Daddy is producing?"

"Irrelevant. It's a good role. Aligned ... mmmm. Yes ... Aligned with your goals."

My goals. I don't think I could find my goals with a bloodhound and a private investigator working round-the-clock. It's not that I disagree with my mother. I probably shouldn't take this nanny part. I should pursue something more relevant, with more depth. I should make my mark, live up to my family's heritage in the film industry, pick up my proverbial machete and clear the way for generations of female actresses who will come after me.

Should, should, should.

My life is a castle built on the foundation of "shoulds." Each expectation settles like an ancient stone on that established bedrock, threatening to dim the appeal of my multi-million dollar views.

"Okay, well. Good talk," Mother declares. "Text me when you've broken the news of your decision to Mitchell. I'll plan lunch with Suzette at Starshine this week. She loves Petit Trois. I'll let her down gently over a niçoise salad and a filet."

Mother laughs lightly. Then she sends air kisses and hangs up before I can even get the word *Goodbye* out.

"Well, that went well, don't you think?" I say to nobody.

Then I collapse back into my leather sofa and grab my iPad, pulling up the *Play on Words* app on my phone. Escapism? Yes. At least I'm not lost in a bottle like so many A-list stars. I prefer to lose myself in a battle of the minds on an online Scrabble platform. Here, no one knows me. I'm simply SaturdayIslandGirl.

The reason for the Saturday in my handle is ridiculous—something from years ago, a time when I didn't carry the weight of the world on my shoulders—when I was Gwendolyn, not Alana Graves, world-famous movie and television celebrity, heir to the Graves Production empire. Back then, I was a girl like any other girl. At least, every Saturday I was.

I log on and wait for a challenge to appear on my game dashboard. I could start my own match, but I'm secretly hoping Wordivore is on here. He—or she—has become a fun competitor for me. I could play against the computer, or a random opponent, but half the fun of *Play on Words* is the social connection. Pathetic as it may sound, this is one of my favorite ways to hang out with other people—anonymously challenging one another to word games.

It's not that I'm completely friendless. I've got a few local people I trust here on the island. And there's my assistant, Brigitte, who lives in Hermosa Beach. If I'm on the set, she's on the set. When I'm here on the island, she and I chat or text daily.

But, when it comes to our personal lives, Brigitte knows everything about me, and I only know her friends by name, as if they are characters in a story. It's not like we can hang out together. Brigitte would take a bullet for me. And she's a straight shooter, often telling me what I don't want to hear and keeping me in line and on time but with a dose of humor and a resilience that's essential if you're going to survive in this business.

Brigitte's not an aspiring star. In her words, "You wouldn't catch me dead living your life." I pointed out she couldn't live my life if she were dead and she laughed that airy, carefree laugh of hers and said, "See. It couldn't happen." I admire her spunk. She's got mad organizational skills but isn't at all neurotic about it like the assistant before her was. That woman needed the vacation she'd never take, and probably a daily dose of Jobert.

Then, just because I was thinking of her, I shoot off a text to Brigitte.

> **Alana**: *Hey. Just want you to know I got the script.*
> **Brigitte**: *You're texting me at dinner time, which means your mom called.*
> **Alana**: *She did, but that's not why I'm texting.*
> **Brigitte**: *Sure it is. You need to be balanced out. Like the pool guy at my apartment.*
> **Alana**: *What are you talking about?*

I smile to myself. Half the time Brigitte only makes sense to herself. She's an excellent translator, though. So, eventually she'll clue me in as to what her eccentric and quirky thoughts mean.

> **Brigitte**: *The pool guy. He tests the water, as pool guys do. If there's too much acid, he has to add alkaline or alka seltzer or alcohol. Something like that ...*

There's a pause. Brigitte knows what the pool guy adds to the water. She's just having fun with me, trying to make me smile since I just dealt with my mother.

Brigitte: *I'm your alkaline. Your mom, beg my pardon, but you know I'm right, she's acid.*

No one—not one soul on this planet or in this solar system—even allows themselves to even *think* the thought that my mother is "acid." And yet, here goes Brigitte. She'd probably say it straight to Mother's face. She calls my mother by her first name, as if they grew up together, even though my mother is nearly old enough to be Brigitte's grandmother.

I can hear it now. Brigitte would affect a cheery, over-the-top voice. "Angelique, you are acid." Then she'd swat her hand in my mom's direction as if they were sharing some private joke.

And Mother would laugh and tell Brigitte she's adorable or sweet and such a gift to our family. It's my assistant's superpower. She can say the most offensive or overly direct thing to anyone, and they laugh and smile like she just buttered their toast. I've never seen anything like it, and I work in Hollywood, so I've seen just about everything there is to be seen.

Alana: *I won't bug you. Just wanted to check in.*
Brigitte: *Awww. You missed me. Well, I miss you too. Cheek kisses and all that other Hollywood mumbo jumbo. Now go eat that rabbit food of yours. Or is it actually a rabbit you're eating? If it is, don't. Eat the veggies. All the veggies. Throw a few in for me. I'll talk to you tomorrow. I've got a hot date.*
Alana: *You can't leave me with your last words being, hot date, and think I'm going to stop texting you.*
Brigitte: *Okay. Okay. It's a blind date. My friend, Sarah, set me up with her boyfriend's friend. He's supposed to be cute and employed, so winner winner chicken dinner, he rings both bells..*

I chuckle. This guy doesn't know what he's in for.

Alana: *Okay. I've got plans anyway. Have a great date.*
Brigitte: *If by plans you mean those word games ... you do
you boo.*
Alana: *I do mean the word games. They calm me.*
Brigitte: *Well, you deserve all the calm. Gotta run. I was
putting on a fake eyelash while I was texting you and it fell
onto my cheek and the glue stuck it there. I look like I'm
being attacked by a very wooly species of exotic caterpillar or
I've got a hairy mole like no other ... and that's not the look
I'm going for here.*

I laugh out loud and it echoes through the living room.

Alana: *Go have fun. Be safe.*
Brigitte: *Okaaaayy, Mom. You be safe too. Don't pop a
blood vessel trying to wrack your brain for those fourteen
letter words. I'll text you tomorrow. You can fill me in on
the script decision and I'll update you on your schedule. It
will be fun times.*
Alana: *(Peace sign fingers emoji)*
Brigitte: *(Kissy face emoji)*

I set my phone down on the coffee table, still smiling.

It's time to see if Wordivore is online. I started playing
matches against Wordivore about six months or so ago. One day,
he—or she—posted in the game chat, *You're going down this
round.* I chuckled and responded, *Not likely.* And the banter
continued as if we were old friends or siblings. Who knew how
much joy trash talking with a total stranger would bring me. Since
then, we've baited one another, and kept the game far more interesting than playing some random competitor.

It's odd that I know nothing about Wordivore—not their
gender, what they look like, where they live, what they do when
they aren't challenging me to an online game. The anonymity of
it all is so freeing. They don't know me either. I'm just another

6

player, an equal, a word-geek who escapes into online gaming when real life feels too weighty to face.

A minute passes with no challenge and I'm about to place a first move for Wordivore to find later and then enter the public arena to look for an opening to another match when my dashboard pings with a notification.

Wordivore has challenged you to a match. Do you accept the challenge?

I hit the "accept" button and a square playing board appears on my screen with my letters lined up at the bottom.

Today is my lucky day. Wordivore types before we even get started laying one word onto the board.

I don't believe in luck. I answer with a revelation more personal than I've ever shared here.

It's true. I don't believe in luck. I was raised to believe we control our own destinies. It's up to me to choose well, work harder than my male counterparts, befriend other women in the industry, but not to the point of trusting them. I'm to climb the ladder, focus on the end game, and eliminate distractions.

Luck has nothing to do with it.

Mother used to say, "You'll hear people talk about lucky breaks. There are no such things in this industry, regardless of the common myths everyone spouts whenever someone shoots up into the spotlight seemingly out of nowhere. There is only diligence and cunning. Being at the right place at the right time with the right people isn't luck. It's strategy."

Oh, what do you believe in, then? Wordivore asks.

Strategy. I answer, only partially cringing when my mother's voice is the one I hear in my mind when I type my response.

I do believe in strategy. It's the key to success. Hard work alone won't get a person where they need to go. Not without strategy. You can apply yourself for years to something. But without strategy, you could apply yourself to the wrong thing, or the right thing in the wrong way.

Ahhh. Well, strategy helps. But luck is a part of everything.

Luck or mystery. There's the part of life we control. And there's the rest which falls outside the scope of our personal influence.

Wow. Wordivore has never been this chatty. I almost wonder if someone hacked the account, but something inside me knows it's the same player.

Deep words for someone who hasn't laid a tile on the board yet, I taunt. *You must have a lot of Zs and Qs in that hand.*

Wordivore's response comes almost immediately: *All the better to spell tranquilizers or quartziest or benzoquinones.*

My barking laughter echoes off my tall beamed ceilings. How long has it been since I've laughed like this? Sure, I laugh at Brigitte's silliness, but not a laugh where I let loose and forget everything but this moment.

Maybe it is your lucky day, I concede. *But I'm not going down without a fight.*

I'd expect nothing less.

I lay down METEORS on the board. The number 10 pops up next to my name in the points tally. It's nothing grand, but it's a solid start, and I have a good draw to replace my tiles. I can build off any of those letters to possibly land a win today.

I wait for whatever Wordivore will place on the board. A text notification appears over the top of my screen. Mitchell, my agent. I swipe the banner out of view and refocus on my game. Mitchell can wait. My life outside this secluded house at the top of a hill on Marbella Island can wait. For now, I'm going to indulge myself in a little online banter with an opponent while I pretend to be just any other girl on a gaming app.

TWO

Stevens

There is nothing wrong with the love of beauty.
But beauty—unless she is wed to something
more meaningful—is always superficial.
~ Donna Tartt

"What is that?" Ben's face scrunches up and he points to the freshly-shaven skin over his own upper lip while staring above my mouth.

I look around the watersports shack as if I'm searching for whatever Ben's talking about when I know full well what it is.

"What is what?" I ask him.

"The piece of furry seaweed over your lip. It looks like a caterpillar gave birth on your face over the last week."

Kai and I laugh.

"Technically caterpillars don't give birth. The butterfly or moth is in full adult stage with wings when it lays and fertilizes eggs."

I can't help myself. I'm a scientist. I'm obliged to correct misrepresentations of nature.

Ben walks closer to me and pretends to study the incoming hair over my lip. It's been four days since I've shaved anything but my beard. Four days I spent assessing the waters north of Santa Barbara for a company that wants to expand development in that area. They are required to have clearance ensuring their expansion won't harm any marine life.

"Is it ugly?" I ask, referencing my burgeoning facial hair.

"It's not exactly ugly." Ben runs a thoughtful hand along his jawline.

"Pretty sure you can't achieve ugly," Kai chimes in. "Did you want to? Because if you were going for ugly, this ..." He gestures to his own upper lip and stares at mine. "... is a move in the right direction, for sure."

"Yeah. I'm just trying to fend off some of the more exuberant advances."

"Poor thing," Ben teases. "Can't keep the women at bay."

Kai adds. "This could backfire. You might end up with a woman who's got a thing for the 'stache. I can't pull one off so I never could try the change you're going for."

"He can't pull one off either," Ben says, pointing at me and confirming my hopes. "You look creepy. Untrustworthy. I wouldn't let you dog sit, let alone care for my child with the look you're sporting."

"All from facial hair?"

"It's a look. One I don't think you should entertain." Ben nods and glances at Kai for confirmation. "It's very, *you should see my collection of doll heads.* Or ... *I mastered every level in Zelda on my couch—alone.*"

I smile. "Great."

Ben looks confused.

As odd as it sounds, I am actually trying to tone down my attractiveness. I'm hoping the facial hair serves as a deterrent to the onslaught of flirty passengers I've had lately. I sound arrogant, even without saying it out loud. But I'm tired of women coming on to me based on my looks alone.

The mustache is an experiment. And, like any experiment, it may need modification over time. Handlebars? Ham hock sideburns? I could try a Dali where the ends are twisted and pointed skyward like symmetrically poised hairy chopsticks. That style wouldn't hold up underwater on my regular dives, though. We'll see. For now, Ben and Kai's responses are data in the column I was hoping for. But the real test will be the single females who accompany me on marine cruises today.

I pass by the mirror outside the dressing room. My eyes do a double take. Yeah. This mustache is horrific. It looks like a yeti lobster loaned me his claw to perch over my lip, only I dyed it black.

"Maybe add a beard," Ben suggests.

"Nah. I'm good. I think adding a beard may trigger a primal response in some women. That's the exact opposite effect of what I'm going for."

"A primal response, huh?" Ben laughs. "That's something I usually aimed for when I was single. Why avoid it?"

"You could always actually date," Kai suggests.

"Date one of the tourists who wants a fun fling with the local marine biologist without even knowing anything about me except that she likes what I look like?"

"It works for peacocks," Kai says.

Sometimes I wonder if he puts in the effort of Googling scientific facts just so he can converse with me on my terms. I wouldn't put it past him. Kai's the kind of guy who wants everyone around him to be safe and happy—and he enjoys playing a role in providing each of us what we need most.

"Male peacocks are irresponsible and hedonistic." I edify Kai with factual evidence. "Peacocks don't mate for life, and they leave the peahen to raise the young on her own while they traipse out to strut their colors in front of female after female. They're good problem solvers, but when it comes to romance, they've got nothing. That's not me."

"Not a peacock. Noted." Kai nods.

Ben barks out a laugh. "Man, the conversations we end up having with you, Stevens."

My ten o'clock group arrives—a flock of women scheduled to take one of my two-hour tours of the harbor. They're here on a girlfriends' four-day weekend, according to the woman who reached out to make the reservation. Along with massages and poolside lounging at the resort, they want to tour the waters surrounding Marbella.

This isn't the evening champagne cruise or the glass-bottom tour which are both more recreational. I hope they know what they're in for. I glance at the hands of each of the women. Manicures. Well, here goes nothing.

"Hi, ladies." I greet the whole group of eight women. "I'm Stevens. I'll be your guide for our marine exploration tour today. And this is Ben. He'll be my first mate. If each of you would sign a waiver and grab a life vest from the pile outside the back door, we'll get going."

Once the women have completed all the preliminary prep, we lead them to the dock at the harbor where I moor my two boats. One is my private sailboat—a blue water pocket cruiser, the *Sea Ya*. And the other is a decent-sized trawler for smaller outings of twenty passengers or fewer. When I have to take a larger group on an educational tour, I'm cleared to use one of the monohulls or motorized catamarans owned by the resort.

"How far out in the ocean will we be going?" one of the passengers asks me on our way down the dock toward *Catching Wishes*.

"We'll mostly be touring along the shoreline. We'll anchor in a few spots along the way. And we'll go a few miles out to drag a net when we're around the north side of the island. That's when we'll pull some sea life up onto the boat."

She stares up at me. Then she blurts, "You're not what I had expected when I pictured a marine biologist."

I wonder if she even listened to my cursory overview of the tour itinerary.

"Do you think of marine biologists often?" I ask her.

"I ... Well, not exactly, I guess. But when Sharon told us we were going on a marine biology cruise, I sort of pictured my high school biology teacher."

"And what was he like?"

"Old. Thinning gray hair. Thick glasses. His teeth were a little yellow. He had a lazy eye ..." She trails off.

I'm tempted to cross my eyes and buck out my top teeth, just for a second. But I don't.

"You're definitely nothing like him," she adds, as if her recounting didn't make her point abundantly clear. "I mean, you're ..." She flicks her hand in my direction and then actually fans her face.

"You okay over there?" I ask.

She titters. "Yeah. I'm fine." Then she blushes a little.

But her embarrassment unfortunately doesn't serve as a deterrent.

"You don't happen to be single?" She looks up hopefully into my eyes.

"I'm in a very committed relationship." I give her my stock answer.

Yes. It's true. My committed relationship is with my boats, my secret project, and my belief that one day I'll meet a woman who isn't intimidated by my use of multisyllabic words of Latin origin —preferably one who doesn't fan herself at the mere sight of me.

Mustache experiment: a total and utter fail.

I'd consider the Dali, but I don't think that would fly with the corporate people I have to interface with in order to support myself. Unfortunately, they determine too many aspects of my life. As Mom would say, *hashtag adulting, am I right?*

Ben's walking a good distance ahead of me, thankfully. If he overheard this conversation between me and my most recent admirer, he'd be making light of it for weeks to come. The guys at the watersports shack entertain themselves by poking fun at me and one another.

By the time the eight passengers and Ben are all aboard my trawler, I've already decided I'm shaving this mustache as soon as I'm home.

My phone pings. I hold my pointer finger up to Ben. He nods.

I pull my cell out of my pocket, tossing the last line into the boat from the cleat on the dock with my free hand.

A text from Mom.

Mom: *It's been three days since we've seen you up here and rumor has it you have a mustache. This I need to see.*

I smile. My mom is a character. She thinks she knows current slang, but misuses it half the time. She job shares as an art teacher at the island high school. Mom and Dad still live in the only house I've ever called home. Yes. I moved out when I went off to college nearly twelve years ago. When I came back, I got my own place, and it serves me. I have somewhere to sleep, shower and eat. My parents' house is still home to me though, even if I only visit once or twice a week.

Stevens: *Who told you I have a mustache?*
Mom: *Your sister.*
Stevens: *Taking a tour out. I'll call you later. But I haven't seen Mitzi in a week, so I'm curious how she'd know.*

Mom doesn't share how my baby sister knows about my facial hair. She heard it somewhere, I imagine. The volume of insignificant gossip around Marbella rivals a pandemonium of macaws in the morning. And my sister runs the most popular taco place on the south shores. She gets plenty of opportunity to hear the island chatter.

My mom and sister are always in cahoots. Mitzi's the middle child and only girl in our family. You'd think having a double X chromosome was an actual accomplishment. My parents act like

Mitzi performed some feat by coming out female. I guess the sperm who won the race during her inception might get an award. And since that half of Mitzi's genetic formulation was ambitious or cunning enough to outrace the other gametes ... Scientifically speaking, she does actually win. Go, Mitzi.

Ben waves me toward the boat, indicating I should board.

Mom: *Pics or it didn't happen.*

I'm not quite sure that's the way that phrase is meant to be used, but I grin, take a selfie, hit send, and hop onto *Catching Wishes*.

I'm pocketing my phone when Mom's last text flashes on the screen.

Mom: *Shave that. Pronto. I want grandbabies someday, and you're far too handsome to have that kind of cringe interfering with your rizz.*

I chuckle. It's relatively pathetic when a thirty-year-old man needs to consult Urban Dictionary just to converse with his fifty-something-year-old mother, but here we are.

Cringe explains itself.

Rizz? I have no clue.

I look at Ben. I might as well ask.

"What's the meaning of the word rizz?" I whisper in a confidential tone.

Ben laughs. "Rizz!"

He nearly shouts the word. All eight sets of eyes turn toward us.

And he doesn't stop there. "Rizz is what you have in spades, man. It's when women basically faint at the mere sight of you. Live it up dude. You're the king of rizz. Am I right, ladies?"

The women collectively giggle and stare at me like I'm a brand new Boston Whaler on the auction block.

And now we've got two hours on the ocean with my unofficial coronation as our send off.

Needless to say, a marine biology tour is not a fit for this group. They squeal and shriek when Ben and I drag the net to pull up various smaller sea creatures for them to interact with up close. The animals, mostly the size of my fist or smaller, are transferred temporarily into large paint buckets filled with ocean water and a rectangular glass aquarium in the center of the back end of my boat.

We've placed a sample of the ocean water on a slide under the microscope at the front of the boat so my passengers can view ocean dwelling microorganisms. I man that station while Ben passes the animals around for the women to admire.

They don't.

Most of them wince and cower as if the nudibranch (aka sea slug) is going to jump from the clear bowl Ben is holding and attack them. I turn my attention to the first woman to approach the microscope. I'm mere inches away, bent over with her as she peers through the scope at the slide where the microorganisms swirl and swim in their miniature universe.

She lifts her head, looks me in the eyes, then places her hand on my bicep and gives it an unmistakable squeeze.

Then she says, "Thank you. I think your eyes are far more captivating than anything else we've seen today."

I'm sure she means it as a compliment. I smile politely and shout toward the back of the boat, "Next!"

Six out of eight women use my proximity to attempt their own form of marine exploration—of me. The next female passenger blatantly rubs circles on my back while keeping her eye fully pressed to the ocular lens. I step away, causing her hand to drop to her side. One woman even gets so bold as to pretend the boat is rocking when we're nearly as steady as if we were docked in the harbor. She wobbles and tips, landing flush against me. Then she uses my cheek to brace her fake fall with her palm. Once she's touching me, she runs her hand along my jawline and hums. It's so bold a move I nearly blush.

Some men would eat this up. Six women all eager to see if they could have a chance with me? It's a man's dream—on paper. In real life, I grew a mustache to avoid this kind of interaction. A mustache that is failing me horribly in my mission to put distance between me and any unwarranted advances. Maybe I'll start wearing a dive suit on tours, flippers and all. Or I might curate one of those old copper dive helmets. I could go heavy on the Axe body spray. That did the trick in Junior High when I actually wanted to attract a girlfriend. No one in my grade went within five feet of me during my Axe phase. I feel like shouting, Eureka! Axe is actually woman repellant. I think I'm on to something.

Ben shoots me a concerned look from the back of the boat where he's supposed to be carefully passing around a vellela vellela in a small dish of ocean water. Instead, he's looking in my direction at the woman who just ran her hand down my jawline, "Ladies, why don't we all gather at the back of the boat to see what we've dragged in today."

After Ben bails me out, I escort the exuberant passenger toward the bench seats that span the stern where the rest of her friends are sitting.

No one wants to hold any of the limpets or spiny brittle stars we placed into the specimen buckets after trawling the ocean. I'm baffled as to why these women scheduled a marine tour instead of one of the glass bottom excursions or a twilight cruise. I might have an uncanny grasp of the natural world. My expertise doesn't always transfer to an understanding of human behavior—especially the females of our species.

After two hours touring with the equivalent of the *Real Housewives of Orange County*, we dock and send the ladies on their way. At least they were generous in making contributions to my "Save the Oceans" dropbox at the stern near the spot where they exit. They have no idea what my secret project is, and I'm certain they couldn't care less. Once one woman opened her purse and dropped in several hundred dollar bills, they all followed suit, one woman even asked if I take PayPal. I do now.

After another tour with a much more interested group—an extended family of ten—I head to my bungalow four blocks from the beach. I live in a small white wood beach cottage with one bedroom, one bathroom and a modest living room.

I'm drained in the sort of way only tours like my first one this morning can render me. The ocean and its creatures are my passion. I know I'm on one end of a spectrum when it comes to my enthusiasm for sea cucumbers and bottom feeders like the leopard shark. I prefer taking people on my boat who want to discover the mysteries of the ocean and marvel at the vast world beneath the surface.

I make my way through my house into my back yard, shucking my shoes along the way and falling into the hammock. The afternoon breeze blows gently through the branches over-head. The sound of gulls and the faintest whoosh and crash of the tides hitting the distant rocks along the shore relax me as they always have.

I don't remember drifting off to sleep, but when I wake, the sun has dipped lower, giving a golden glow to my tiny back yard and the surrounding trees.

It's not quite dinner time, but I'm already hungry, so I warm some leftovers in the microwave. Then I pull out my phone and open the *Play on Words* app while I sit at my dining table to eat.

Is it wrong to hope SaturdayIslandGirl will be online? I play with other competitors, but our games are the ones I look forward to the most. She doesn't know what I look like, or anything about me, really. I can be myself with her in ways I can't in the real world.

I wait a few minutes, nearly succumbing to the disappoint-ment that I'll have to initiate a match and leave it for her to respond later. Just before I accept a challenge from an unknown competitor, SaturdayIslandGirl's gamer tag pops up on my side-bar. A few seconds later she's challenging me to a match.

Are you ready to rumble? She types while both of us receive our tiles.

I smile. It's the first time I've genuinely smiled all day besides the amused grins Ben drew out of me over my mustache—which I'm shaving as soon as I finish playing this game.

So ready. I was born ready. As a matter of fact, I think this is my night to shine. I type my response, still smiling the whole time.

Big words. Let's see if you can back those up.

I bark out a laugh. She's fun.

I analyze my tiles. She may be right. But one thing I've learned in this game is that you can't tell where it will lead until you play it out. Just when you think you couldn't possibly win, you pick up a J and two Zs and you're able to spell JAZZ, earning yourself twenty-nine points with one seemingly innocuous four-letter word.

We play while I eat, and then I place my plate in the sink and move to the couch in my living room. It turns out SaturdayIsland-Girl was right. This may not be my night to shine.

She's kept her lead the whole game and is currently ahead by six points. Normally, I'd feel a surge of competitiveness. But with her, I'm just glad to be playing—enjoying our ongoing banter and smack talk as much as the actual game itself. She lays down four letters. It's not a word we use in America, but I know I'm going to let it pass as soon as I see what I can build with my tiles on what she's set down. Maybe my luck is turning.

THREE

Alana

It's not so important who starts the game,
but who finishes it.
~ John Wooden

F-O-U-D.

I set the tiles down on the virtual game board on my screen, pretty proud of myself for remembering that's an actual word in Britain. I nearly cross my fingers in hopes that Wordivore doesn't call me on the fact that foud isn't actually a universally used word in all of English. I lean back on my couch, tucking my legs under me on the cushion, waiting for Wordivore's response.

I earned eight points for that word, and I'm ahead by six already, so that makes my lead fourteen.

Wordivore wastes no time adding ROYANT to the end of the tiles I just laid, creating FOUDROYANT and earning my eight plus nine. Seventeen!

Bam! The message comes through almost as quickly as the tiles show up on our shared game board.

Are you using a computer assistant to discover words? I ask.

Are you accusing me of cheating? Where would the fun be in that?

I have to agree. Half the fun, or maybe ninety percent of it, comes from knowing you won by your wits.

Well done, then. I concede. Are you sure foudroyant is an actual word?

I am.

Why do I long for more than those two words from my opponent?

What does it mean then? I ask instead of Googling the definition.

Sudden and overwhelming in effect; stunning; dazzling. It comes from the French word for lightning. As in, my opponent's word choice was foudroyant.

I chuckle at the double entendre.

Ah. Foudre. Oui. I don't know why I answer with the actual French word for lightning.

My response reveals something personal. Not that I am French, I'm not. I just exposed the fact that I speak the language. Maybe I shouldn't have.

Tu parles français? Wordivore asks while our game board sits idle.

Of course my statement would prompt the question as to whether I speak French.

No. I answer with a falsehood.

I really don't want to lie to Wordivore, even though we'll never meet outside this game. The reality is, I'm better off not being open about anything personal. Any hint at who I am would ruin the anonymity I have here—this rare place I can come to be unknown and known at the same time.

Ah. Well, good guess as to what the French word for lightning is, then. And also at what my question meant. My opponent adds a winking emoji. *And, also a surprisingly accurate use of the word oui. Though, I guess most Americans would know that word. But many wouldn't know the spelling. Spelling French words threat-*

ened to be the death of me in high school. Luckily, I had a cute tutor.

This is a conversation. Not merely comments on the game. A part of me thrills at the opportunity to learn more about Wordivore. For one thing, I'm sensing he's a man, not that it matters. But maybe she's a woman? For some reason that detail feels tantamount to all others. The winking emoji in the middle of the last comment feels like one Brigitte would give me when she says something particularly over the edge. Friend to friend, goofing off. But if he's a man ...

I wonder. What does he—or she—do all day? Do they work, are they married? Do they have pets? Children? What color is their hair, their eyes, their skin? Where do they live? What are their hobbies, passions, dreams, fears, concerns? All those questions are the very ones I'd rather not answer about myself, so it's obvious I can't ask them either.

Instead of continuing the conversation, I play off the N in FOUDROYANT. I lay down A-NEX and make the word ANNEX for twelve points, thanks to my X.

Great comeback, Wordivore types. *Gotta love that X.*

Thanks, I type, while watching my opponent add, -ATION to my ANNEX to gain five points plus my twelve, ending with an eight point lead over me in the process.

I can't help but smile. There's something satisfying in finding a worthy opponent.

It's your lucky day, I goad.

Must be, Wordivore answers, and then adds, *So now you believe in luck?*

Touché. I smile. Wordivore remembers our brief conversation about strategy and mystery—one I've been pondering ever since.

More French, Wordivore types.

Maybe I know un peu, I admit.

Admitting I know a little isn't like saying I know French. Besides, over three hundred million people speak French around the world. Finding me through that one clue would be needle-in-a-haystack level detective skills. I'll simply be careful not to admit I also speak Spanish, German, Italian and enough of three Asian languages to get around in Japan, China and Vietnam, places I've been for extended movie shoots on location.

Well, big things often have small beginnings. Wordivore types.

I recognize the line immediately.

Lawrence of Arabia? I ask.

Maybe the quote is a coincidence. Wordivore may not know the origin.

A classic film.

I stare at those three words.

I know very well that *Lawrence of Arabia* is a classic film, starring Peter O'Toole as T. E. Lawrence. The plot is based on one man's role in a war and the book *The Seven Pillars of Wisdom.* Will I admit my extensive knowledge about the film here? No. Not if I can help it. What modern person would know that much about movies, especially ones shot over sixty years ago? Maybe Wordivore is a senior citizen. Someone who could be my grandmother or grandfather.

Instead of disclosing my knowledge, I type, *A classic. Yes. So I've heard.* Again with the lies.

I'm a horrible liar. Not that I'd want to be a good one. You might think being an accomplished actress would mean I excel at deception. But acting isn't deceiving, it's portraying. I can embody a believable character in a riveting scene all day long. Lying, not so much.

You've barely heard of the movie you just named out of the blue after I quoted only one line? Incredible.

I laugh. I can almost feel the smile on Wordivore's face. I don't know if it's a man's face or a woman's, young or old, but whomever it is, they're smiling at my ridiculous attempt to conceal my identity.

I know the film. I admit, since it's obvious.

Wordivore types the shocked face of a cat emoji.

Maybe my opponent is a woman. Do men use that emoji? I

don't know. The only texting I do with men has to do with filming and business meetings and not one of them uses emojis at all. Not even the thumbs up, which seems business appropriate.

I draw my tiles, ready to end this tempting interchange between me and my favorite opponent. Then I spot the word I can play from the tiles in my hand, and I smile. I lay down FEED-ARD around the Y in FOUDROYANT to make FEEDYARD.

Sixteen points! I type, gloating unabashedly.

Why do I sense you doing a victory dance right now?

I'm doing no such thing.

I'm not even finished typing when Wordivore sets an S at the end of my word, gaining all my points plus one, and earning a nine point lead over me.

The game continues for another thirty minutes in a similar trend. Every time I think I've gotten ahead, Wordivore bests me. Our banter continues too, though it's more about the game than anything dangerously personal.

It's past what should have been my scheduled dinner hour by the time we end. I run out of tiles and the game goes to Wordivore.

Well played, I say.

You too. Really.

You're a gracious winner, I taunt.

I'd say you were a gracious loser, but I get the feeling you're dying a little inside.

I'll survive. If you lived through learning to spell in French, I'll live through this defeat. I'll live to fight another day.

That's a relief.

I smile. *Goodnight, Wordivore.*

Bonne nuit, SaturdayIslandGirl.

I don't know why I didn't realize until just this moment that my gamer tag gives away my gender. Well, I know what I'm asking Wordivore the next time we play. It's only fair that we both know one another's gender. A playing field should be level, even though most are not.

I'm heating up my baked chicken breast with quinoa and wilted spinach when there's a knock at the door. I'm not supposed to eat this late, but I lost track of time playing our game. The knock sounds again. My brain sorts through the options of who it could be. My front gate has a code, so whoever it is got as far as my porch without buzzing me. That means it's a friend, employee or family member—narrowing it down to a handful of possibilities.

Oh! Wait. Sunday evening. It's my Trader Joe's groceries. And, no. We don't have Trader Joe's on the island. I have a private delivery scheduled once a week from the mainland. The same guy, Joel, who pilots my water taxi when I need to go in to Hollywood does a weekly delivery. He's signed an NDA and he does random errands for me—for a sizeable fee. It's worth it. If I have to sequester myself like a hermit simply to enjoy a modicum of peace, at least I can use my wealth to pay people to shuttle whatever my heart desires to my secret hideaway.

I check the feed from the front security camera on my cell while I walk to the front door. I learned the habit of double-checking the hard way. More than once in my Hollywood condo, I thought someone I knew was at the front entrance, only to find a bevy of paparazzi silently awaiting my appearance. It's amazing how utterly still they can be—like lions awaiting the movement of a gazelle. At the click of the lock, the silence turned to a frenzied chaos and my pursuers pounced with a ferocious hunger for one image, one word, one facial expression to feed their endless craving.

My face breaks into a wide grin when I see it's actually not Joel with my Trader Joe's delivery. I open the door for one of my closest friends on the island—actually, she's one of my closest friends on earth.

Phyllis.

I don't even get a greeting out before Phyllis is pushing past me, a plate covered in Saran in hand. I know what's under the plastic wrap and I trail behind, my mouth nearly watering.

"Lemon bars?"

"Of course, dear. I have to make sure you don't wither away on wilted greens and air or whatever they have you eating these days."

"You know how it goes." I follow Phyllis into my chef's kitchen and watch her move through the room as if this were her own house. "Did you drive yourself up here?"

"You don't see my chauffeur anywhere around here, do you?"

I laugh. Phyllis should not be driving. Even a golf cart. The woman is like the female version of Mister Magoo. But I know better than to argue with her. No one tells her what to do.

Phyllis did a stint in Hollywood years ago. Married a director. But she got out of the business in her thirties. She grew up on Marbella and came back here permanently after her acting career and marriage came to an end. She doesn't talk about what happened. I get the feeling she's worked through most of it and doesn't want to dig up skeletons.

Phyllis sets the plate on my imported marble countertop and grabs down two dessert plates, chattering away the whole time.

"Mila and Kai set a date. And of course Noah's going to be a groomsman. None of this carrying the rings for that boy. No sir. He told Kai, 'I'm going to wear a tuxedo and stand up front with the other guys.' I think Kalaine is trying to talk Kai into having Shaka take the rings down the aisle. A dog in a wedding. That's something you'd never have seen back in my day."

I settle onto one of the barstools, content to hear Phyllis talk about anything, her niece's wedding, the weather, whatever.

She plops a lemon bar on my plate and slides it in my direction. Then she pulls up the stool next to mine.

"You know what's divine with these? Strawberry tea." She takes a bite and hums.

I glance toward the microwave. Phyllis, being as perceptive as ever, follows my line of vision.

She stands and walks to the microwave, opens the door,

furrows her brow and holds my now-room-temperature dinner out in front of her.

"Is this what you're supposed to be eating?"

I nod.

"Well ..." Phyllis pauses. Her eyes flit between the plate in her hand and the one sitting on the counter in front of me. "Dessert first!"

I laugh. "You're a horrible influence. You know that?"

"I'm a magnificent influence and you know it. Those studios would have you looking like a skeleton with skin. If I've told you once, I've told you one thousand times. And I'm going to keep telling you. They'll steal your soul if you let them. You have to draw your lines. At the end of the day, it's a job."

She stares at me, her eyes warm with concern and love. "A career. I'll give you that. It's more than a job. But it's merely what pays the bills. You could sell popsicles at the Corner Market or you could portray characters on film. One pays a bit better, sure. But it also demands a whole lot more. And it will take all if you allow it. So, don't. You're Alana Graves. Act like it."

Phyllis' slightly wrinkled hand comes up to cup my cheek. In a soft voice, full of emotion, with the sweetest smile on her face she adds, "Act like it, Gwendolyn."

She utters my childhood name like a secret we share. And it is one. Gwendolyn's a perfectly great name for an actress. I was named with my future in mind. But, just before I had an audition for a life-changing role in my first sitcom at age twelve, my mother learned that another up-and-coming child actress named Gwen was also trying out for that same show. So, we fixed that. My name was legally changed before auditions even started. I got the role. Gwen got a walk-on for one episode. I've been Alana ever since, both in my childhood home and in the public eye.

I smile at Phyllis.

"I'll act like it," I assure her, knowing full well her idea of what that means and the reality of what I'll do are worlds apart.

"I never did agree with them changing your name," she mutters around the next bite of her lemon bar.

"It was for *Around the Block,*" I defend, even though I know she knows.

"Hmph." She rolls her eyes.

Around the Block ran for five years. Giving up my name turned out to be a great move. Not that they wouldn't have hired me without the name change. Who knows. With my family's legacy in the industry, they might have given me the advantage unspoken nepotism often does. Either way, that show was the springboard we had been working toward. It ran long enough for me to get my feet wet and become an established actress.

I made a name for myself, meaning I was given preferential auditions for other sitcoms when *Around the Block* finished filming, and we had our choice of what I'd do next. I landed the key role as the live-in nanny on *Are You Kidding Me?* When that series ended, I already had my first movie lined up. And the rest is history.

My career has been like a whitewater rafting trip. I stepped onto the boat, looking for something to grab on to. Newsflash: rafts don't have handles. You have to go with the flow from the first shove off shore. I've been sloshing, peaking, dipping, and careening forward, propelled by a force much greater than me ever since my pre-teen years. The current has swept me along, and there's no end in sight.

Phyllis may think this is merely a career, and I appreciate the way her wisdom always feels like a warm bath after a particularly long day. But she doesn't know what it's like to be me—a woman born into this destiny like a princess birthed into royalty. Apparently, Phyllis had a choice. I'm happy for her. I won't argue with her, either. Instead, I'll enjoy one of my favorite things on earth—time with my friend and the rare treat of her delicious lemon bars.

Joel arrives with my groceries. Phyllis helps me put them away while she reheats my meal in the microwave. Then she shreds the chicken over the quinoa and places the spinach on top. She digs through my refrigerator and finds some salsa.

"You're allowed to eat this aren't you?"

"I just had a lemon bar. I'd say all regulated eating is out the window when you're around."

"Good. As it should be." She nods definitively, scoops some salsa into the bowl and stirs it in. "If only you had cheese in this house."

"You're incorrigible." I chuckle.

"You're in need of a whole lot of incorrigible. I'm here as a service to you." She smiles over at me.

Incorrigible. I store that word in my memory bank for Play on Words. It's a good one with B, C and G. Thinking of the game draws my mind back to Wordivore. Next time we play I'll know if my opponent is a female or male. My money's on a guy, and I can hardly wait to see if I'm right.

FOUR

Stevens

Life is more fun if you play games.
~ Roald Dahl

"Hey!" Kai shouts from the rear doorway of the watersports shack.

I wave to Ben, who is helping a customer at the moment, and then walk through the shop.

The rear of the shack opens onto the end of a wooden dock. From here it's just views of the ocean, the beach, and the harbor to our north with all the sailboats and smaller motorboats lined in slips and tethered to moorings.

"Long time no see," Kai says, lifting a wetsuit from the stock tank and hosing it down.

It's been three days since I've been around the shack. I arrived home from work on the mainland late last night and woke early to take *Sea Ya* out for a solo sail while the mist was still thick across the ocean. I snorkeled along a portion of a cove, checking on my project. My head is clear and I bet if we had taken my pulse when I got home from serving corporate America, and then again right now, my heart rate would have dropped after a morning doing what I love most.

"I had a job off the coast of Gaviota. Pipeline being extended."

I always stay on the mainland when I'm working there. No use in making two trips across the channel daily when I can knock out a job and come home to stay once my obligation is fulfilled.

My face must reveal my true feelings about my occupation. Kai's next comment isn't even posed as a question. "Not your favorite assignment."

"It's not what I anticipated doing with my degree." I smile despite the truth. "But my job affords me a life I love, so I really can't start complaining any time soon."

"I didn't exactly picture myself running a watersports rental and giving lessons for a living," Kai says, lifting another wetsuit and going through the same ritual to clean the saltwater off it before draping it over the wooden railing of the dock.

"Were you going to surf forever?"

"I still surf."

"Right. But were you originally planning to stay on the pro circuit? Isn't there a cutoff for that sport as your knees and body age?"

"Yeah. Of course. I left when I was at the top of my game. I knew it was time. This opportunity came up, and I'm glad it did. I would never have met Mila if I hadn't moved here."

"Funny how life works."

"It's like the waves."

I wait for my friend to expound on his thoughts.

Kai looks up from his task. "The waves seem to wash up the most random collection of seaweed, shells, animals, and trash. But the ocean is also surprisingly consistent. The moon directs the ebb and flow of the tide in a steady rhythm; the water rarely encroaches on the shoreline past a given point; each portion of the sea provides a home to certain species. Those things are constants. Life is like that. Both predictable and random."

"Like the waves."

One thing I appreciate about my friendship with Kai are these types of talks. Most surfers and divers have an innate respect for the ocean. But Kai's a deep thinker, and I think our friendship is one of the few places where he gives voice to his more profound thoughts.

Ben walks out back, apparently finished with his customer.

"What are you two pontificating about?"

Kai smirks. "The way life mirrors the ocean."

Ben takes both his hands and pinches his fingers together, placing them next to his temples. Then he blows his hands wide open. "You two philosophers are way over my pay grade."

Kai smiles at me.

"On to more mundane and normal topics," Ben says. "Are you coming to Bodhi's Saturday?"

"The barbecue?" I ask. Bodhi extended me an invitation two days ago.

"Yeah. We'll all be there." Ben tips his chin toward Kai. "Kai and Mila, Cam and Riley, Bodhi and Kalaine, Summer and Me."

"Is there such a thing as being the ninth wheel?" I half joke.

"We know women," Ben wags his eyebrows. "Giselle's still single. That yoga instructor friend of Riley and Summer's, Aria, is still single, I think. Want us to invite some women?"

"No. No. I'm good."

Ben chuckles. "It's a waste of all that good rizz, my friend. You should be blessing the women of Marbella with some dates at the very least."

Kai shakes his head. "Leave him alone, Ben."

Kai's forehead wrinkles with confusion when he looks at me. "Rizz?"

"It's nothing. Trust me," I glance at Ben, and Kai seems to read the room.

"It may be a bunch of couples at Bodhi's, but we'll just be hanging out," Kai says. "These gatherings usually end up with all the girls on one end of the yard and all us guys around the grill anyway. Come over. We'd love to have you."

"I just might." I concede.

Eventually, I may just have to give in and let the guys set me up with someone. My thoughts flick to SaturdayIslandGirl. I looked up Saturday Island the other day, hoping it was a location I had never heard of before. It's not.

There's an old 1950s movie with an island by that name located in the South Pacific. And there's a book too—about a shipwreck near Jamaica. That doesn't narrow things down at all. If I employ deductive reasoning based on those two pieces of information, my online friend either lives in the Caribbean or Bora Bora. Those two spots are nearly six thousand miles away from one another, and they each are three or four thousand away from me. I'm probably not going to end up dating her. Well, let's be practical here. I will not be dating her.

For some inexplicable reason, SaturdayIslandGirl is the one woman I have any interest in pursuing even though I know nothing about her outside the ease of our connection, her wit, and the way she draws out my desire to banter. For now, I'd rather not date. I'm happy with my boats, my friends, and the curious relationship I've formed with SaturdayIslandGirl.

I have dated women in the past. I even had a pretty serious girlfriend in grad school. She dreamed of touring the world drumming up grants to fund research trips focused on furthering ocean conservation. She met an ecologist one summer and broke things off with me when she returned home from that expedition. I barely grieved. She was more of a companion than the love of my life. It was then I landed on an important discovery about myself. I don't want a relationship that's basically a convenience.

If I'm ever going to invest in something committed and romantic, I want the woman to be someone I can't live without. I need to be swept away by her. She needs to challenge me and settle me. That woman may not exist, and that's fine. I'm pretty good at being single. But if she does exist, I'll pursue her until she's mine. And she'll be worth whatever I have to do or sacrifice to be with her.

Until then, I need to spend at least as much time with the actual people I know in real life as I do with anonymous acquaintances online.

"I'll be there," I tell Ben, snapping out of my spiraling thoughts about relationships.

He whoops enthusiastically. "Atta boy. And let me know if you change your mind. I'm sure we could come up with quite a few females who would want to show up if they knew the elusive Stevens was coming over."

"I'm good," I assure Ben. "I'll see you two later. I've got to stop by my mom's for a bit."

"Give her a kiss on the cheek for the boy she wishes were her actual son," Ben says. "I love that woman."

"I'll do just that." I chuckle.

My mom unofficially adopted Ben once she found out his family lives in the Midwest. She's always been like that, collecting stray friends of mine and treating them like extended family. Her extroversion knows no bounds.

The air outside the watersports shack is warm on my skin. A light breeze blows in, tempting me to consider taking my sailboat out for a second trip today. I don't have any tours scheduled. I need to finalize my formal report for work. Otherwise, I'm a free man—until Bodhi's barbecue, at least. Here's hoping Ben doesn't invite a random woman.

I pedal my bike back toward the north shore. When I arrive at my childhood home, Mom's voice filters through the house out to the front porch. She's singing an Adele song. My father can sing. My brother can sing like he was born to make music. I might be able to carry a tune. Mom ... can't. The women in our family are spunky, delightful, beautiful ... and horrible singers. She's giving it her all. And when she sings the word, "Hello," I sing back "It's me."

"Ren!"

Mom shouts my childhood nickname. It's a shortened form of my full name, which no, I'm not disclosing to you, or anyone for that matter. I follow the sound of her voice to the screened-in porch off the back of the house. Our home is in a hilly section of the island, about two-thirds of the way up the street. We have a small front yard, but a decent sized back yard with a porch up on stilts off the back of the house. Mom often sets up an easel or table out here, depending on her project, and loses herself in whatever she's creating for hours.

She stands from the easel and sets her brush into a cup of water.

"What a sweet surprise!" Mom exclaims before squeezing me into one of her notorious hugs. She warned each of us kids when we entered our preteen years, "I'll be hugging you. You're my children and I'm going to hug you. That's not negotiable. Get over any awkwardness you have right now. Some kids go through this, *Mom, you're embarrassing me* stage. Not in our family. I'm a hugger and you need hugs."

I believe each of us rolled our eyes at her when it was our turn to hear the speech. I distinctly remember trying to arrange for Mom to pick me up at discreet locations throughout my high school years so no one would witness her hugging me. Looking back, I now know I was one of the lucky ones.

When she steps back I glance over at her painting.

"What are you working on?"

"It's a painting I started last weekend."

"San Simeon?"

"You recognize it."

"I'd probably be able to identify any part of the coast from Big Sur to Redondo Beach. That's my office, so to speak."

"What an office." She sighs.

"I prefer Marbella."

"Of course you do. Who wouldn't?"

Mom loosens her paint apron and drapes it over the back of the easel.

"Have you seen your brother? I wasn't sure if he made it back yet."

"Dustin?"

"Do you have another brother I'm not aware of?"

I shake my head and chuckle.

"No. Just Dustin. I haven't heard from him, but that's how it is when he's out on a fire. And when he comes back, he usually crashes. So we won't hear from him right away anyway."

My brother isn't a full-time firefighter yet, but he's a volunteer here and gets called out when there are wildfires in the California forests or other high-frequency areas. His life outside firefighting involves writing country music, singing at local bars and other venues, and working part-time as a bouncer at two of the clubs in Descanso on the south end of the island. How he ever came to love country music is beyond me. We're a California island. Surf tunes. Pop. Even some R & B. Not country. But that's Dustin. It's like he was imported from the south.

"You might hear from him between naps once he's home," I assure my mom. "Since he has the typical short-term, post-traumatic symptom including an inability to regulate sleep due to the cortisol his adrenal glands over-emit during the fire response, he's bound to wake intermittently. Maybe he'll get the urge to let you know he's home during one of his bouts of wakefulness. The maternal-child bond means he'll think to call you first before anyone else in the family. So, you can relax."

Mom stares at me. That same stunned expression passes over her face every time I lapse into scientist mode.

She squeezes her eyebrows together momentarily and then she asks, "Do you want some tea?"

"Sure. I'd love some. I came here just to hang out with you. I get bonus son points for that, right?"

She smiles at me. "Your points are maxed out. No need to earn more. And I see you've shaved that horrible thing off your lip. You're such a handsome guy, Ren. Some people were not meant to sport the mustache. I'm just sayin'. Full facial hair? Maybe. But not the 'stache. Not for you."

"Agreed."

The 'stache. My mom.

"Well, good. Speaking of your mustache, I wanted to talk to you about painting."

"Painting? What does painting have to do with my ex-mustache?"

Mom doesn't clarify her poor segue. Instead she veers into a completely unrelated subject. "There's this painting class. Do you remember Harry?"

"Harriet Symes?"

"Yes. That's her."

Harriet and I have one thing in common. Our parents must have been smoking crack when they named us. Again. I'm not telling you my name. Ever. At least I can go by my middle name. Harry was forced to choose between a name that makes her sound like a seventy-year-old with knee pain and hearing aids that squeal when they aren't properly adjusted, or that man who met Sally in the classic romcom movie.

"Yeah. I know Harry. She was two years older than me in high school. We didn't really hang out, but I see her around the island from time to time."

"Yes. Well, Harry's single and self-employed as an art teacher. Did you know that? And she just started hosting outdoor painting classes in the cove every weekend. It's called plein air painting. It means outdoors in French."

"I know, Mom. I took French. Remember?"

"I know. I didn't, as you well know. But I can pick things up here and there, like plein air. Which, to be fair, sounds like plain air. So, it's logical. If only all French were logical. I'd be a whiz at it."

"I'm sure you would," I smile at her.

She wouldn't. Mom has one of the most American accents I've ever heard. Even when she says things like burrito or salsa, she's so obviously not Mexican. She says sahl-zah and breeto. We've tried to correct her. I mean, we live in California. Mexican food is as common as burgers and salads out here. Over half our state speaks Spanish. My mom is clearly not in that half.

And it didn't pass by me that Mom mentioned Harry's marital status. Mom always has to throw in when any female is single if she's talking to me or my brother. Mom can be discussing the most irrelevant fact about a woman, and she'll slip the detail of how this particular young woman is unattached. Like, *Oh, did you know Susan Stearns fell while she was hiking the back side of the island? She's single. And she sprained her ankle.* If she's feeling extra pushy, she might add, *Poor Susan, she'll have to recover all alone. It's so much better when you have your person to go through life with.*

"I'm just glad Harry can support herself with her art," Mom says. "It's hard on these single women, you know. And she's just so pretty. And talented. Sweet too."

There you have it. The push.

"That's great for Harry. I'm glad she's making a living with her art."

"Well, I want you to come to Harry's class."

It's not the oddest request my mother has ever made of me—not by a long shot.

"Because ...?"

"Because nothing. Can't a mom want her son to spend an afternoon outdoors with her?"

"She can. But you are not just any mom, and I think you're up to something."

Mom puts her hand to her chest and makes an overly dramatic face. "Moi, up to something? You wound me."

"I'm sure. And you are definitely up to something. I just don't know what yet."

"But you'll come? Saturday?"

"Sure. Why not?"

I follow Mom into the kitchen. She pours me tea and we spend the rest of the visit on the porch. She paints and I watch her while I sip my tea. I pull out my phone and open *Play on Words.*

Might as well start a game even if SaturdayIslandGirl isn't online. I can leave a board open for her to respond to and then we'll finish the game later. It's not as fun playing that way, waiting for her to play and answering with my own move. I far prefer when we're online together for hours, bantering and trash talking.

I initiate a game, am dealt tiles, and lay down the word EAGLET. It's not a strong start: seven points for a six-letter word, but I can play off a lot of those letters if I get the right tiles.

To my surprise, SaturdayIslandGirl responds right away.

A midday game? Okay, then. I'll slay you in the sunlight as well as I do at night.

"Well, hello there," I say out loud without thinking.

"Hello to you, too," Mom says from her stool by the easel. "Who's that?"

"Who's who?"

"Whoever got you to speak in that tone of voice."

"Oh. It's nothing. Just a gamer. Online."

"Oh."

The disappointment in Mom's voice is palpable. Poor woman wants daughters-in-law, a son-in-law, grandkids and all the chaos of extended family running around her at all times. The three of us have failed her utterly so far.

SaturdayIslandGirl uses the G in EAGLET and adds E-Y-S-E-R-S, making GEYSERS.

Eleven points right out the gate.

Well played. I smile.

I feel like asking, *Are you by any chance in either Bora Bora or the Caribbean?*, but I obviously don't.

I'm surprised at what appears next in the chat box next to our board.

I'm studying my tiles for my next move when SaturdayIsland Girl types, *I want to ask you a personal question. Is that alright?*

I temporarily abandon my thoughts about letter combinations. *Maybe. What would you like to know?*

Her response pops up immediately. *Right. Of course. It's*

nothing too intrusive. I just realized my gamer tag reveals that I'm a woman. To level the playing field I wanted to know ...

She pauses and her sentence stops at the three bouncing dots. I'll spare her the suspense.

I chuckle and type, *I'm a woman.*

Oh. Good. Okay. That's what I was wondering. Well, now I know.

I'm smiling, wondering if she thought I was a woman all along.

I'm kidding. I'm a man.

Seriously?

I am.

Now I have to wonder.

I was just joking around. I am a man.

Maybe I shouldn't have joked. Now she can't believe me. I was just having fun, the way we do. Short of offering to send her to a website where she could see a photo of me after I won an award for my field of work, there's no way to assure her. And how would she know if the photo I sent her to check out was actually me? I could be one of those guys posing with a poodle, roses and a yacht. You just know the guy behind that kind of picture actually drives a beater car and has a beer gut. No. I have to think of something else. The board sits idle while I wrack my brain for proof.

My mom is blissfully painting in the corner of the porch, unaware of my self-inflicted predicament. Then I hit on the perfect thing to say, or at least the best I've got short of a video chat which would probably not be something SaturdayIslandGirl would agree to. Besides, could you imagine a video chat with my mom in the same room? No. Not happening.

Remember how I told you I thought my French tutor was cute?

Yes. I do.

Well, she was a grade older than me. A girl named Charise. She lived a few blocks over from us. My parents hired her because my grades in my French class were going to decimate my GPA. I did think she was cute—had a serious crush on her. But she had a boyfriend. Does that give you enough proof?

SaturdayIslandGirl answers me. *For this platform, short of you showing me a photo of yourself, which you could drag up from anywhere on the web and pretend is you anyway, I'll have to take your word for it.*

I thought of a photo, but you're right. I could pull up any random picture and claim it's me. Is the playing field level now?

Never. I've got a distinct advantage. Four points and growing.

She boasts as usual. Even when she's losing, she's got confidence to spare. I love that about her. It reminds me of Mitzi a little. But the unusual feelings I have about SaturdayIslandGirl are not the kind of affection I feel for my sister. It's a problem, but not one I want to dwell on. We share this online space. It's fun. I'll enjoy it for what it is.

Advantage depends on what tiles you're holding, I retort.

Maybe it's not the tiles, but how you use them that matters.

She adds a winking emoji.

It's the first time she's virtually winked at me. Is this flirting? Will something change between us now that she believes I'm a man?

FIVE

Alana

"You are not leaving this tower EVER!"
~ Tangled

Joel is waiting at the private dock bright and early to take me across the channel. I've got a meeting in Studio City mid-morning today to go over a script in person with the casting director and producer. I'm wearing a hoodie, jeans shorts, deck shoes and one of probably one hundred pairs of sunglasses I own.

The movie star sunglasses are the equivalent of an ostrich sticking his head in the sand. That bird and I both believe hiding one small part of ourselves means we're incognito, when we both should know we're the only ones being fooled. Still, I feel safer behind my Jackie Ohh Ray-Bans. They're one more layer of protection between me and the insatiable world around me.

"Good morning, Layna," Joel says as he extends his hand to me so I can board his motorboat. I hand him my duffle filled with a change of clothes, my makeup bag and hair supplies.

Layna is such an unimaginative pseudonym. We could have gone with anything from Marge to Bambi or even Aphrodite.

Layna is so similar to Alana, but so far it has worked. I even use it when I stay in hotels. Layna Vargas. I've had so many personas in my life between the characters I've portrayed and the shifting of my own name, it's a wonder I even know who I am anymore.

"Good morning, Joel. Thank you for arranging to take me on such short notice."

"I live to serve," he jokes, taking a half-bow to emphasize his words.

I settle on the cushioned seats at the back of the boat. Joel stands at the captain's chair, turns the key and reverses away from the dock. Then he turns the boat and we're off, the bow tipping up over cresting waves, and the spray softly misting across my face.

"Tell me about your normal life," I shout to Joel over the roar of the engine and the slap of the water against the sides of the boat.

"Come sit next to me so we don't have to shout." He looks back at me with a friendly wink.

Joel was hired by Brigitte. She's a finder of people and solutions. Somehow she managed to discover this guy who's in his late twenties and has never seen one of my movies and never wants to. He's completely unimpressed by me. He's also signed an NDA and went through whatever other security checks we needed before he was granted clearance to be my water-taxi driver and my grocery delivery person, among other random tasks he does for me.

I'm hard pressed to decide whether I should indulge myself in a conversation with Joel or simply sit back here and enjoy the feel of the wind and water on my face. Joel wins out. He's entertaining and always has a fun story for me if I'm in the mood to hear it. When I'm not feeling so chatty, he respects my privacy and leaves me alone to my thoughts.

I stand and make my way to the passenger seat next to the captain's chair at the front of the boat.

"Want to drive?" he offers.

I've never taken him up when he asks. Maybe one day I'll

confess that I don't know how to drive—a car, a boat, or any other motorized vehicle. I've never needed to. I live on an island where we get around by bike, golf cart or foot. And I spend most of my days on Marbella enjoying my privacy on my property. When I'm in LA, I have a driver. And here's Joel, shuttling me across the water.

"Nah. You drive," I answer. "I just want to hear what you've been up to. Give me a peek into some normalcy."

"You want a peek into normalcy? I'd take you out with me to Club Descanso if you wanted."

"That dance club that only holds one hundred and fifty people?"

He nods.

"I don't see what could possibly go wrong there. I mean, stars do that all the time—showing up at a local club and fitting right in."

"We could get you a wig." He looks so sincere. "And one of those big oafs of yours could come over to the island for the occasion, just to be certain no one messed with you. My buddy's brother is a bouncer there a couple of nights a week. I'd make sure he was there. He'd keep the fans at bay. You'd have fun."

"Fun." I stare out at the mainland shore in the distance. "I'm not sure if having fun is in any of my contracts. I'll have to read the fine print."

"Let me get this straight," Joel teases. "I'm offering you a night out with all this," he waves his hand from his chin downward. "And guaranteeing you not one, but two bodyguards, in addition to my expertise in a very specific martial art. And you are declining?"

"Martial arts? Which martial art do you know?"

"I'm a master at Ah Ah Chi Yu."

"What is that? I've never heard of it."

"If someone gets too close to you, I sneeze like an elephant breathing in a vat of baby powder. They won't know what hit 'em. Ah ah chee-ew!"

I laugh at the dorky joke and Joel smiles. He's extremely pleased with himself.

His face grows serious. "Give it some thought, Layna. You could use a day out with the little people. It's not healthy for a woman your age to live like Rapunzel in her tower."

"I have people in my life."

"I'm sure you do. But you haven't lived until you've danced the *Cupid Shuffle* on a crowded dance floor with this guy. Some men have moves like Jagger. I've got moves like Psy."

"The guy who made up Gangnam Style?"

"That's the one."

I chuckle. "This I have to see."

"Then come out. I'm just asking as a friend. You know that. You're so far above my pay grade and we don't have that kind of chemistry. Sorry for you, but it's true. Besides, I have my eye on someone, as you know. She's not a rich starlet who keeps herself locked in a tower, but hey, sometimes a guy's gotta settle for second best."

He smiles that playful, carefree smile of his. It's like medicine. Being on the water, having him treat me like I'm just another person, it's always so good for me. What awaits me on the other side of this boat ride, well, that's another story.

"How's that going?" I ask, hoping to drag my thoughts back to something more light than picking my next script.

"With the woman of my dreams?"

"Yes. Any progress there?"

"If I could introduce her to my influential friend, maybe she'd see what a catch I am—by association. But, alas, I signed an NDA so I can't even mention that I know you, let alone the fact that you pine for me so deeply it wounds you."

"Yeah. That is a bummer. You'll just have to rely on your good looks and charm to win her heart."

"Well, then I guess it's hopeless before it's begun." He winks again.

Joel knows he's good looking and charming. I hope this

woman figures it out. Joel feels like the brother I never had. The ease between us is unexpected—and necessary. I guess I could have a water-taxi pilot who was stoic and responsible—someone who was more like a human vault. I'm glad I have Joel instead.

"Oh! I forgot to tell you." He looks over at me. "I'm going to Wisconsin for a family wedding all of next week. I won't be here to drive you. But your girl, Brigitte, has things in hand. She asked me if I know anyone I'd trust with my life who also can captain a boat. Turns out, I do. So I'm going to approach my buddy and he'll sub for you while I'm gone."

"Are you sure you can trust him?"

"With my life. He's a bit quirky at times. Smartest guy I know. And kind. He'd do anything for anyone. Keeps to himself mostly, but not in a weird way." He pauses. "Like some people we know." His smile is big and teasing.

"I don't keep to myself in a weird way."

"Who says I was talking about you? But now that you mention it ..." He laughs.

We chat the rest of the one hour boat ride, and far too soon, we're pulling up alongside the dock in Ventura.

Ken, one of the bodyguards who works for our family, is standing outside the metal gate, waiting for me. He's the embodiment of the ex-military man he is: built like a tank, rigid, unyielding. I wouldn't mess with him, though, I do. He's an easy target for teasing. But I'm on his good side, if you want to call it a good side. I've never seen Ken smile in all the years I've known him. Not even a twitch indicating he's suppressing a grin. It's a secret life's mission of mine to get Ken to break down and actually smile.

Before I walk down the dock to where Ken is waiting for me, I catch Joel's eyes. "I actually know that dance."

"That dance?"

"The Cupid Shuffle."

"See?" He smiles at me. "Destiny."

I spontaneously start humming the tune and Joel starts

singing the *down-down* background line and then he's rapping, "The Cupid. The shuffle," over and over to a beat we're both hearing even though there's nothing but the sounds of shorebirds and boats in the water around us. I start doing the moves on the dock and Joel mimics them inside his boat exaggerating and adding ridiculous swagger. I turn when we say "walk it ..." and Ken comes into view. His face is set in the typical unreadable expression of what I affectionately call *resting bodyguard face*. He raises one eyebrow and crosses his arms over his chest.

Joel and I both stop dancing and singing. The power Ken wields with the small patch of hair over one eye. It's remarkable.

"I think your babysitter is getting restless," Joel beams at me like the Clyde to my Bonnie. "Better go ask him to join us at Club Descanso before he makes other plans that won't be half as fun."

My tone drops to something more serious. "I can't, Joel. You know that."

"I know no such thing. You're Layna Freaking Vargas. Or whomever we both know you really are. You can do what you want. Call the shots, Miss Hollywood. Have some fun outside that secret lair of yours."

He's joking, but there's a seriousness to the way he holds my eyes with his stare. He's challenging me. And we all know how much I love a challenge.

"We'll see," I say, before I grab my duffle from his outstretched hand and turn to walk down the dock toward Ken.

I slip into the back seat of the black Town Car and Ken takes shotgun once my door is shut. Our driver, Miguel, greets me and takes off for the offices in Studio City. The drive to LA goes quickly, but once we're within the city limits, traffic slows to a crawl. Our windows are tinted, so I roll up the divider and change into my dress and heels while we're moving slower than a sleep-deprived snail.

Miguel parks in front of the nondescript office building and Ken exits the car, holding my door for me. In my opinion, I could slip through LA far more stealthily without Ken, the tank, by my side. Ken draws attention. He's massive and magnetic, like a boulder of lodestone. People turn and look at the two of us, but no one stops, snaps a photo or rushes us. Celebrities are a dime a dozen in this part of LA. We're close enough to the studios to be a common sight.

Once we're inside, Ken remains in the hallway while I enter the room where the creative team fills a table much like any other board room. Casting calls happen on studio lots, in trailers, in offices like this one, and even at directors' houses sometimes. There can be couches and charcuterie boards, which no one will touch, or we can be seated around tables. General auditions are more like cattle calls than casting calls, but there are tiers to this process. Thankfully, I am well beyond the point of nervously huddling along hallway walls reciting lines next to other anxious wannabes.

An advanced, offer-only meeting like this one only happens for those of us who have made a name for ourselves. The director hand-picks his A-listers and gives them first dibs. The producer has a type in mind. An actor or actress is invited if they fit the type. Sometimes a script is even crafted around a lead. The creative team gets lucky if that actor or actress accepts the role by the end. If not, the search is on for the closest approximation.

My seat at the table is empty. I settle into it wordlessly and glance around at the faces of the men and women present. Some I know. A few are new to me. A young woman places a glass of ice water in front of me. I thank her. She blushes and scurries toward the back wall.

At my level in the industry, I'm not here to audition, per se. If anything, this meeting is a type of informal screening for both parties. I'll listen to their vision for the film and the role they want me to fill, making sure we're on the same page creatively. They won't make a formal offer until after this meeting has occurred. On their end, this meeting is more of a formality. They want me. Mother has made that clear. After all, my father's company—our family's company—is producing the film. But, thankfully, they didn't pick me solely based on nepotism. I have to carry my weight. And I always do. My name and reputation along with my skills make me a sought-after commodity. I'm aware of how many people long to be in my shoes every time I walk into one of these curated, invite-only audition sessions. Still, privilege often comes with some steep price tags.

"Welcome, everyone," Stan, the casting director, calls out once we're all seated.

We go around and make introductions. People smile at one another politely, or not.

"We're here to discuss *Only the Remnant* with Alana, specifically we're talking about the role of Ember, the lead female. Alana, I take it you've read the script."

"I have." I smile at Stan.

"You'll be among the small population of humans who survived the decimation of Earth. The role would require you to hone your martial arts skills and sword handling." Stan pauses and looks down at his iPad. "You know Taekwondo and Kendo?"

"Yes. Black belt in each. And I've studied Capoeira as well, but I only have an azul marinho belt."

Stan looks confused, so I clarify. "I have the mid-level belt—in a Brazilian martial art combining a variety of movements for both show and actual fighting. Depending on what you're going for, the dance element of that discipline works well on film."

Conversation after this minor clarification flows as if I'm not there. People talk about me, and occasionally I'm addressed. Stan's seen my work. But he wants me to read with the actor who's already locked in by contract to play the male lead part of Jericho. About a half an hour before we adjourn, Benson Stiles shows up. We've never officially worked together, but we're familiar enough with one another's bodies of work.

"Alana Graves. What an honor." He takes my hand and grasps it firmly while shaking it gently.

"Same here, Benson. Congratulations on the SAG award.

That's one I'd place in the center of my mantle. Oscar could sit next to him."

Benson laughs a full laugh. "Well, the awards from our peers do mean more, that's true. And thank you."

We get down to business. Benson and I feel one another out as we read our respective lines. He's good. A natural with training and experience, obviously. And our professional chemistry works. I'd cast us. But I'm secretly pining away for another role right now. And that's the trouble. As much as this film might be a big blockbuster and could even result in an actual coveted golden statue on my shelf, I want something else even more.

I'm privately considering a script for *She's Impossible*, a film based on Shakespeare's *Taming of the Shrew*. It's not as prosaic as the typecast nanny role I already turned down last week. It's a good middle ground. I'm not sure I want to perpetuate my notoriety as an action-adventure star.

The meeting wraps up with everyone saying things like, "We'll be in touch," and "Let us know what you think," and "I'll be calling Mitchell this week."

On the car ride home, I purposely talk Ken's ear off. He sits quietly staring out the front window.

"Meryl Streep morphed into multiple roles. She was fluid and able to do whatever a director set in front of her. No one typecast Meryl Streep. You know who she is, right Tank?"

I call Ken by the nickname Tank when I want to get under his skin. I'm the equivalent of a little sister poking at her older brother. I think he secretly loves it.

Tank's silence fills the car like a resounding boom.

"I know. I know. You're right, Tank. Meryl's roles were nearly always dramatic. Good point."

He doesn't budge. I know he's still alive. His chest rises and falls, but otherwise, he's a statue.

I catch Tank's glance in the rear view mirror. Stoic. Unflinching. Neither upset, nor amused.

"Okay. What about Julia Roberts and Scarlett Johansson?

You know them, don't ya, Tank? Those women. Iconic actresses. I bet you watched Black Widow more than once." I study his face. He stares at me. "You've got a crush on her, don't you? Oh yes, you do. You actually have the lines memorized from every movie she's been in. Tank. You and Scarlett. Who knew?"

Nothing. He's good. And it just makes me want to poke the bear all the more.

Miguel laughs, though. His eyes crinkle up around the edges.

"Miguel, you like Scarlett?"

"Who doesn't like Scarlett? She's the queen—funny, beautiful, and she could kick your ... Yeah. I like her. But she's married, no?"

"Tank here likes her too," I say. "And yes. She's married. Sorry, Tank. I'm a dream crusher, I know."

I wink at him when he barely glances at me in the rearview mirror. He knows I'm playing around. I know he knows even if he doesn't show an iota of emotion.

Miguel laughs, looks over at Tank and stops laughing immediately.

"Don't let him intimidate you, Miguel. He's a big teddy bear. Besides, we're all on the same team. You have nothing to worry about."

Miguel gives me a small nod in the rearview mirror, but he doesn't laugh again.

"All I'm saying is, these women have managed to straddle multiple genres. And let's not forget Sandra Bullock! She primarily does humorous roles, yes. But she also took on mysteries, thrillers, romance, and she excels in dramas. Why can't I have a career like that?"

"You can, Miss. You can," Miguel says enthusiastically.

Tank says nothing.

SIX

Stevens

You look familiar. Do I know you?
~ Madagascar

"So, this movie star is pretty private," Joel says.

I met Joel a few minutes ago at the dock where he parks his motorboat in one of the coves on the North Shore of Marbella. He climbs aboard the boat and I follow.

"I emailed the papers yesterday, including the NDA," I say. "They got me cleared in record time."

"Let me tell you," Joel starts the engine and backs out of the slip. "Working with Hollywood people is sort of like being in an alternate universe. What they want, they get."

I hum, considering what it would be like to snap my fingers and have anything I wanted or needed. I wonder if that level of instant gratification and power is actually beneficial long term. Most healthy systems in nature are interdependent, even if there is a natural hierarchy of organisms. When one species takes up more than its share of resources or dominates the ecosystem, the entire dynamic shifts to an imbalance which threatens the well-being of all the organisms.

"Whatcha thinking?" Joel asks.

"About ecological balance."

"Of course you are." He smiles warmly at me.

I like that about Joel. He gets me. He'll be the first to say he doesn't follow my train of thought at any given moment, but he never judges me for being who I am.

"So, you're not going to tell me who I'm driving?" I ask.

"She requested that you not know in advance. There's less chance of a leak that way, I guess. You'll be contacted by her personal assistant when you're needed. Like I said, this star is very private. Just call her Ms. Vargas. I never even call her by her actual name. It's one of those things—alternate universe, I'm telling you. Besides, you won't need to strike up a conversation. If she wants to talk, she'll let you know. Sometimes she just wants to ride in silence. Other times she'll ask you things."

"What kinds of things? Like personal things?"

Joel laughs. "No. Not personal things. She's just ... I don't know. She might ask you what you did over the weekend. Or she'll ask about ... probably nothing since she doesn't know you. I've been driving her for a few years now. So, she asks me all sorts of stuff. We talk about music, her life, my life, the woman I've got a thing for, her movies. Don't worry. You'll be fine. It's just a few trips back and forth across the channel during the coming week."

"Can you give me a hint?"

"As to who she is?"

"Yeah."

"No can do. That's what I signed an NDA for. Any stipulations she places on me, I follow, unless it's something unethical or illegal. So far she's been neither of those things. If only she would be just a little more ..." Joel trails off and a warm smile overtakes his face.

"Do you have feelings for her?"

"Nah. Not like that. She's like a big sister, or a good friend. Only we're not really friends. I'm just her lackey, getting her groceries, driving her around. You know, like that old movie? Driving Miss Daisy." He chuckles. "Anyway, thanks for doing this. It's hard on her, you know? Being in the spotlight, not trusting anyone unless they've been screened. It's not all glitz and glamor."

I nod. I imagine it's not easy. She must be pretty big to go to these lengths to avoid being in the public eye. Her assistant told me she can't even take the ferry—*too much exposure and people can be unpredictable.* Who lives like that?

"It's no problem. I'm glad to help. And, tell your sister I said congratulations."

"I will. I still can't believe my baby sister is going to beat me to the altar."

Joel has me take over driving the boat around for a bit, even though I pilot larger boats than this one all the time. We chat about a lot of nothing and spend about an hour or so tooling around on the water. At one point, we cut the engine and I free-dive off the back of the boat, intentionally submerging myself for a few minutes in the cool blue depths of our ocean. I have friends who practice this way more often than I do. They can stay under for nearly ten minutes without tanks or a snorkel. After three minutes, I emerge, refreshed, my mind clear and peaceful.

We motor back to the slip in silence. I have just enough time to finish responding to some grant emails, shower and meet my mom at Harry's painting class after Joel and I dock.

I'm surprised to see so many people on the beach when I get there. Mom's waving like we're in a crowd of a thousand, and shouting my name as if we aren't looking right at one another. At least she calls me Stevens when we're in public.

"Stevens! Stevens! Yoo hoo! Over here!"

"Coming," I answer in a normal volume, since there are only twenty people milling around in a relatively secluded cove. A couple is off in the distance laying on towels on the sand. A family runs in and out of the shorepound at another spot. But otherwise, the painting class has taken over the beach, four rows of five easels per row, each with their own folding stool propped in front of them, staggered so we can each have a clear view of the scenery.

I walk up to the front row and take my seat behind the easel next to Mom's.

"Harry!" Mom shouts nearly as loudly as she called out my name. Harry walks over.

Mom beams at her. "You remember my son, Ren, er ... Stevens. Well ... we call him Stevens now. Anyway, he's single. A marine biologist. He does tours out of the Alicante harbor. And he does important evaluations of marine life whenever a company wants to expand along the coast. Reh ... Stevens, this is Harry. Of course you know her. You two went to Marbella High together. Isn't that amazing? A shared history." Mom sighs. "Harry's an accomplished artist, and our teacher. Also single. Isn't that a coincidence?"

Mom glances between us. I smile at her and then give Harry an apologetic smile.

"Subtlety was never her forte," I explain.

"It's fine. My mom isn't much better."

"Oh! See! You two have that in common," Mom says in an incredibly glee-filled voice. "Meddling mothers. What a coincidence! The second thing you've had in common in only a few moments. That could mean something, you know."

"I need to start the class," Harry says, smiling an amused smile at my mom and then smiling kindly at me.

"Oh, yes," Mom says to Harry. "You go. We'll be right here. Me and Stevens. Painting. Admiring you as you teach. All that."

"Mom," I smile softly at her. "Maybe dial it back to fifty percent."

"Okay. Okay. But she's cute, right? I told you she was."

"She's an attractive woman."

"So, you'll ask her out?"

Thankfully, Mom's voice has shifted to a conspiratorial level.

I lean toward her. "No. I will not ask her out. I don't know her. And I'm busy this week with a job."

"So? Dates are for just that. You get to know one another. You could ask her out for sometime the following week. That will build the anticipation."

So help me, Mom wags her eyebrows suggestively.

"One day I might meet a woman. And if I do, she'll be the one. We'll date and fill your house with grandbabies at the holidays and on weekends and you can even babysit them when I take my wife on a date. Today is not that day. So, let nature take its course. Please."

"That is not how it works, Ren."

Mom's whisper-hissing while Harry explains the history and intention of plein air painting.

"How does it work, then?" I regrettably ask.

I should keep my mouth shut in hopes that she realizes we're here to paint. Though, it's obvious now, we're not really here to paint.

"How it works is that you let your mom do some of the preselecting. It's faster that way. I know Harry's family. They're good Marbella people. Harry's sweet and beautiful. I already screened her." Mom looks wistfully in Harry's direction, then back at me. "You won't feel all that warmth and chemistry when you first meet someone. The sparks usually aren't instantaneous. Trust me. Love grows from familiarity."

"Love is a byproduct of chemicals," I explain to my dreamer of a mother. "Initially, serotonin, norepinephrine and dopamine determine our reaction to someone we find remotely attractive and eligible. Then oxytocin solidifies the bonds those other chemicals initiated. We're not talking about pheromones, though the debate rages on about the possible role of those in human attraction. We can't force these relational chemicals, Mom. They're either present, or they aren't. It's science."

She shakes her head at me and mutters, "I'm going to be one of those old women who can't recognize her grandchildren because her children all waited far too long to settle down and she went completely senile by the time they had any babies."

I place my hand on her back and smile softly at her again. "Let's enjoy an afternoon of painting together. What do you say?"

She's pouting, but she says, "Bet," which I've come to learn means yes among the high school crowd.

There's a small disturbance in the row behind us. A woman in a ball cap and glasses takes the stool behind Mom. She's wearing extremely dark sunglasses which block not only her eyes but half her cheeks. I'd imagine wearing those might interfere with her choice of paint colors, but I'm not an expert.

Harry glances over at the new arrival, waves as though she knows her, and says, "Hello, Layna. Let me know if you need anything."

The new arrival nods at Harry and smiles a reserved smile. Her teeth are the whitest I've ever seen in person.

Mom, being Mom, turns around and starts chatting with the new student while Harry goes over how we will sketch our concept before painting with the oil paints she's provided as a part of the lesson supplies covered by our registration fee.

"Layna, is it?" Mom asks the tardy classmate behind us.

The new student nods and then diverts her attention to the blank canvas in front of her.

I stare at her for a moment, trying to figure out if I know her from somewhere. Maybe she took a tour? I doubt it, though. I usually remember every face of every person who rides on my boats with me. She looks so familiar, which isn't too odd for Marbella. But usually when someone looks that familiar, I can place them pretty quickly.

"Are you new to the island?" Mom asks.

The new student shakes her head lightly to indicate she's not new, and then shrugs like she's playing some understated and mysterious form of charades.

"We've lived here since I married my husband," Mom continues. "R ... Stevens here was born at the Marbella Island Medical

Center, as were my other children. I have two grown sons and a daughter. All single."

No. She. Didn't. I'm starting to think my mother's going to try to pair me up with anything that moves. We don't know this woman behind us, even though she looks familiar in a way that nags at me like a puzzle I need to solve. The woman obviously doesn't want to be known. She's out to have an uninterrupted afternoon of painting—without having the local bachelor scientist foisted on her.

"Mom. Let's focus on what Harry's saying, huh?"

"Sure. Sure." Mom shoos me off.

Then she asks the woman, "Are you single, dear? I don't see a ring."

"Mom." I speak more loudly this time.

"Right. Well. Nice to meet you dear. Layna, was it?"

The stranger nods again and smiles what might be an amused grin at Mom. Thankfully, we're instructed that we'll have five minutes to roughly sketch the scene we've chosen to paint—something we're looking at on the beach, either the whole cove, or an aspect of it. Harry's directions temporarily distract Mom from her self-appointed role as Marbella's own yenta.

SEVEN

Stevens

*I just want to apologize in advance
for having chased you down the street.*
~ FRIENDS

Just as Kai predicted, the women are gathered in the Adirondack chairs around the fire pit while the guys huddle around the barbecue. Bodhi's yard is the perfect spot for a barbecue.

"Does it bother you if we cook shrimp?" Ben asks me with a playful smirk on his face.

"Why would that bother me?"

"They live in the ocean. You know. They're your little underwater buddies."

"You're joking, right?" Bodhi says with a chuckle.

Ben holds his hands up in a gesture of innocence. "Just checking. Just checking."

I laugh along with the rest of the guys. We exchange stories about memorable guest interactions we've had this week. Kai's at the center, manning the grill, browning marinated chicken and shrimp, skewers of vegetables and some pineapple dipped in brown sugar.

When the platters are piled with everything we've cooked, we carry them over to a large farmhouse style table set under the trees. Twinkle lights are strung overhead and tiki torches line the edge of the yard. The couples find seats on the benches around the tables, paired up next to one another. I don't really feel as out of place as I had expected to. Conversation flows among all of us as we dig into the meal.

"Summer, when does your next film start shooting?" Kalaine asks, rubbing her abdomen.

Kalaine and Bodhi are expecting a child any day now, but here they are, hosting a barbecue like they've got all the leisure time in the world.

Ben places his hand on Summer's back. Summer looks up at him and they exchange a private conversation through a series of glances and facial expressions.

"Well," Summer says. "I've got a contract to start an eight week project in New York in four weeks." She looks at Ben again and they both smile. "Then I'm going to do a few local commercials and cameos ... and then take some time off because ..."

Ben shouts, "We're pregnant!"

Kalaine squeals. "Our babies will be besties!"

The table breaks into mayhem, everyone shouting congratulations, the women standing to give Summer hugs. I study Ben and Summer. They have that thing I was describing to Mom—a tangible love so strong it radiates to anyone around them. That could be said for every couple at the table. You can feel the devotion and connection between each pair. I'm right not to settle for someone sweet and pretty if there's not that innate attraction and a feeling that I can't live without her. I've seen what's possible every time one of my friends found their match. For me, it's finding the love of my life, or nothing.

Once we're all digging back into the food on our plates,

Kalaine announces, "I heard there's a new Alana Graves movie out. You know her. Right, Summer?"

"I do, though mostly only through our agent. And Alana helped me get a role a few years ago when I was breaking into the business. We don't hang out or anything."

I'm holding a piece of shrimp midair in front of my face when Alana Graves' name is mentioned. I'm a massive fan. My mom puts me to shame with the way she fangirls over Alana. She's watched Alana ever since her days in TV sitcoms. I saw the shows, of course. They were on in the family room. I only became truly interested in Alana once she started starring in action-adventure roles. Those are more my speed.

"Look at Stevens." Ben nudges Bodhi. Then he announces to the whole table, "Stevens is a *huge* fan of Alana's movies."

"I'm not a *huge* fan. I enjoy her work. That's all. Not really a huge fan at all. Average. I mean, we're all fans, right?"

Everyone stares at me.

Then Summer breaks the silence. "Oh! We should introduce you to her."

"No. No. That's fine."

I can only imagine meeting her. I'd make a complete idiot of myself, I'm sure.

"Why?" Ben teases. "Are you afraid you'll freeze up with starstruckness?"

"Nah. No. She's just another human, right?"

"Exactly," Summer agrees. "She really is. She's like the rest of us. You'd love her."

"Oh, he loves her alright," Ben continues to rib me in his usual way.

"I love her body of work ..." I feel heat creeping up my face. "Her movies, that is. I admire her acting."

"Artistically speaking," Kai teases, obviously enjoying my moment on the hot seat.

"Yes," I agree. "Artistically speaking. Of course."

"She's gorgeous. I'm pretty sure you noticed." Ben teases.

"Not as gorgeous as you, sweet mother of my child," he leans in and plants a kiss on Summer's temple.

"Yeah. Yeah. I hear you," Summer swats playfully at Ben. "It's okay. She is beautiful. I was starstruck when I first met her too, and I don't get intimidated easily."

"She is pleasant looking," I say. Then I add, "She has good bone structure and incredibly symmetrical features."

Symmetry is a proven measure of beauty. The more symmetrical the features, the more likely other humans will assess the person as beautiful. Alana is nearly perfectly symmetrical, and since there's no such thing as absolute perfection in nature, she's as close as one can get. I've noticed her beauty when I watched her films, along with admiring her skills as an actress, of course. She's not only beautiful, she's very talented. And she does martial arts, if that is actually her in those scenes. It could be a body double. Whoever it is, she's impressive.

Summer bursts into laughter. "Yeah. Maybe it's not the best idea for you to meet her in person. I don't know how she'd respond to being told she's symmetrical."

"It's the highest form of beauty to the human eye," I explain.

"Well, if you want to meet her, let us know," Summer says. "She likes to keep to herself, but sometimes I can coax her out to an event with enough begging and cajoling. If you're interested, I'll make it happen."

"I think I'm better off admiring her from afar."

"If you say so. But she's just a normal person—like me or you."

"Babe," Ben says, wrapping his arms around Summer's waist playfully and possessively. "You are anything but normal."

He kisses her temple and tugs her near.

"Anything but normal? That's almost as bad as symmetrical," Summer smiles playfully in my direction.

Ben nuzzles his face in Summer's hair and murmurs, "You're amazing, babe. Beyond amazing."

I arrive at the boat a full hour ahead of schedule. Today's the day I meet this elusive movie star. Her assistant, Brigitte, called two days ago to explain the need for a water taxi today and a few other times this week. I'll have to remain on the mainland once we're over there because her meeting is only a few hours long. It wouldn't be worth coming home and heading back out. I'll go to Costco for Mom since it's one of the stores we don't have on Marbella. I won't mention why I'm in Ventura to my mother. It really wouldn't matter what star it is, Mom has no chill when it comes to situations like this. She'd probably be down here on the docks trying to board the boat right now if she knew I was taxiing anyone famous.

A woman approaches the end of the pier. Her nearly white-blond curly hair spills over her shoulders. Considering this cove is private and only used by people who dock their boats in this harbor, I assume she's my passenger. She's a little too far away for me to tell who she is, but the closer she gets, the more sure I am. She's wearing sunglasses, but not the gigantic ones she had on Saturday. These perch high enough on her face to fully reveal her cheekbones. She's Layna ... from paint class. And I know where I've seen her now.

Layna is Alana.

Alana Graves.

The sudden urge to jump ship rolls through me like a physical force, and I have to fight the desire to catapult myself off the back of the boat before she gets any closer.

Alana Graves. *The* Alana Graves.

Alana Graves is walking toward me, and I'm her driver, and she's going to sit with me in this boat, alone, for an hour.

Get a grip, Ren.

Great. Now I'm talking to myself and using my childhood nickname. This is bad. So bad. And amazing. So amazing. But mostly, it's bad.

She's getting closer and my pulse is quickening, my mouth going dry, my palms, just the slightest bit clammy. Not good. Not at all.

She's just a human.

Human. Just human.

"Just human!" I shout from out of nowhere when Alana is barely ten feet from the boat.

She jolts backward a step.

So, I do the next best thing and start singing Rag'n'Bone Man's alternative rock song, *Human*, as if screaming "Just human!" was somehow the crescendo to an anthem about humanity I've decided I need to belt out in the early morning hours, here, alone, on this dock, in my very mediocre singing voice.

Alana will never board this water taxi. I'm sure of it. I wouldn't. I'm supposed to be stable, reliable. The man she can trust with her life and her privacy. I don't know if I can even recommend myself at this point.

I close out the line from the song, figuring my humiliation is already at a record low. I won't be able to come back from this, and the singing is only making things worse, like bleach on a red stain that turns the whole garment pink.

"Oh, hi," I say. "Hello. And welcome ... and ... Good morning. Right. Yes. Hi. I'm Stevens. And, well, so ... you're Ms. Vargas, I take it?"

She nods, eyeing me like I'm a rabid racoon or one of the island's rogue monkeys perched on her garbage cans. Rightfully so. Unhinged isn't even an apt enough word to describe how I'm acting.

"Can we just ...?" I run my hand through my hair. "Forget I reacted like that? I'm a certified dive instructor, not actually certifiable. I spend more time on or under the ocean than on land whenever given the choice. I could drive this boat in my sleep. And I don't spill secrets—ever. If someone tells me something, I'm as sealed and unreachable as a chest fallen from the Titanic and lost to the depths. Well, unless someone finds that chest and digs it up. But let's imagine the other chest—the one no one finds, ever. That's me. I'm that chest. So. Yeah. Welcome aboard!"

I literally slap a hand over my face. When I dare to peek at Alana, or Ms. Vargas as she wants to be called, she's smiling just a little.

"I need to get going, so ..." She gestures to the spot where I'm blocking the point of entry to the boat.

"Right. Right. Of course. Hop on."

I extend my hand. *AND SHE TAKES IT.* Alana Graves is holding my hand. My hand. Her hand. We're touching and I'm instantly reduced to teen girl status at a Taylor Swift concert, trying not to faint or lose my ever-living mind because Alana Graves is touching *me*.

I tuck my lips in to keep from saying something ridiculous like, *I've always wanted to hold your hand.* I haven't, officially. I mean, the idea never occurred to me, or I would have very much wanted to hold her dainty, soft, perfect hand. But I don't, of course, say that. Thankfully.

She releases our connection and walks to the back of the boat like she's done this a hundred times, and I guess she has. Joel is *friends* with her. They shuttle across the channel together regularly. He talks about the girl he has a crush on with *her*. I, on the other hand, can barely breathe or focus. And I need to, since, you know, I'm the captain at the moment.

"Okay. I'll just ..." I thumb toward the captain's chair and walk toward the helm. With my back to Alana and my hands on the steering wheel, I close my eyes and imagine I'm forty feet under water, tankless and floating. Fish are swimming around me. The water muffles all the noise of what's above. I'm still. Suspended. Weightless. I take one deep breath, let it out, check my surroundings, and turn the key.

We ride in total silence, me glancing at Alana occasionally. Okay, more than occasionally. She often closes her eyes, seeming to enjoy the way the wind whips her hair all over and the slight spray of mist coming up from the water as it spritzes her skin. Once in a while, our eyes catch, but Alana always glances away with this effortlessly elegant movement. She's not abrupt or annoyed. It's obvious from the simple turn of her head what our positions are here. She's a world-famous actress. I'm a guy who's driving a boat.

We've probably got about fifteen minutes left before we reach Ventura Harbor. I'm in the zone, observing the water all around us, enjoying the feel of the boat under my control. I haven't even glanced at Alana in at least five minutes. She could have fallen overboard and I wouldn't know.

I check. Just to be sure.

And she's doing the most surprising thing.

She's walking toward me and taking a seat in the passenger chair right next to me.

"So," she says, nonchalantly. "You and Joel are friends?"

"We both grew up on Marbella. I've known him forever. I guess you could say we're friends, even though I'm a bit older than him so we had different friends growing up."

Maybe it's the effect of the water on me. I just got a full, coherent sentence out—more than one, actually. I fix my eyes on the horizon to make sure I don't break my streak and start acting like a crazed fan again. Maybe if I don't look at her beautiful windblown hair, her bright gray-blue eyes, the perfect line of her jaw or those rosy lips, I'll be safe.

"Joel's a good guy," she adds.

"He's a lot of fun. And sincere. Yeah. He's a good guy."

I should hang out with him more, maybe. Maybe not. I've already got the guys at watersports when I need some human connection. And I have my family. I sort of thrive on time alone. People tend to drain me if I'm around them too often or in large doses. I prefer smaller, intimate gatherings over large crowds. I'm a classic introvert, but definitely not averse to being with people—in moderation.

"Joel said he'd trust you with his life." Alana looks toward the horizon as she speaks.

I study her exquisite profile. She's mussed from the wind and water, but that only amplifies her attractiveness. She's like a red crowntail betta among all the other fish. Some creatures are simply more stunning by nature. Captivating. Rare. Elevated above the rest of creation.

"So, you're a marine biologist?"

"Yeah. Yes. That's my line of work."

She smiles, obviously picking up on the nerves that haven't fully settled in her presence.

"What exactly does a marine biologist do?"

"Well, we can do hundreds of things. It's a pretty broad field —considering the ocean takes up nearly seventy-one percent of the earth."

I don't laugh at the subtle joke hidden in there, but, surprisingly she does. It's a light giggle, but still, it's musical and sweet, like a concert floutist playing Rampal.

I made Alana Graves laugh. I tuck that little nugget of truth away to take out later.

"So, what do you do within this broad field of yours?"

"Me? I ... well, I work for corporations as a marine consultant. When they want to expand, they call me. I go in, assess the situation, report to them what species are in the area, ensure they go forward with minimal ecological impact. That sort of thing."

"So, you dive for work. Do you dive recreationally? Around Marbella?"

"Yes. I dive with tanks and without."

"Free-diving?"

"Yeah. But I'm not as good as a lot of the guys I know. I can only go down for three to four minutes tops."

"Without any oxygen?!" Her eyes go wide and a swell of pride fills my chest accompanied by a pleasant buzz that travels through me. I impressed her.

"Yeah. That's what free-diving is, essentially. I have friends who can go down for ten minutes. But they practice and devote themselves to it. I usually dive with tanks if I plan to stay down for any length of time."

"I've never dived before. I've snorkeled all over the world. Asia, the Caribbean, Hawaii ... but never diving."

"Would you want to?"

Whaaaaaat? I'm not offering to take Alana Graves diving. I can barely breathe around the woman. I mean, I'm doing okay right now, but underwater, there's a serious possibility I'd take in water and drown.

"I really would love to learn. Do you teach?"

She looks directly at me and I feel her gaze like a spear to my heart. It's piercing and light. Her translucent, intelligent eyes study me.

"I do teach. Also, I think you know my friend, Ben. He's Summer Monroe's husband? He teaches at the Alicante."

She stiffens a little, and I immediately discern why. "I haven't told anyone I'm driving you this morning. They don't even know I'm out here. I'm the chest, remember?" I wink at her.

I winked. At her.

It felt like the most natural thing in the world. But I don't know what made me think I could actually wink at Alana Graves.

She smiles. "Yeah. You're the chest. From the Titanic. I remember."

We both chuckle—together. And I can see now why Joel treats Alana like a friend—why Summer said Alana's just human like the rest of us. For a moment, as fleeting as it is, we're just a man and a woman out on the water while I taxi her to work.

But that passes, don't you worry.

I'm beyond aware that she's Alana Graves. And I'm just ... me.

EIGHT

Alana

You're a beautiful woman.
You deserve a beautiful life.
~Water for Elephants

The substitute water taxi driver is funny. And attractive. I don't mention his appearance for any reason except that he's one of the beautiful people. And I don't think he even knows it. He could easily co-star in a major picture. Until he opens his mouth.

I grin to myself thinking of how he stumbled over himself when I approached the boat. Thankfully, this isn't my first rodeo. People lose their marbles over me all the time. I don't usually have to contend with the fan freak-outs from my inner circle of drivers and bodyguards, assistants, makeup artists or other people who are employed to surround and sustain my life. But someone having an attack like this guy, Stevens? Yes. I've dealt with more than my share of stuttering, screaming, and even fainting. Thankfully he didn't faint. Things were awkward enough without that added bonus feature.

I finally decided to put him out of his misery. It was either going to go one of two ways. He'd crash the boat when I came up to sit next to him, or we'd talk. I'm glad we ended up in an easy conversation. I miss Joel. He reads me. And he knows when to initiate a conversation. Also, Joel was never ever impressed by me. Not even a little. But, to this guy's credit, he's made up for the heavy case of nerves with his sweetness and sensitivity. I really believe he's "the chest."

I smile again thinking of that whole interaction.

Stevens pulls into the slip and kills the engine. He walks to the side of the boat and extends me his hand. I grab my duffle, rest my palm in Stevens' and step from the boat to the dock. His hands are strong and big, slightly calloused, clean. Nice hands. He watches me, and I'm pretty sure he's more focused on my safety than my appearance. That's more refreshing than I can say.

"You have a car waiting for you?" he asks.

He pockets the key to the boat and steps out next to me.

"I have a car. And ..." I point toward the end of the finger of slips where Ken is standing in his typical stoic stance, doing a stellar impersonation of a statue entitled, *Beefy Bodyguard Awaiting Starlet.*

"Is that your security detail? Oh. Wow. Okay. Yeah. That makes sense." Stevens assesses Tank for more than a few seconds. Then he glances back at me. "He's big."

I chuckle. "He is. Massive. And he literally never smiles."

"Never?"

"Not that I've seen, and he's worked for our family for years."

"Huh."

I almost don't say the next sentence, but history has shown me even the most seemingly trustworthy people can turn on you or be the opposite of what they appeared to be. Though, this guy seems pretty reliable. Still ...

"I'm sorry. I just need to remind you. Please don't tell anyone about me—or today."

"No. Yeah. Of course. I won't."

"No one." I repeat, feeling instantly bad for insisting so hard.

I look up into his eyes—brown and warm, compassionate, even.

"You'd be surprised how many people say something about being with me or spotting me to that one person they can trust, and before you know it, one hundred people and the local press know where I am."

"Wow." His brow furrows with definite concern. "That must be horrible."

I can only nod. I can't explain it, but the way he's looking at me could nearly draw up tears.

"I mean it. I'll keep this whole morning a secret," he assures me. "It sounds like you have no privacy. You can't even ride over on the main ferry. That's a big price tag for the life you live."

I search his face for any hint that he's being sarcastic.

Finding nothing but warmth in every feature of his, I answer, "Thank you. Yeah. There's a heavy price tag."

He looks me dead in the eyes. "I won't tell anyone. Not even my mom, who loves you. I mean, she's a superfan. She watched your shows religiously when you were on television. And she has every older movie of yours on DVD. She kept her DVD player just so she could have a full collection of your movies. Well, you and Jude Law. She loves that man. But that's beside the point. She'd die if she knew I took you to the mainland today."

It seems to suddenly dawn on both of us that I've already met his mom. She actually seemed to have tried to set Stevens up with me.

"Your mom. Yes. I remember her. Painting class?"

I feel my eyebrows pinch together. I know this guy means to keep my confidence. He did sign an NDA, but I really, really don't want to have to sue him for breach. I'm not even sure I would. But it would stink if he talked to his mom, even though a part of me wishes I could offer to officially meet her—as Alana, not Layna, hiding behind sunglasses and a ball cap just so I could get out of the house and do something creative for once. Brigitte set that painting class up too. I'm glad she did. On one hand, it was a great way to spend an afternoon. On the other hand, I could have been identified and that would have had ramifications I don't even want to entertain.

I can't officially meet any fan. Especially not when we both live on the island. Marbella is my sanctuary. I can't afford to have rabid admirers knowing I'm residing there whenever I'm not filming.

Stevens reiterates his mom's love of me. "She'd go crazy. Like ... so crazy. I think you got a small sample of that Saturday. And she had no clue who you were then. I'm surprised, honestly. I guess your disguise did the trick."

I muster up a smile. "If only I could pull off a mustache."

Stevens smiles back. "It's not just you. Most people can't. Trust me."

I laugh. It feels good to laugh a little, and I'm honestly surprised he's drawn one out of me two or three times this morning.

It's an honor to be loved by fans. I know that deep down. There's also a fine line between love and psychotic idol worship. I don't have the luxury of testing to find out which side of the line his mom lives on where I'm concerned.

"I won't tell her," Stevens reiterates. "Trust me."

He smiles again. It's a casual smile—handsome and soothing. He's getting used to me. And I like the idea of that a lot. If he's going to be my driver this week, I'd far prefer him to act like I'm just another passenger, and to lose the nerves. They make me edgy and I need my boat rides to be a place of solace.

"You're the chest," I say.

"I am."

He winks again. It's a great wink. His wink is one of those types that seems so easy to pull off but really isn't. Winks can so easily cross the line to being downright creepy or try-hard.

His isn't. It's just sweet and a little sexy.

Single guy. Self-employed. Flexible work schedule. Recommended by Joel. Reliable and familiar with all aspects of boating. That's all I know about this man who can wink like it's his job. It's all I need to know. He's just another temp employee in my life.

"I'll be here when you're finished," Stevens assures me. "Just running to Costco for my mom ... My mom, who has no idea why I'm over here or who came with me. I promise."

"I believe you."

There's a clearing of a throat at the end of the dock. Tank.

"Hold your horses, big guy. We're just working out the details of my return ride," I shout down to my stern statue of a bodyguard.

Tank doesn't flinch. He just stares.

"That guy. Whew." Stevens whistles.

"Yeah. He's good at what he does."

"Okay then. I'll see you when you're back here."

"Thanks. Enjoy Costco."

He chuckles. "Enjoy Hollywood."

I turn and walk away to attend the meeting that will determine the trajectory of the next two years of my life. My father wants to talk about the film. He's got ideas. And I'm going to either comply or decide to go rogue and do what my heart is yearning to do.

∼

This day was ... whew. I type in the chat next to my invite to Wordivore. I'm starting a new match, and secretly hoping he's online.

I haven't texted or spoken to Brigitte since I got in this afternoon. I will. She'll want to know the upshot of the meeting from me before she hears it from someone else. I collapsed for a half hour on the couch when I got back from my day in LA. I went straight to my indoor pool and swam laps, and then I did a session of yoga with Aria. She's my private yoga-pilates instructor and she comes up here three or four days a week to give me a workout that keeps me remembering her the following day.

Bad day? Wordivore types.

My smile is instant. He's here.

It started out interesting. And then ... yeah. Went from interesting to difficult within hours.

Sorry to hear that. Wordivore answers. *I, too, had an interesting day. Not bad. Definitely interesting. Want to talk about it?*

Our board sits idle. My initial word, FROGS sits out there with the F on a double point spot, giving me thirteen points right out the gate. I can't even bring myself to gloat, I'm so preoccupied with the events of the day.

Do I want to talk about it? With Wordivore? I could. I'll just keep everything super generic.

I'd like that. But, ground rules first: No sharing the specifics of where we live, what we do for a living, our names, our dates of birth, our appearance or cultural identification. Here, we're just Wordivore and SaturdayIslandGirl. Deal?

His cursor moves immediately. *Deal. I'm great with anonymity.*

I smile thinking of how Stevens said he was the chest. This morning feels like light-years ago. So much has happened since that boat ride.

I stare at my keypad, and then I type, *Have you ever felt like you're living your life for everyone else around you? Like you are meant for one thing, or maybe a whole bunch of things, but you have to do what's expected of you instead? And if you don't there's a world of people who will feel let down by you?* I stare at what I just typed, take a deep breath, and hit send.

A rush of relief flows through me immediately. I don't even know what Wordivore will say, but getting that out of my head feels like dropping a weighted pack. I'm taken aback by the lightness I experience just knowing someone else now knows all the thoughts rattling around in my head.

I definitely know what that's like. I'd say more, but it would give specifics away. Suffice it to say, I'm disappointing my mother deeply by not living up to certain dreams she has for me. I have a job I am qualified for, but it's something I would never have chosen for myself, exactly. It pays the bills, but it goes against the bigger reason I even started pursuing the field I'm in. So, yeah. I get it.

If I thought I felt relief when I hit send, that's nothing compared to what I feel reading Wordivore's response to me. I feel seen.

Today, I had a choice to make. If you want to call it a choice. On one hand, I could do the expected thing, the thing everyone wants me to do. On the other, I could choose to veer a little and do this other thing that is really what I think I want to try. Option two feels right to me. I can't explain it any other way. I had a meeting with an influential person—one who matters deeply to me. And by the time we were sitting together a half hour or so, I had conceded and let him talk me into the expected thing. Thing one, not thing two. (And now I'm thinking about Cat in the Hat!) Option one isn't bad. It's just one more time where I said yes to the pressure, yes to being what others want of me. And those yes answers feel like a no to me. I sacrificed my current dream and my preferences to make other people around me happy—again.

I stare at the screen after I hit send. That paragraph says more than I've ever shared with a therapist or even with Brigitte.

Wordivore's cursor blinks. I wait eagerly to see what he'll type. And then it comes: *I'm sorry you let yourself down.*

Yeah. I did.

Can I say something? I love that he asks that instead of barreling forward like so many men do, mansplaining and solving before even wiping their feet on the proverbial mat.

Sure. Shoot. I sit back, taking a long pull from my water. I read along as Wordivore types out his thoughts.

We tend to view things as this or that. Option A or B. No middle ground. Most things in life aren't that cut and dry. We also expect ourselves to change overnight. It sounds like you have a history of bending to please the people who matter to you. And that's not bad—not until you feel like you're selling out (preaching to the choir over here, and I know I need to hear this as much as I need to say it).

So, let's say we both decide we've had enough of the back-bending, conceding, disregarding ourselves and our dreams for the sake of the bigger picture. What if we decide we matter enough to pursue a goal or a dream that is a little unpopular (or a lot)? We won't make those changes in leaps and bounds. Change happens over time —like the seasons. Like a plant growing. Like a child becoming an adult. We don't change overnight. We change by increments.

So, you decided your dream matters. That's huge. You listened to yourself. Next time, you might stand your ground a little more. And the time after that, you might even say no to a part of something—find a compromise, or at least let your voice be heard. In time you'll be the woman who chases her dreams with both hands. But for now, you did a big thing. You listened to yourself and you decided your dreams matter.

I feel the warm prick of tears behind my eyes, and I don't even swipe them as they swell, forming a watery lens and blurring my view of the screen slightly.

Wordivore sees me.

The one person who has no idea who I am or what I do just affirmed me in a way I don't think anyone ever has before. And the patient tone of his voice came through even though I've never met him in real life.

And I never will.

I can't, of course.

And tonight, that feels like a bigger loss than the starring role I wish I had taken in the modern Shakespeare adaptation.

NINE

Alana

You don't marry someone you can live with,
you marry the person you cannot live without.
~ P.S. I Love You

"It's an all white party," Mother announces over what sounds like her car phone.

"Okay. All white. I'm assuming I'll need something new to wear."

I'm on my deck this morning, my yoga mat unfurled beneath me, surrounded by the view of treetops and rooftops and the ocean beyond Marbella. Our call is on speaker so I can continue through my poses while we talk.

"Of course—a new dress. Hair, makeup. Some teasers in the press before the event. You've been out of the public eye for too long. I spoke with Caroline yesterday. We need to build a little buzz around you before *Blasted* releases."

Caroline is my publicist. I like her, and she's one of the best at what she does. But Mother and Caroline talking? That's never a good sign. They cook up schemes, and I end up doing things that make me question all my life choices.

"Are you driving?" I ask.

"I am. I have nails and waxing followed by lunch at the club. I felt like driving myself today."

My mother actually often drives herself around the Palisades where she and my father live in their primary residence. They also have a condo nearer to the studios for convenience, and homes in Banff, Lake Como and Maui which are maintained, but only occasionally inhabited.

"And you'll be expected to come with Rex."

"Rex?"

"Your co-star and ex-boyfriend? Don't play coy, Alana."

I sigh. So this is what she and Caroline have worked up? "The tabloids already leaked our breakup over a year ago. We're old news."

Rex and I co-star in a trilogy of films, *Twisted*, *Combusted* and *Blasted*. The plotline follows two spies in love, so of course a real-life romance became a speculation over the course of us working together. Eventually, our publicists—and my mother—determined it would be brilliant to give the public what they wanted. #Faves (Fordham + Graves) became yet another identity I had to sustain. I despised every facet of that pretense, except Rex. He's a decent guy and a hard-working actor. Liking him was a plus. At least if I had to have a fake boyfriend, he was someone I tolerated.

Fans went bonkers for our love story. We had to stage meetups where we could be seen exiting a deli in Beverly Hills, or boarding a private jet in Burbank. People Magazine, TMZ, Page Six, and E! News all ran interviews, which we faked our way through while holding hands and looking adoringly into one another's eyes, saying things like, "It was inevitable that we'd fall after spending that much time together filming."

Our faux relationship had a scheduled end date, like all good time-limited contracts do. We officially announced our breakup, stating we'd remain friendly. We cited the pressure of working on different projects as our reason for ending things. The public bought it all. I was relieved when I could go back to being more authentic with my fans. I abhorred the idea of deceiving them, even though this sort of publicity stunt is done all the time in Hollywood.

That year of deception had a few perks. The world thought I was attached to someone. Online proposals from total strangers died down. I didn't have to entertain the thought of another man. Rex actually was in a secret, real relationship with a model he met in Milan the whole time we were fake dating. I felt for them, having to hide just so we could go public with our charade. His agent and publicist were livid when they found out about Rex's girlfriend. I couldn't have cared less, obviously. I knew if his real relationship came out we'd spin it. As my publicist, Caroline, always says, bad press is still press. On paper it is. In real life, bad press is a bitter pill you either swallow or avoid.

Mom's chatting on about where this screening will be held and how I need to meet her to go dress shopping.

"After the premier we'll slip out for the party at Rooftop by JG atop the Waldorf Astoria." She barely takes a breath before she quips, "I hope you're minding your weight. I told Brigitte to give your size to the shops on Rodeo so they can have dresses set aside for us this afternoon."

"This afternoon?"

"We need to get first dibs on these designs. We'll make a statement, Alana. You will, especially. And the world will eat up this reunification story just in time to set the stage for the premier."

"I don't like it." I speak up. Maybe I'm a little bolder after Wordivore's encouragement.

"I know, dear. I know. But you have to realize, this is simply a form of advertisement. Your product is *Blasted*. You want fans to put that movie on their watch list. What better way than for them to reinvest in your love affair with Rex?"

My love affair with Rex.

My mother would like nothing more than for that "love

affair" to actually materialize. A Hollywood wedding and marriage? Her dream.

I'm not fully opposed to the idea of marriage, or even marrying another actor if I fell in love. A commitment to someone in Hollywood would double the time I spent on red carpets, attended special screenings, and participated in fundraisers. If I were truly in love, all that would be worth it. But, since I'm not in love, I'm not interested in the equivalent of a merger. I've already given enough of myself to this career and lifestyle. I've also gained a lot—and for that I am grateful.

But I have lines. And I've been ignoring them far too long.

Wordivore is right. I hadn't anticipated spilling my guts to him. His compassionate, challenging answer was everything I needed and didn't even know I was waiting to hear. I was drowning. He threw me a life ring. He has no ulterior motive. I'm not paying him. I'm not the heir to his legacy or the key to his next blockbuster. He's just some guy on a word game.

Who would have thought a stranger could end up being the first person to ever truly be in my corner?

TEN

Stevens

We can only sense that
in the deep and turbulent recesses of the sea
are hidden mysteries
far greater than any we have solved.
~ R. Carson

I'm sitting on my sailboat in the harbor admiring some rare underwater shots my friend sent me of the Pacific Hagfish *Eptatretus stoutii*. It's a primitive fish that lives below 600 feet and often far deeper. Gene and I went to grad school together. He's into mixed-air tank diving to extreme depths. He sends me shots like this out of the blue every few months. I'm never disappointed.

I'm so focused on the photos I barely notice Ben climbing aboard my boat.

"Hey, man. What's up?" he asks.

"Hey. Just looking at some photos a friend sent me."

"Photos of ... a girl? His dog? His vacation?"

I turn my phone around and Ben's face is priceless.

He rears his head back and an expression of disgust overtakes his features. "What *is* that thing?"

"It's a Pacific Hagfish. Otherwise known as a slime eel."

"And your friend sent you this pic?"

"Yes."

"Time to get some new friends, my man. That's not the kind of pic friends send friends."

I chuckle. Then I decide to have some fun.

"The slime eel has five stomachs."

"For what?"

"Digestion, of course. And ..." I wait for maximum impact. "They can emit a bucket-full of slime instantaneously when they are frightened or threatened."

"Dude! Gross! And you wonder why you're single. There are some things that should just not be discussed. Even between friends. Buckets of slime are definitely in that category. You do wonder why you're single, don't you? If not, I don't. Not anymore."

He's shaking his head and smiling, but then he shudders and says, "Gross, Dude! Gross!" while he flicks his hands as if they have slime on them, followed by a dramatic demonstration where he sticks his tongue out in sheer disgust.

"Man. How do you expect me to even get in the ocean after your slimy overshare?"

I'm laughing. I flash Ben another photo. I'm an older brother. I know how to poke fun when I'm getting a reaction out of someone younger than me. And this? This is more entertaining than it should be.

"This isn't funny, man." Ben makes a disgusted face again, but then he smiles and shrugs off his reaction. "I'm going to have nightmares of that creature sliming all over me. And to think. I came here to apologize for teasing you about your fanboy crush on Alana Graves."

My laughter dies down at the mention of her name.

"Uh huh. That's what I thought." Ben points at me. "You need to put that phone away."

If he only knew I spent two whole hours with Alana yesterday.

"I'm going to pretend you didn't just show me the world's weirdest creature right now, and do what I came to do."

"That isn't the world's weirdest creature by a long shot," I assure Ben.

"You need to get out a bit more, Stevens. I'm not kidding. Get a dog. Date someone—preferably a human."

"Is that what you came to say?" I stand and walk to the mini fridge in my cabin. "Want something to drink?"

"Do you have pop?"

"I do." I grab a soda and bring it up to Ben. "Sorry. I ... nah. I'm not sorry." I laugh again.

"You've got a dark side, bro. I never knew. You actually enjoyed making me squirm like that."

"I did. I'll admit it."

Ben chuckles and opens his can. "Look, I know I teased you about Alana, but I don't want you to miss out on meeting her just because I was being ... well, me. Summer's serious. If you want to meet Alana, we'll invite her over to a barbecue or something. Just say the word." He pauses. "But you can't talk about that stink eel with Alana—at all."

"Slime eel."

"Whatever. That gigantic sea worm is not up for discussion. Talk about ... normal things. Her movies. Your ... nah. Just her movies, I think we're safe there."

"I appreciate the offer, and you coming out here. I really do. I think I'm good, though."

"She's really not that intimidating. Just keep it in mind."

She is one hundred percent that intimidating. At least, she was at first. On the boat ride home I managed to keep things quiet and chill so she could unwind. She looked like whatever happened in LA took the wind out of her sails, so I just put the boat in motion and did the job I was hired to do.

"I will keep it in mind. Thanks. Want to take the boat out for a bit?"

"Nope. I've got to go. Summer gets really tired these days, so I'm cooking her dinner tonight. I've got to stop by the store to pick a few things up and then I'm going back for a few lessons before I cut out for the day."

"You're a good man, Ben."

"I'd say the same about you ... but, then there's the whole showing your friends inappropriate underwater pics ..." He laughs.

Ben hangs around a little longer. I don't taunt him with photos of creatures who live on the ocean floor. Instead, I ask how he feels about becoming a dad and he gushes. I know I'm smiling the whole time. He's going to be a fun father, for sure. His heart's all in for his family, as it should be.

My phone pings with a text.

"Just a second." I hold my finger up to Ben while I check my cell.

Brigitte: *Layna needs a last-minute ride over to LA this afternoon.*

This afternoon? It's already mid-morning.

Stevens: *When does she need to leave?*
Brigitte: *As soon as you can be ready.*
Stevens: *Give me an hour to clean up and meet her at the dock.*
Brigitte: *Done. And, thanks! (and, just a reminder to delete this conversation now).*
Stevens: *Gotcha. Doing that.*

I hit send and then erase the message thread.

"Who was that?" Ben asks.

"Uh ... Oh. Work."

"You leaving us again for a few days?"

"No. Nah. Just gotta run over to Ventura for a thing. And then I'll be back tonight."

"A thing, huh? Don't you sound all mysterious."

"Uh. Yeah. I guess. Well, I better run. Thanks for coming by."

"It was good to hang out ... all except that eel thing ..." He makes a face. "But seriously, if you want to meet Alana, please let me know and I'll have Summer work something out. It's not every day a man gets the opportunity to meet one of his Hollywood faves. You should take us up on it."

"Yeah. Right. Maybe."

"Okay. Well, travel safely. I'll see you around."

"You too. I mean, I'll see you around. Not travel safely, since you're walking home and then walking back to the shack. So, safety's not exactly an issue for you ... Yeah. I'll see you, Ben."

Ben shakes his head at me and turns to walk away.

He looks back over his shoulder and adds, "I recommend the less is more approach in front of Alana to be safe, though. I'll carry the conversation if we end up getting her to come over."

"Yeah. Agreed."

Ben leaves. I take off right after he does. Less than an hour later I'm on Joel's boat, waiting for Alana as if I meet her every day of my life. No biggie.

She comes speed walking down the dock and starts talking to me before she even tosses me her duffle. "Thank you. I know this is last minute. I hope you weren't doing something more important."

"Than driving you? No." I shake my head. "I was just on my sailboat with a friend. Not sailing. Just hanging out at the docks."

"Sounds lovely."

"It was ... interesting."

Her lips turn up in a half-smile. "This, I have to hear."

I head to the captain's chair, fully expecting her to take the seat at the back of the boat, but she follows behind me, her curls wild from under the ball cap she's wearing—a different one than the one she wore to art class. Her sunglasses are aviators today. They don't do much to hide her identity, but I guess she's only seeing me and then that massive security detail of hers. And she's wearing a pair of jeans shorts, a white T-shirt and a loose coverup with Converse tennis shoes. Her legs are extremely distracting, so I keep my eyes trained on the ocean.

"So?" she asks once I start the engine and back up.

"So, what?"

"The story. What made your time with your friend so interesting?"

"I'm pretty sure you don't want to know."

"Guy stuff?"

I nearly choke on my laugh. "No. Not exactly. I just shared a few pictures a dive buddy of mine sent me. They grossed my friend out. I was teasing him with them."

"What pictures?"

"No. Nope. I ... probably deleted them."

Alana does this thing I've seen her do in a movie. It's a move I've memorized. It's sexy and disorienting, and she's doing it here, now, at me. She pinches the stem of her glasses and slowly lowers them, incrementally unveiling her crystal blue eyes one millimeter at a time. And then she's smirking at me.

"You deleted them?" One brow pops up into a disbelieving arch.

"Okay. I didn't. But, I'd kind of have to jump overboard and never surface if I showed you, so ..."

"Come on!" she teases. "You can't say you showed your friend a gross picture and not share it. That's just wrong."

"Really?"

Am I really going to show Alana Graves a slime eel?

"Yeah. Really. Hand it over. Show me the pictures."

I guess I am. Ben would literally die. Or kill me. I grin

thinking of all he said. He's not wrong. I probably should have kept my mouth shut. Well, there's no turning back now.

Keeping one hand on the wheel, I pull out my phone and stare at it to unlock it with facial recognition. Then I hand it over to Alana.

"It's in my photos. Most recent pics."

She taps a few things and then she starts laughing.

When she speaks, she surprises me. "It's almost so ugly it's cute."

"Really? You're calling a Hagfish cute? Do you know what their nickname is?"

"No. What is it?"

"They're called slime eels."

I hear Ben's voice in my head shouting, *Nooooooo!*

"A slime eel. Do they slime things?"

She's so serious.

"They do, actually. As a defense mechanism."

Look at me, not mentioning the quantity. *Chill out, Ben. I've got this.*

She glances up at me from the photos. "Aren't defense mechanisms fascinating?"

Are you serious? Alana Graves is talking with me about defense mechanisms as if we're on a project together, studying marine life and marveling at it in a moment of shared wonder.

"They are. I think it's fascinating to see all the ways creatures morph or adapt to defend themselves."

I turn my head so I can keep my eyes on the water.

"I guess it's true for us too," she says.

"Humans?"

"Yeah. We learn to adapt and morph."

I nod, and then I glance over at her. She's staring off at the horizon with a pensive expression on her face. I get the feeling she's morphed and adapted a lot over the years. Maybe she's thinking about all the ways right now. Our conversation seems to have stalled, so I stand next to her, and we ride along to the coast-line in silence for the rest of our trip.

ELEVEN
Alana

Life is an improvisation.
You have no idea what's going to happen next
and you are mostly just
making things up as you go along.
~ Stephen Colbert

Brigitte meets us for dress selection on Rodeo Drive. Tank isn't even walking around with us. Rodeo's a place where you'll regularly see celebrities and high-end influencers, business moguls, famous athletes, and wives of the elite Los Angeles crowd. No one cares that I'm Alana Graves here.

We spend a few hours in and out of shops, trying on dress after dress. We finally land on an asymmetric midi-dress by Oscar de la Renta with floral guipure lace overlay. The lace is all that covers me in spots. It's discreet but sexy, and of course, it's white. I feel beautiful in it. And Mother approves. Four thousand dollars later, I'm set for the party.

We say our goodbyes to Brigitte, and I think I see Mom slip Brigitte a hundred dollar tip before she leaves to retrieve her car from the valet. Miguel pulls up not a moment later. The front door of the Town Car swings open and Tank exits the passenger seat to hold the back door open for me and my mother.

"Well, now. I thought I wasn't going to get to show you my dress, Tank. I know you were dying to see what I ended up picking, weren't you?"

I wink just for fun.

Tank nods nearly imperceptibly, but he doesn't crack a smile.

Mother chides me once we're all buckled in. "You really shouldn't tease Ken, darling. He's one of our best."

"We're just having fun, aren't we, Tank?"

I nearly have to scoop my jaw off the floorboards when he actually speaks to my mother. "It's fine, ma'am. She's just having fun."

"If you say so. But you let me know if my daughter makes you uncomfortable. We can't afford to lose you."

"Yes, ma'am."

His voice has notes of something slightly southern. Like he grew up in the south, but left years ago. I'm itching to hear his story. Now I have two bucket list items with Tank's name on them.

"Where to, Mrs. Graves?"

"The Henry, Miguel. Thank you."

We ride along surface streets, out through Beverly Hills and into West Hollywood. Tank gets out once we're at our destination and opens our door. The area is nondescript. The restaurant is one you could nearly overlook amidst white buildings, some one-story, like Chanel across the street, some ten stories high. The Henry has striped awnings and an outdoor patio that faces a clean metropolitan courtyard. The interior is spacious, with a coffee bar and seating, a comfortable lounge area with leather sofas and chairs around trendy wicker petal tables. Past that is the bar and the roomy dining room.

Tank follows us inside and watches until we're greeted by the hostess, then he heads out to sit with Miguel, I guess. A few people stare as Mother and I walk to our table. We're not the only notable people here. I'm wearing designer jeans, a floral top and heels. I've got my Jackie Ohh glasses back on—my shield—but I remove those once we're at our table.

Our waitress approaches and starts into "Welcome to The Henry ... Oh. Wow ..." She quickly composes herself and starts her spiel over. "I'm sorry. Welcome. Can I get either of you a drink before you order?"

Her eyes flit between Mother and me, then she says, "I'm such a huge fan. I've seen all your movies twice. I can't wait for *Blasted*. I know I'm not supposed to say anything. I just couldn't help myself."

"It's no problem," I tell her with a smile. "Would you like me to sign something? Take a photo?"

"Oh my gosh. Would you really? We're not supposed to take selfies with customers, but I'd be so stoked for an autograph." She brings a hand up to her cheek. "I swear I'm not like this with most customers. Famous people come in here all the time. I'm just such a huge fan. I don't even like action movies. My boyfriend got me into them. But I love you and every single film you've been in. You're just ... awesome."

Mother is beaming from across the table. She slides me a piece of thick white paper she just took out of her purse. When I lift it, I realize it's a photo. Of me. My mother is literally carrying around my publicity shots. I shoot her a look of disbelief and she returns it with her version of a self-satisfied smirk.

"Well, look at this, Samantha. It's your lucky day." I glance at my mother again. She's still smiling that supervisory smile of approval. I shift my focus to the waitress whose name tag tipped me off as to what to call her.

"Oh my gosh. Oh my gosh. Ohmigosh." Samantha's fanning herself slightly as I scrawl my name in a flourish and add, *So nice to meet you* underneath.

I hand her the photo and she stares at it with a look of awe in her eyes. I smile up at her, forcing myself not to glance at Mother so I don't feel like such a puppet. I love moments like this. They are sweet, and sincere, and a reward and compensation for so much of what I deal with in other aspects of this lifestyle and career.

"Thank you so so much. You have no idea. My boyfriend is going to lose his mind over this."

"You're not giving it to him, are you?" I ask out of curiosity.

The way she's clutching that photo, he'd better be one heck of a boyfriend to get that from her.

"No way! Are you kidding me? This photo's the first thing I'm grabbing in a fire. He'll have to have his own sighting and accidental meet up. I'm just going to show it to him. And gloat."

I laugh. And Samantha smiles, settling in a little after the initial amazement wears off.

"Can we get our drinks now, dear?" Mother says.

"Oh, yes. I'm so sorry. Please forgive me. I ... Yes. Of course. What can I get you?"

Mother orders for both of us. Something with lime and watermelon. Then she orders our meals. Both vegan and gluten free. The food here is excellent. I smile to myself thinking of Phyllis and her lemon bars. Mom would pop an artery if she had seen Phyllis feeding me the other night.

No sooner has Samantha turned to walk away than a man starts to approach our table from the front of the restaurant. It takes my mind a few beats to register that he's not another fan. No. He's definitely not a fan.

Mom follows my line of vision, turning and grinning and then standing to greet him, lightly grasping his upper arms and placing an air kiss to his cheek.

"Rex! How wonderful!" She exclaims as if she's surprised. "Do join us. Alana, dear, how long has it been since we've seen Rex?"

"A year," I deadpan. "Hey, Rex."

"Alana." He sits next to me, glancing over almost apologetically.

He doesn't seem nearly as disturbed as I definitely am. Obviously my mother picked up on my hesitancy to commit to anything that perpetuated yet another fake relationship with Rex, so she took it upon herself to arrange for us to be seen out together.

"Please, Rex. Order some food and join us." Mother beams at him.

"Thank you."

He looks at me again. "You're looking well, Alana. Rested. How have you been?"

It's not his fault, I remind myself. "I've been great, hiding out, away from the madness."

"That explains it. You look refreshed. I'm glad you're well."

"How is Ingrid?" I ask.

He purses his lips slightly. "We called things off last year. About six months after you and I broke up."

"Oh. Sorry."

"It's fine. She deserves better."

"You do too," I say, meaning every word.

We all deserve better in some ways. We are the privileged, the elite. Rex doesn't elaborate as to what happened between him and Ingrid, but I can guess. Their relationship went the way of so many in our business.

"So," Mother says. "Now that we're all here."

I shoot her a look that makes me feel like I'm thirteen again. I'm a grown woman. I turned thirty last year. I joke around with Joel and with this new water taxi guy. I treat Brigitte like a younger sister. But I'm an adult. And yet, my mother somehow seems to always reduce me to a rebellious teen.

She clears her throat. "I wanted to discuss the details of how this will play out this time."

"Do I get a say in this?" I ask, shooting Rex an apologetic look.

He smiles compassionately at me. He gets it.

"Of course, dear." Mother smiles a tight smile. "And keep your voice down, please."

It occurs to me this setting isn't an accident either. She knows she can make me behave here. Otherwise, the tabloids will run amok with stories of how I came unhinged on Roberts Avenue at an upscale neighborhood eatery.

Rex places a hand over my mother's. "Let's let Alana have a say."

I could kiss him for standing up for me. Of course, me kissing Rex would end up being photographed. Not that I would *kiss him*, kiss him. I'd just plant a friendly kiss of gratitude on his cheek. Like I would a brother, if I had one.

Rex is drop-dead gorgeous. It's an effortless beauty, but with much polishing and some slight augmentation over the years. If you didn't know he was in film, you'd know anyway. He's that beautiful. But I don't feel anything toward him that goes beyond a workplace friendship. It would be highly convenient if we could feel something for one another. I could march along with the Graves parade right into my rightful place as the head of production with Rex at my side.

Instead, I'm that one trombone player, off-key and out of step. The one you notice because she can't quite get with the flow of the rest of the band.

"All I want to say is this," I take a breath and collect myself. "I'm fine being seen with Rex. Fine with some rumors starting—officially. If we plant the seeds for those—whatever—I'll go along. But I'm not doing a whole year of *we're back together* and *are they getting married this time?* A year is too long and it's unnecessary. Our premier comes and goes, we break this off, amicably as we did last time. And then we never pull this sort of stunt again. For one thing, it's not fair to our fans. They get all worked up over something that's never happening. I don't want to feed the machine.

"And secondly, what if one of us actually falls in love with someone, but the world thinks we're with one another? It's messy and inconvenient. So, for now, I'm glad to be seen with Rex here and there. We can do the premier. We'll go out a few times before that. But I'm not doing this for a year ..." I pause, look my mom in the eyes and say, "And that's final."

Rex smiles kindly at me.

Mother takes a sip of her water. She's about to say something when Samantha shows up with our drinks.

"Oh. Wow. Um. You're here too," Samantha says to Rex. She looks between the two of us, obviously drawing a false conclusion —one that thrills my mother deeply. "Wow. Okay. Well, can I get you something to drink?"

"Sparkling water is fine," Rex says with his dazzling smile. "Thank you."

"I'll be right back with that."

When Samantha leaves, I nudge Rex. "She drooled over me. Got an autographed photo she says would be the first thing she grabs in a fire. Sorry you're not her favorite."

He chuckles. "I never could outshine you, Alana."

"True. True," I tease him.

And just like that, we've fallen right back into our comfortable friendship.

I'm glad we're reconnecting. Making movies with other actors is so different from what the public imagines. They picture us all hanging out at one another's houses, raising our kids together, going on vacations with one another. The truth is, a major motion picture takes about two months to film. We're just getting to know one another well by the time we wrap up production and go our separate ways. Of course, Rex and I have done more than one film together, so we have built a rapport and casual friendship.

"See," Mother says from across the table. "You two have chemistry to spare."

"What we have," I say. "Is a friendship."

"Agreed," Rex says. He can't say more or he'll tip the delicate balance that is my mother's good favor.

"Well, friendship can deepen," she states, not so subtly.

The subject of our publicity stunt is abandoned for the duration of our lunch. I'm nearly giddy with the outcome of my newly-stated boundary. And for some reason, I can't wait to get online and tell Wordivore about my success. Only, I can't divulge details about the lines I've had to draw to keep a fraction of my life untouched by fame. In what other universe would two co-workers be forced to put on this kind of a charade? Only in Hollywood.

Over lunch, Rex catches us up on the projects he's been working on since we finished filming *Blasted*. I fill him in on my next role. My mother manages to keep things delightful. She is able to be extremely charming and sweet, usually when she's had her agenda met, but still.

Rex insists on paying. We stand to leave, and I sense a phone being raised in our direction before I even see the person across the room, seated at a table with a friend, snapping a shot of Rex and me. Rex places his hand on my back and leads me out of the restaurant. I fall into my role. This is a show like any other. I just have to follow the script and look believable.

I'm slipping my sunglasses on, Rex still has his palm to my lower back. The door swings open and cameras flash. The din of shouting is like the moment you click the remote and discover the volume was accidentally left at full blast.

The paparazzi are here.

This is not an accident.

We're at a restaurant where influential people come to eat, but many other local residents dine here too. And the surrounding area isn't especially bougie. The press were tipped off.

Rex guides me to Tank who is standing directly down the small set of concrete steps, just outside the waist-high, black wrought iron railing surrounding The Henry. Tank nods to Rex as he opens the gate to let me through. Cameras flash and voices overlap with shouts intended to get me to turn their direction. Rex bends and places a chaste kiss on my cheek. I turn and look up at him.

He leans in and whispers into my ear. "It's going to be okay. This is publicity. It will boost the film. Hang in there." When he pulls away, I smile up at him. Not because I'm in love, but because I'm not alone in this chaos. He's here. We'll muscle through. My boundaries are clear, for once. And Rex is right. The frenzy around our alleged reunification will boost the film.

As soon as we separate, the shouting punches through my awareness. People are screaming my name. "Alana! Alana! Are you and Rex back together? Alana!"

"Rex! Did you leave Ingrid Lund to get back with Alana?"

"How long have you been back together?"

"Look over here!" "Rex!" "Alana!"

Tank swoops his gigantic arm around my shoulders and Rex steps back. I'm ushered into the car, where somehow, my mother already has taken her place in the back seat. The door slams. Tank slides into the front seat. Miguel hits the gas and pulls into traffic, and the sound of people shouting my name dims into the background as we drive away.

TWELVE

Alana

*You can't complain about the pressures,
the paparazzi, the madness.
Because that is the job.
I've always understood that's the deal.*
~ Avril Lavigne

Fatigue sets in on the drive from West Hollywood to Ventura. I must have fallen asleep during the ride. I wake to Tank nudging me.

"Time to go," he says in his deep voice.

"You talked three times today, Tank. I think you just hit your quota for the year."

He stares at me, neutral and wordless, as if his customary nonverbal presence is proof enough that he agrees with me. Still, there's this inexplicable kindness in his non-expression. I can't explain it.

"Thank you." I stand and look up at him, taking the duffle he's holding out. "You did well today. And I don't thank you enough."

"It's my job." Three words. Powerful and sincere.

I nod and smile. Tank walks me to the gate, uses his key to let me onto the dock and shuts it with a clang behind me.

I wonder, as I make my way past the boats to the one that will take me back home. Does Tank have a family? I picture him on a battery charging stand like the one I set my toothbrush on at night, powering down and re-energizing for the next day of serving my family. He and I aren't that different, actually.

Stevens is sitting at the stern of the boat, his feet extended out along the cushions of the bench seating. He's holding a book.

I walk slowly, breathing in the ocean air. Today is behind me. I'm heading home.

"Hey," I say, boarding the boat before Stevens stands to give me his hand.

"Hi. Sorry." He stands and walks over. "I didn't hear you coming."

"What were you reading?"

"Oh. That? Just a book."

I chuckle. "You don't say. What book?"

He laughs. "It's ... uh ... Gone With the Wind."

"What? Really?"

"Would I kid about that?"

"I guess not. Wow."

"Wow that I didn't make up something more manly really quickly? Or wow that I'm reading that book?

"Maybe both?" I smile.

He walks to the front of the boat and I take my spot at the back. "I'm not avoiding you," I shout as the engine starts up. "I just need to space out for a bit."

"Take your time. I'll just be up here, driving."

About halfway across the channel with the wind in my hair and the spray misting my face, my heart finally settles. The crowd of paparazzi feels like a dream I woke from—vague and blurry, insignificant.

I take the seat next to Stevens. He looks over and smiles. It's a far cry from the blundering interaction we had when he first met me. I have to give him credit for getting over his nerves around me so quickly.

"So, hard day?" he asks as if I just got out of any job and am weary from the grind of my work life.

"Yeah. Paparazzi. It's always draining when they show up."

"What's it like?"

I look over at him. He's seriously curious. "Blinding lights in rapid succession. So many voices shouting over one another you can barely make out what they're saying. It's overwhelming, even after all these years."

"How could it not be?"

"I don't mean to sound like a whiner. I'm grateful for my life and career."

"I haven't heard you whine yet."

"Well, it feels like I should just suck it up."

"Being harrassed? Having so little privacy? Everyone wanting a piece of you?" He pauses and looks over at me and then back at the water. "I don't see where anyone should suck that up."

"Yeah. I guess you're right."

We ride along for a little while longer in this silence that's weirdly easy between us. I get the feeling this guy makes everyone feel comfortable. It's in the way he doesn't seem to care what anyone thinks about him.

"You could have made driving me around awkward," I tell him. Then I laugh lightly. "Well, you did."

"I definitely did." He laughs along with me and shakes his head.

"But you moved on pretty quickly. I'm grateful. I usually spend these boat rides across the channel either gearing up for what awaits me or decompressing from whatever just happened. I need my time on the water to be distracting or comfortable. And you've made it both."

"I'm sure Joel is good at helping you get what you need. He's a jokester, but he's got a big heart. And he's a people person."

There's this unspoken sentence hanging in the air: *not like me*. "Joel is great." I look over at Stevens, his brown hair, strong face, kind eyes. "There are lots of ways to be a people person. Not all of them include being the class clown or having been voted most likely to have fifty best friends."

Stevens studies me and then nods as if he's still digesting my words.

I look out across the water. The sun is setting behind Marbella in the distance, smearing a pastel watercolor across the sky. I glance behind me at the shoreline of California.

Everything's smaller from here.

∽

My dinner is in the refrigerator, prepped and left for me as if by a magic fairy. In reality, I have a service drop off healthy meals that fit the parameters of my dietary regimen and I eat off those a few nights a week. I pull the foil tray out, pop it in the convection oven and pick up my phone.

Wordivore left a game open for me to play with him earlier today. His first word sits abandoned on the center of the board. MAXIM, with the X on a double point square. Seriously? Twenty-four points out the gate?

I type: *Are you trying to kill me before I even have a chance to look at my tiles?*

I don't expect an answer, but his cursor roars to life and the three taunting dots appear.

Kill is such a vicious word. I prefer maim ... or even, subdue.

I laugh. I carry my dinner into the living room and curl my legs under me on the couch. The world is a deep blue-gray outside, the sun long since set. Trees form black silhouettes in the night, making me feel like the only things that exist in the world are within this house. My dress went home with my mother. The paparazzi are having their dinners, submitting their photos of me and Rex to their publications or websites and not giving another thought as to how the ripples of their seemingly innocuous stones will impact our lives and the hearts of our fans. And Rex is somewhere in Beverly Hills, running on his treadmill or watching TV with his two yorkies.

Rex.

I push our situation out of my mind, stare out into the treetops and remind myself what my yoga instructor is always reminding me: *be here now.*

Rex isn't here. My mother isn't here. Wordivore is here.

I look over my tiles. Then I smile.

Using Wordivore's X, I add Y-L-E-M. Xylem. It's a plant term. I forget what it means. Playing word games means gathering the oddest collection of vocabulary and stashing it for future use like a cache of weaponry.

Take that. I type.

Oof.

I'm up by one point. And it feels like one hundred.

This is why I choose you. His words are sweet.

Because you're a masochist?

Ha. Possibly. Mostly because you are a worthy opponent. I enjoy a challenge.

I've been accused of being challenging more than once in my lifetime.

We're all challenging in our own way.

I smile. We play for another hour, bantering about the game, but veering away from personal comments.

I've only got a few tiles left when Wordivore types: *Can I ask you a question?* Then he adds, *It seems only fair since you asked me a question.*

I asked you a question to level the playing field. You knew I was a woman. Now I know you are a man.

So that's a no?

Depends

On the question?

Yes.

Well then, I'll have to ask it so you can see if it's one you'll answer.

I smile. *Okay. Ask.*

Do you have any siblings?

Seems harmless. I'll answer.

I don't. I ask him, *Do you?*

Ah ah ah. He mocks me. *If you ask another question, I'll get another one.*

No. We're not even anymore. You know one thing about me I don't know about you. To make it even, you answer me.

He doesn't argue. He simply types an answer, and as his cursor moves, I eagerly await this new revelation about my online mystery man.

I do. I have a brother and a sister. We all live near one another. Always have.

Are you close? I'm suddenly hungry for everything I can find out about him and his family.

There's a pause and then he types: *Pretty close. I'm ...*

The dots blink while I wait to see what he is. He's what? Adopted? An heir to a throne? A red-headed stepchild?

Finally he finishes his thought.

I'm a bit of an introvert. So I don't always initiate time with them, or anyone. But knowing they're right here in the same town as I am is comforting. I think I take them for granted.

Were you hesitant to tell me you're an introvert?

Is that another question? If I'm counting correctly, you already asked one more than I did by asking if I'm close with my siblings. And now this question. If I answer you, do I get to ask another one?

I laugh. This guy.

I don't think those two count as questions.

Beg to differ. But, let's make this simple. Since I told you I was an introvert, you tell me. That's fair, right? Are you? I'm guessing there are more introverts on this app than extroverts. He pauses and types. *And, yes. I guess I was nervous to admit I'm an introvert. I'm surrounded by a lot of extroverts, and my family consists of four extroverts and me. They can treat my introversion like an ailment I'll get over or grow out of one day. I'm sort of the odd one.* He pauses again. Then he types: *Not odd, as in you should run for the hills and block me. Odd as in different from the majority.*

I am a bit of both, I admit. *Introvert and extrovert. I love people. But I need a lot of time alone and I enjoy solitude. People can burn me out. But too much time alone and I get all up in my head, which is not a good place for me to hang out in unsupervised for extended periods of time.*

I hit send and look back over what I wrote and then immediately type: *Now I sound creepy. I promise I'm not.*

So, you're an ambivert. That's what it's called when a person has strong leanings toward both introversion and extroversion.

Well, now you know. I should be a little freaked out by this new level of disclosure, but I'm not—at all. I find myself wanting to tell him more. But I won't. I can't, really.

Now I know. His answer is so simple, but it makes me smile anyway.

THIRTEEN

Stevens

Nothing brings people together like a group chat.
~ Unknown

I have one dive tour this afternoon, but my morning is free, so I'm on my boat in the harbor, reading the last few chapters of *Gone With the Wind*.

I smile thinking of Alana's reaction when I told her what I was reading. I enjoy stories and poems that have spanned generations of readers. It may not be the conventional choice of most men, but I'm not exactly conventional in most things.

My phone vibrates with a text alert. It's the family chat my mother created.

Can I just take a moment to say whoever created group chats should have a close encounter with a slime eel? Not only do you get a notification of the original message, but that's followed by all the thumbs up reactions from every single member of the chat. Then another comment is made which instigates the flurry of hearts, LOL comments, and various emoji reactions. I might feel differently if something significant were actually being said.

Trust me. There isn't.

Mom: Hey, my fam. I'm hoping we can hang for supper.
Dustin: Is this my mother or the teen boy from down the street?
Mitzi: Seriously, Mom. It's not cool to use slang at your age.
Mom: And by my age, you're implying I'm some sort of Karen Boomer?
Me: A what?
Mitzi: I'll translate later.

Against my will, I put a thumbs up emoji in response to my sister's message. See what these group texts do to a person?

Mom: So, are we all down for picky bits?
Dustin: Lost me there, Mom? Could you speak English?
Mom: Bruh. Picky bits. A meal you eat in hot weather that consists of cooler food so you don't sweat trying to cook in the kitchen. Get with the times.
Mitzi: Is anyone else snort laughing?
Me: I'm not. I'm getting a headache, though.
Dustin: Lighten up, bro. And yes, Mom. That's a yes to dinner.
Mom: I'm stoked!

I shake my head.

Me: I can be there.
Mom: Yay! Mitzi?
Mitzi: Do you want me to just bring tacos from the shop?
Mom: Could you? Dad and I will reimburse you.
Dad: #facts

I laugh at Dad's text. My dad is outgoing and a great host, but when it comes to Mom, he steps back and lets her do her thing.

He's probably at work. He goes into Ventura a few times a week to meet with clients. The rest of the time he runs his marriage and family therapy practice here on the island.

Mom: Peace out, fam.

All the heart and thumbs up emojis filter through, and even a GIF from dad of a guy frantically waving from the back of a boat with the caption *BON VOYAGE*. The responses keep pinging until my family wears themselves out and gets back to whatever each of them were doing.

Peace out, fam. I chuckle. My mom. The thing is, she's not trying to be something she's not. She's just prone to picking up the culture around her. And right now, that culture is high school.

I text Mitzi.

Me: Let me know if you want me to bring anything to dinner.
Mitzi: Just yourself. Unless you want to bring a date.
Me: Ha. I'll be solo.
Mitzi: Me too. Seems to be a thing with us Stevens kids.
Me: We do single well.
Mitzi: Poor Mom.

I smile.

Me: She'll survive. I've got a plan. Let's get Dustin a girlfriend. Then Mom will leave us alone.
Mitzi: Bet.
Me: Did you just say, bet?
Mitzi: Hahahaha. Just playing with you. But I am down for fixing Dustin up so we can get off the "when are you going to start dating someone" radar. Let's give this some serious thought.

Me: You know lots of people. All my friends are couples.
Mitzi: On it. See you tonight.
Me: See you. Love you, Mitz.

I set my phone aside, kick back and finish my book. After a light lunch, I head to the shack to meet the group I'm taking out for a dive in a cove just north of the resort. We use one of the Kodiak inflatable rafts provided by the Alicante for these kinds of tours.

Kai's in the watersports shack with Jeremiah and Bodhi when I get there. I greet the three men.

"I've got your tanks out already," Kai tells me. "Want to check them over and top them off?"

I nod and follow him through the shop and out the back door.

"So, you've been MIA this week," Kai says.

I pull the first tank over to the air compressor and start to work.

"I've been working some per diem jobs, privately. And I had an assignment in Avila checking radiation impact from the Diablo plant over the past two days."

"You're such a stud," Kai says casually. "And you don't even know it. Do you?"

I study his face to see if he's teasing me. He looks sincere. "I guess not."

"It's impressive—all the things you know. We need to find you some nerdy woman who likes to talk about marine life and play word games in her spare time."

I instantly think of how Alana Graves reacted to the photos of the slime eel. Of course, she's not nerdy—not in the least. And she's also obviously not the one for me—not at all, considering I nearly lost my mind when I first met her. Besides, according to my mom, Alana's got some celebrity romance rekindling, anyway. I always take all of that kind of information with a grain of sand.

Rumors need to be substantiated by proof, and not merely an image in a tabloid which could mean anything.

My mind shifts to SaturdayIslandGirl. If she didn't live in Bora Bora ...

"You're thinking of someone," Kai says—perceptive as ever.

"It's no one."

"Oh, no. No one is someone. Who is this girl?"

"Really. It's inconsequential. Basically an impossible situation."

"You think you get to say, impossible situation, and then take off for a dive tour without filling in the blanks on that? No. Just tell me about her."

"She's a woman on the word game I play. We compete regularly. Sometimes we're on there for hours together."

"You're spending hours playing the equivalent of online Scrabble with this woman?"

I nod.

"Like, once a week? Or more often?"

"Four or five nights a week, and then we leave games open for one another to play on when the other person isn't available."

"Four or five times a week? You're spending eight to ten hours a week with this woman. Do you two chat?"

"We do. But we just recently started sharing significant details about ourselves. Before that it was just banter about the game. Smack talk."

Kai laughs hard. "Smack talk over a word game. Oh, man. That's rich."

"It's cutthroat."

He laughs some more.

He doesn't get it. He's physical—an ex-pro surfer. Competition for him involves his body. For me, it's my mind—and hers.

"She calls herself Saturday Island Girl. I think she lives in Bora Bora or the Caribbean."

Kai raises a brow. He knows the oceans of the world. He's

surfed over half of them. "Dude. That's a broad range of possible locations."

"I haven't narrowed it down."

"Obviously." He chuckles.

"I've gathered data. I'm still in need of more information before I can determine anything conclusive."

"Are you cyberstalking this woman?"

"What? No. I'm just developing hypotheses from what she gives me."

"Sounds like you like her."

I can't help but smile. "I can be different with her."

Kai's quiet. He passes me another tank and I turn the compressor on to fill it.

"I'm not nervous around her at all. Besides, she has no idea what I look like, so I know everything we say is authentic."

"Authentic?" Kai chuckles. "She could be an eighty-year-old man. Or a lonely housewife who lives in sweats and has ten kids, but is actually married to a man who's too busy with work to pay enough attention to her."

I'm horrified. "She's not."

"You don't know that."

"I do."

"You. The man of science? You are going on what? A hunch?"

"Hunches are some of the best starting points of science. We sense things outside our awareness. It's a fact that the brain only raises a fraction of what we see and hear, smell, touch, taste to our awareness. The rest filters in. We simply don't acknowledge it. So, hunches aren't so mysterious. And I know she's a woman. She's actually beautiful."

"How do you know that?"

"I just know."

"Then she knows you're not ugly."

"Nah."

"I bet she does. Does she flirt with you?"

"Flirting? I don't know if you'd call it flirting?"

"Tell me this. Did she always know you were a man?"

"No. She just recently found out. My gamer tag on Play on Words is Wordivore. No gender is evident. She had to ask."

"And she asked. That means she was thinking about you." Kai's eyebrows lift quickly and he flashes me a grin. "And did she act more flirty—warm, open—after that detail was revealed?"

I consider Kai's question. He may be on to something. It doesn't matter because SaturdayIslandGirl lives so far away. This is not a realistic line of thought to pursue.

"It really doesn't make a difference. It's not like we're going to start an actual relationship."

"You never know. Weirder things have happened."

My dive group shows up after Kai and I finish filling the last of the tanks. We spend three hours in the water, plus the short boat ride over to the cove and back. Once the equipment is cleaned and stored, I head to Mom and Dad's for family dinner.

Mom greets me at the door. I'm the last one to arrive. The sounds of Mitzi and Dustin's voices carry through to the front room from the kitchen.

"Everyone's here." Mom's face looks less cheerful than I'd expect considering all three of her grown children are under one roof for the evening.

"Are you alright?" I instinctively reach out and pull her into a hug.

She clings to me and takes a deep breath. I think I hear a sniffle.

"You'll know soon enough," she mumbles her words into my chest.

Dad comes out from the study.

"Everything okay?" I ask him over Mom's head while she still has a death grip on me like a barnacle to a barge.

"You'll hear about it at dinner." Dad pries Mom off me. "Come on, Judith. Let's enjoy dinner with our three kids."

I leave Dad to comfort or cajole Mom, whatever it is she needs, and walk through to the kitchen where Mitzi's laying out an assortment of tacos from her restaurant onto a platter next to a massive tin pan of beans and another of Spanish rice.

"Hey," she says to me. "Grab the salsa and guac out of that bag, would ya? And put a spoon in each."

I get busy following my sister's directions.

"I might be called out on the wildfires near Malibu this week," Dustin says by way of greeting.

"Is that what has Mom so worked up?"

I wouldn't think she'd get upset over Dustin going on fires. He's a volunteer here on the island and often pitches in on the mainland when needed. His primary job is split between solo music gigs at local bars and nightclubs and other events, and being a bouncer. Where I'm tall and lean, Dustin is built like a house.

Dustin and Mitzi share a look. Then Mitzi says, "You'll hear soon enough."

"That's what Mom said," I tell her. "I'm ready to hear now, thank you."

"I'm leaving," Dustin says.

He and Mitzi glance at one another again.

"For the fires?"

"Yes, and no. I'm ..." .

Mom walks into the kitchen with Dad right on her heels. "He's enlisted."

"In the military?" My confusion carries through in my voice.

My brother never even liked getting into the usual scrappy fights boys would pick with one another in elementary and junior high school. He's a bouncer, but his gift in diplomacy is how he handles ninety-nine percent of the situations that other men might handle with force. Besides, this is Marbella. The usual night for a bouncer involves telling a teen who's here on vacation that they can't enter Club Descanso.

"Not military," Dad supplies.

"Fire," Dustin says. "I've been accepted to a station in a small town called Waterford."

"I've never heard of it," I tell him.

"You've never heard of it because it's in Tennessee!" Mom throws her hands up as if Tennessee is also in Bora Bora. Maybe we can make a trip of it and I can meet SaturdayIslandGirl while we visit my brother.

"I think we had a little heads up that this was coming," I say in my talk-you-down-off-the-ledge tone of voice. "Maybe when he got his bachelor's in fire technology?"

"I'm right here," Dustin says.

I nod at him, but I keep on. He's diplomatic, but I'm the family balancer. I usually step in when things are off-kilter and help everyone see each others' sides of a situation.

"And also when he spent summers volunteering on wildland crews. I'd say we had more than a fair amount of data to lead us to conclude that Dustin was going in this direction. Objectively speaking."

Mom makes a "pfft" sound. "You've been doing all those regular gigs around the island, and even those few in Oxnard and Ventura. I thought you wanted to get into music. I'm fine with you choosing a career in firefighting, but why Tennessee?"

She looks up at my Dad who's standing right behind her. "It's so far. We've all been here on Marbella since before Ren was born."

Mom's face contorts with sadness. My brother looks equally distraught, like he's five seconds from breaking into tears.

"Mom, it's not that I want to leave you. It's not always easy to get a position at a fire station. You have to wait for an opening, and they have to accept you. You know all this. I'd love to stay here. But I also want to explore other places. I've spent my whole life living in this bubble. I want to see what other parts of the world are like while I'm still young."

"You don't need to. Your father and I have done that for you. We traveled before we had kids and found the best place of all here on the island." Mom's voice has a note of finality to it, even though she knows Dustin is not going to be swayed—or at least, I think she knows.

She's being unreasonable, grasping at straws. We all know it. I can't blame her. This is a bomb dropped and detonated. I've never lived further than ten miles from my brother. Sure, he leaves to volunteer on fires or to play the occasional off-island gig. I have to leave a few days a week to assess something underwater. But we always come back here—to Marbella—back home.

Mom dabs her eyes with one of the paper napkins Mitzi brought from the restaurant. Mitzi and Dad immediately flank Mom.

"It's just a lot to swallow," Mom sniffles. "I know I'm being delulu thinking you'd all be here with me and Dad forever. I'm just full of beige flags."

"Delulu?" Dustin asks.

At least I'm not the only one who needs a translator for Mom's hip lingo.

She scoffs. "Delusional."

And ... dare I ask? I have to, though. "And beige flags?"

"They're between green and red," Mitzi explains.

"Huh?" Dad asks.

"It applies when you're thinking about dating someone," Mitzi tells us. "There's green flags. Red flags. Beige flags. The beige flags aren't green or red."

"Why mention them then?" I ask.

Mitzi shakes her head like I'm hopeless. No one points out how Mom totally misused the term and I'm surely not about to—not after Dustin dropped the news he did. I am going to have to talk with him. I would have liked a heads up. I wonder if Mitzi already knew. Nope. I don't even have to ask. I'm sure she knew. She didn't even flinch when Mom brought it up. I'm almost always the last person in the family to know about things like this.

One person comes to mind. It should bother or surprise me. But it doesn't.

I can't wait to chat with SaturdayIslandGirl about this new development in my family.

FOURTEEN

Alana

Don't grow up too quickly,
lest you forget how much you love the beach.
~ Michelle Held

A week of being back on Marbella since our day spent shopping on Rodeo has been nearly utopian. Mother called the day after we were hounded by the paparazzi to rave about the publicity stunt she orchestrated. The media gobbled the story up like seagulls at a spilled trash can. Now, as far as the public's concerned, Rex and I are either getting back together, actually already engaged, or his body was taken over by an alien and I'm carrying his alien love child.

Gotta love the tabloids.

I put all that out of my mind since my mother's call and have spent my days doing yoga, gardening my flower beds, reading, and playing on the online game. Wordivore hasn't been on in person for three days, and I weirdly miss him.

I just finished swimming laps and I'm curled on my bed in my fluffy robe.

I pull up the app on my phone.

Wordivore's profile says, *Online.*

I open a board and my tiles spill into place at the bottom of my screen. Then I hit *Invite.*

Wordivore shows up. I'm studying my tiles when he types a sentence in the chat.

Remember how I told you my siblings and I are close?

Usually we open with some taunt about the game, or another more neutral comment. I'm not averse to him making conversation. A part of me actually likes the fact that he feels comfortable to open with something this personal. And, I'll admit it, I'm intrigued as to what he's going to say.

Yes. Did something happen?

It most definitely did. Tonight, we were having a family dinner. My brother dropped a bomb. He's moving away to another state here in America.

He pauses and then he types: *Everything will be different when he leaves.*

So, Wordivore's in America. I figured as much, since we play in English. But with online things, you never know. I toss around whether I should answer him with what's in my heart or keep things a little more neutral. Wordivore helped me so much with my last struggle. I sort of owe him the same kind of encouragement he gave me.

I decide to go all in. I won't tell him who I am or what I do, but I'll share from the heart.

In my line of work, I do a lot of short-term projects that last only a few months at a time. Just when I'm starting to get to know the people (who I'm spending ten to twelve hours a day with), my workload changes and I'm surrounded by a new group of people.

There are those people who are with me through it all, but I am constantly moving from one project to the next. My situation is not the same as having siblings. I just want you to know I do sort of relate to having to let go of someone before you're ready to. And I don't know where your sibling is going, but I imagine you can still visit. Am I right?

You are. And now you have me very, very curious as to what you do for a living.

Next question, please. That's one I'm definitely not answering.

Are you a mural painter?

No. I chuckle.

Do you travel from farm to farm training goats?

No. My smile spreads across my face, filling me with an odd warmth.

You can't be in the circus. Those people travel together. Maybe you're a traveling saleswoman. Door to door sales of cleaning supplies, miracle diet products ... No! Solar panels. Tell me you're not a solar saleswoman. I don't know if we could still be friends. Those people show up at all hours asking if you've considered solar.

Not solar, I type.

You're in the rodeo.

Sorry to disappoint. Not in the rodeo. I turn the tables on him. This line of questioning has to be shut down. *How about you? What do you do for work?*

Ah ah ah. He playfully chides. *I won't show mine if you don't show yours. Maybe you need to ask me something else.*

Maybe. I think that's enough disclosure for one night, though.

Fair enough, he answers.

I wouldn't mind learning what he does—and a lot more about him. But I can't tell him what I do because that will lead to who I am. And he can never know that.

We play for nearly two hours without any other personal conversation. Wordivore beats me by twelve points in the end. I'm more relaxed and content than I've been nearly all week.

When we go to say goodnight, he types: *Have fun training goats tomorrow.*

And you have fun doing whatever it is you do.

I'll give you a hint, he says.

Okay. I sit up a little straighter waiting for one more detail about his life outside our online interactions.

He types: *It's not training goats. I leave that to the experts.*

I smile. *Goodnight, Wordivore.*

Goodnight, SaturdayIslandGirl.

～

Brigitte arrived an hour ago like a cloud of rainbow smoke fireworks. She's loud and bold and beautiful, filling my home with life.

"I love the dress you're going to wear to the premier!" she lets out a low, appreciative whistle from her spot on one of my wicker porch chairs where we've been relaxing with homemade smoothies I whipped up for us. "Can't wait to see it on you with your hair and makeup done. You are going to rock that thing like ..." Brigitte raises both hands in the air and shimmies while she says "Come on ... wobble wit it ... Uh. Uh. Uh."

I crack up. "You're crazy. You know that."

"That's what my date said."

"In a good way, I hope."

"Jury's out. He literally said some version of, 'You're crazy,' like five or six times during our date. I started out agreeing with him, like he was complimenting me for my unique brand of personality. But by the end of the night I thought I might need to look over my shoulder to make sure he hadn't called in the guys in white coats."

I chuckle. "If he did, his loss. You are a catch and a half."

"Right? Plus. I work for this awesome movie star."

"That's not your appeal. Trust me. You don't want a guy that would want you because you're close to me."

"Which is why I tell people I'm a personal assistant. I don't say to whom, and I definitely don't divulge how actually I'm such a bad mammah jamma for keeping your life in order." She curls her fingers into her palm, brushes her fist just below her shoulder and pulls her hand back to blow across her nails.

"You are the baddest mammah jamma," I agree. "I don't know what I'd do without you."

"As you should wonder. It would be a flaming hot mess. I even take calls from Mother Gothel all week long for you. That alone deserves a raise."

I shake my head at the thought of my mother hounding Brigitte. "Do you want a raise?"

"Shut up. Just hush. If I wanted a raise, you'd know it. I'd say, 'Alana, give me a raise.'"

She rolls her eyes like I'm ridiculous for not knowing better. I love her unapologetic presence. She's so unaffected by people.

As always, Brigitte shifts subjects like a roulette wheel, "I'd literally die to go a white party."

"Well, I'd love it if you were at this party."

"To see you with Rex?"

"Ugh. Don't remind me. He's great, and I'm thankful that he's the one I'm shackled to. We could have done way, way worse. But ... I hate that we're back in this dance of faking it for the press."

"I hear you. Really. But stop and see things from the point of view of one of the people who does their own dishes."

"I do my own dishes," I protest.

Brigitte rolls her eyes. "And laundry?"

I have no answer.

"That's what I thought. And you do your dishes after you eat a meal curated and prepared for you by someone else." She pauses. "I'm not berating you for that. You earn all of it. If you had round the clock servants, which you could obviously afford, and one of them had the sole job of filing your nails and picking your nose for you, it would be justified."

"Ewww. And, no thank you. I'll pick my own nose, thank you very much."

We both laugh.

A breeze blows through the treetops—the kind that only blows in off the ocean, just to remind you how close the water is to wherever you are on this island. I breathe it in, closing my eyes for a moment to let Marbella work its magic on me.

"Anyway, from my POV," Brigitte says. "Here you are, getting to dress up in this gorgeous gown, have your hair and makeup done by other people, and walk into an exclusive premier and then a rooftop party on the arm of one of the hottest bachelors on the planet. I'm not crying for you. Not even a drop."

"Well, when you put it that way."

"Right?! Suck it up, buttercup. Have some fun being the princess, even if you are locked in a tower by the evil mother. Just keep a frying pan with you at all times."

"A frying pan?"

"Duh. *Tangled?*"

"What?"

"Do not even tell me you don't know what *Tangled* is. The cartoon adaptation of the Rapunzel story?"

"Oh. Yeah. I heard of it."

"Heard of it? Heard of it! What?!! You haven't watched it, like a minimum of ten to one hundred times?"

I laugh at her outrage.

"Stand up. We've got a movie to watch. And then you're taking me hiking so I can have a sighting of those wild monkeys that live on the uninhabited side of this island."

After a few hours curled up on my couch watching a movie, that yes, does bear an uncanny resemblance to some aspects of my life, Brigitte and I take the golf cart she acquired at the resort and drive to a trailhead where the path traverses along hills and cliffs on the back side of Marbella.

It's true, rogue wild monkeys inhabit this portion of the island, along with other non-native species who were brought here for a film years ago and now have populated the area.

Brigitte has her binoculars and is searching for wildlife while I'm along for the ride, hiking down the switchback that leads to a cove at the bottom of the trail. The coastline feels more rugged here and we seem to be the only two people out right now. It's a fact that many residents of the island have never even been to this side of Marbella. They prefer staying on the developed side that faces California rather than the wilder areas facing the wide-open ocean.

We reach the bottom of the trail where jagged cliffs form a perfect semi-circle around a white-sand beach. Tide pools line one side of the cove and the water laps up onto shore and washes back out in a soothing rhythm.

"I want a selfie—the two of us!" Brigitte says. "This is the perfect spot with the crystal-clear water in the background. Come here."

Brigitte climbs onto a large, flat rock near the water's edge and strikes a dramatic pose, then she curls her finger, inviting me to join her.

"Okay. Okay," I concede.

I never mind taking photos with Brigitte. She doesn't post them, and she always sends me a copy to keep for myself.

I hop up onto the rock next to Brigitte. But the surface is slicker than I anticipated. I start flailing around and lose my balance. Brigitte grabs for me, but that only serves to throw her off too. We cling to one another, screaming, eyes wide.

"Ahhhh!" I topple into the shallow water on the other side of the rock with a splash.

"Ohhhh my gosh! Alana!" Brigitte follows me only seconds later.

I sit up, my hair and clothes soaked.

Brigitte looks over from where she's sitting up to her waist in water and starts laughing.

She holds up her phone. "I got that on film! And my camera's still running!"

I try to stand, but I'm laughing too hard, so I fall back down, which only makes me laugh harder. My hair is dripping water down my face and neck. My shirt and pants are soaked.

Brigitte and I look like twin drowned rats, but we're both cracking up.

Brigitte jumps up. "Something tickled me! Or nibbled! What is it? What is it? It's near my ankles. I'm being attacked!" She snaps up and then she's doing some sort of high-knee run out of the waves, flailing her arms and squealing. "Ahhh! Is it following me? What is that slimy tickle fish? Get it away from me!" She runs onto shore and turns to look back where she came from.

I walk toward the spot where she had landed and see her "assailant" just beneath the surface.

I grab a hold of it and hold it in the air. "This?"

"Uh. Yeah." She places a palm on her abdomen and bends in laughter.

"Seaweed, Bridge. It's seaweed." I chuckle, tossing it back where it came from.

A deep male voice surprises me. "Yes, but that's a particularly dangerous variety. The seaweed around here has a reputation for sneak attacks on unsuspecting women."

I turn toward the voice.

Stevens, the guy who has been taxiing me from Marbella to the mainland this week is waist-deep in the gentle waves, shirtless. The top of his board shorts are just barely visible above the sloshing of the water around him. A snorkeling mask is perched on his wet hair while the snorkel dangles next to his face.

He looks different. Relaxed. Scrumptious. *What?* No. Well, yes. But, no. Obviously, no.

Brigitte is looking between me and Stevens, realizing we know one another.

She sticks her hand out. "Hi. Brigitte. And you are?"

Stevens sluices through the water with purposeful strides. He'd never fall off a rock. He's far too surefooted and seemingly built for the ocean. He's like Poseidon, emerging from the depths with a swagger and confidence that belies the fifteen minutes of our first encounter at Joel's boat. This man is not that man—not at all—and yet, he is.

"Stevens," he says, shaking Brigitte's hand. "Wait. Brigitte?"

"Stevens?"

"Yes!" They both exclaim at the same time.

"Alana," he smiles broadly at me. "Forgot your suit?"

I laugh, tipping my head to the side to wring some water from my hair and then scrunching it out of habit, to shape the curls as they dry.

"We weren't exactly planning on swimming," Brigitte says, beaming up at Stevens.

"We were taking a selfie and I slipped," I explain.

He smiles and his mouth tips up on one side, revealing a dimple I hadn't noticed before.

"Did you get the selfie?"

"We did!" Brigitte exclaims.

"Good. Good. Well, next time you want to check out this cove, let me know. I'm glad to take you two out in proper gear."

"Snorkeling?" Brigitte asks.

"Yeah. Or diving. Whatever you want."

"Sounds amazing." She looks over at me. "Doesn't it, Alana?"

"Yeah. Amazing. Right. That would be great."

Stevens looks at me with a question on his face.

"We'd better head back," I say. "Brigitte has to catch the ferry this afternoon."

Stevens nods in that calm, steady way of his. "Sounds good. I'll see you later, Alana. If you need a ride, that is."

"Nice to meet you," Brigitte gushes.

We're only halfway across the sand when my assistant turns and glances over her shoulder at Stevens again. "That man is beautiful. Why didn't you say something? You've been riding back and forth across the channel with him all week and you never told me he was a hottie."

I chuckle. "It didn't seem relevant."

"Oh, it's relevant, alright. Gah. Did you see him coming up out of that water like some merman returning to land? What a vision. He's gorgeous. And he seems so kind."

"He is," I agree.

"Too bad," she coos.

We reach the trail and turn up the first switchback, giving me the perfect vantage point to watch as Stevens grabs a towel that was sitting on a rock where I didn't even notice it before. He runs it across his hair, ruffling it dry and then shakes the rest of the droplets loose while he drapes the towel over his shoulders. Then he turns and picks his snorkel and mask off the rock where he set them. I'm imagining he's going to follow us up the trail, but he stays on the beach, staring out at the ocean with the look of a man in love written all over his face. He loves the ocean. And the feeling seems to be mutual.

"What's too bad? I ask Brigitte, shaking myself from watching my substitute water taxi pilot.

"Too bad you're a movie star. He couldn't take his eyes off you. And I'm certain it wasn't because you're Alana Graves. He likes you."

"He's been good to me this week. I think that's just his way with everyone. You did it again, Brigitte. As always. You found a great man to transport me."

"Hmmm," she hums thoughtfully. Then she adds, "Stinks to be you sometimes."

I don't even ask her to elaborate. Instead, I take one more glance down into the cove to see Stevens sitting on the sand in his swim trunks, his arms wrapped loosely around his knees as he gazes off into the ocean.

FIFTEEN

Stevens

I can't see anything that I don't like about you.
~ Eternal Sunshine of the Spotless Mind

S*o, I couldn't sleep last night.* I start typing before our tiles are even dealt.

SaturdayIslandGirl answers me: *Really? What kept you from sleeping?*

The first move is mine, so I pause, leaning back in my hammock to consider my options. But my mind drifts to the relaxing afternoon I spent snorkeling on the back side of the island. And then, the biggest surprise of all, I bumped into Alana and her assistant. Seeing her away from Joel's boat was momentarily jarring. And, she wasn't just anywhere. She was in my cove —not mine, mine, but the one where I go regularly for a private snorkel.

After Alana and Brigitte left, I sat on the beach, watching the waves roll in and out, enjoying an afternoon with no agenda. Then I stopped by Dustin's so he could tell me about the plans for his move to Tennessee. He and I ended up grabbing burgers, and now I'm here, in my back yard laying in my hammock, watching the sky turn colors as the sun starts to set.

SaturdayIslandGirl types again: *Are you going to tell me what kept you from sleeping, or are you just throwing your insomnia out there and leaving me hanging?*

I smile. She always makes me smile the kind of smile that starts somewhere behind my rib cage and spreads to my face. It's a blend of contentment, intrigue and desire I've never felt before.

Why does she have to be on the other side of this screen—and this planet?

Sorry. I was studying my tiles so I didn't answer you. I couldn't sleep because I kept wondering what you do for a living.

I lay down AQUEOUS, placing the Q on a double point space.

Hold that thought, she types. *I have to focus after you laid down twenty-six points to start the game.*

I smile. She's a true competitor. Whatever she does, I have no doubt she's the best at it. It's funny how much I know her, and yet, I don't know her at all.

Not even a minute later, she types: *Aha! Take this!* and she lays down CUMQUAT, using my Q and gaining a four point lead, just like that.

How did you do that? I marvel.

I'm a woman of many talents.

One of which is your mysterious career path, I retort.

And you actually lost sleep wondering what I do for a living?

Okay, maybe only a few minutes passed while I was wondering about it before I settled in and got my usual eight hours.

Ha. Okay.

So, permission to ask … What do you do? Because, to be honest, I've narrowed it down to a few more options than my original guesses.

Oh? Do tell.

I smile. She sounds flirty. Maybe Kai was right.

I've been planning what I'd say to SaturdayIslandGirl for most of the day. Here we go ...

First: CIA or a spy. You go on missions for a few months at a time. Then you're reassigned. You can't get emotionally invested because your country needs you. You sacrifice romance for patriotism. Of course you can't admit this to me, or you'd have to have me hunted down and captured—or worse.

The dots appear on her side of the chat box. *I just snort-laughed and inhaled a part of my smoothie.*

I have that effect on women. I joke. It's something I'd probably never say in person, but here, online, I'm less inhibited—or maybe it's just her.

You make women snort and choke?

Now I'm laughing. *Not exactly. That didn't end up sounding as smooth when you repeated it back to me as I thought it did when I typed it.*

Neither of us type anything in the chat box for a moment. I spell TREBLE off her T in CUMQUAT.

Eight points? She types.

It's the lack of sleep, I joke. *It's throwing off my game.*

The lack of several minutes of sleep you lost imagining I'm a spy?

Exactly. And I'm gathering from your answers that I hit the nail on the head. You're a spy.

She lays down BACCHIC, using her own C in CUMQUAT to build the eighteen point word. She's fourteen points ahead now.

Bacchic, what is that? It's new to me.

It's something about being riotous. And, I've got a confession.

Oh. I'm all ears. Is it that you're a spy?

Ha! No. It's not that. I've been reading up on vocabulary words ... and I subscribed to the Word of the Day on four platforms.

Mm hmm. Stockpiling weapons, I see. Well, you wouldn't be a competitor if you didn't arm yourself properly.

Then, without missing a beat, she types: *You are eerily close in one odd detail of what you guessed I do for a living, but if I say that as my official answer, it will throw you off.*

Well, that's not cryptic at all.

Stop making me laugh.

Nevahhhhh! (Insert evil laugh).

She types a laughing emoji. And then asks: *What's your other guess?*

Guesses. Plural. More than one guess. I've been giving this a significant amount of thought.

Okay, well, what's your next guess?

I chuckle.

You are a bank robber. Or jewelry thief. You work heists in various cities. Can't stay still or you'll be caught. You are on America's Top Fifty Most Wanted list. You actually work for the mafia. No. No. You're related to the head of the mafia. You have a strong accent, much like the Godfather, but you're a female, so ... the Godmother?

It's dead silent on her end. Did I go too far?

Then the dots appear. *Oh. My. Gosh. I literally ... no. I can't tell you.*

All these secrets are killing me slowly. I tease. *You know that, don't you? What did you just do?*

Okay. Okay. I laughed so hard, I spit out what was in my mouth and dribbled smoothie down my shirt. I had to get up and go to my bedroom. I'm grabbing a clean shirt to change into. Give me a minute.

I smile, loving the fact that I made her laugh that hard.

The screen goes dead on her end for a minute. Then she comes back. *So, I'm not sure I can take many more guesses at this point. You're dangerous. I may have to wear a bib, or hire someone to come steam clean if we keep this up.*

Alright. My final guess. I smile as I type. *You teach indigenous tribes TikTok dances. Your official title is Ambassador of Funk and Groove. You roam the earth spreading the viral trends to unreached people groups. You're out there on a mission until every person knows how to dance the Toosie Slide and the Whoa.*

Oh. My. Gosh ...

The cursor just blinks. Then three dots.

You ... guessed it!

I knew it! I'm laughing. I hope she is.

I couldn't breathe through my laughter for a minute. I wish you could hear how hard you had me laughing.

I hesitate, but then I type. *Me too.*

It seems like I'm simply agreeing, but this urge to hear her laugh feels strong enough to spur me into investigating what it would take to travel to the South Pacific for a quick visit.

Where did you learn about the Toosie Slide and the Whoa? she asks.

Maybe I'm a traveling TikTok instructor too. It's destiny that we met.

She doesn't respond to my destiny comment, but she types: *I'm getting T-shirts and merch with that title: Ambassador of Funk and Groove. It might not have been mine before, but I'm claiming it now. And, after all the effort you obviously put into those guesses, and to spare you the insomnia, I'll have mercy on you.*

There's a long pause as if she's deliberating. I'm seriously curious why she's so hesitant to simply tell me what she does for a living. It's not like I'll actually be booking a flight to the Caribbean or Bora Bora to meet her once I hear her profession. That would be fruitless. Our situation is strictly online. I'm honestly a little disappointed.

I'm going to tell you, she writes by way of a preface. *I ...*

There's another pause.

The suspense is excruciating.

Why? Why do I care so much? It's not as if we're going to meet—ever.

Finally, she writes, *I'm in theater.*

Theater? Like doing plays? Like acting on stage? Or directing?

Or are you a stage hand? A gaffer? (I don't know what that is. I just heard the term. Or is that in film? Anyway, are you a gaffer?)
Something like that.
Something like being in plays or directing? Or something like a gaffer—which I just looked up? They run the lighting and electricity on a television or movie set, in case you didn't know. Great word to keep handy if you have a G and two Fs.
We've abandoned the game and are just chatting for now.
My job is something in the wide world of theater. And that's all I'm giving you for now.
I've always wondered if working in theater makes enough to live on. No offense.
I get by.
She lays down I-V and then S to build HIVES off the H in BACCHIC and the E in AQUEOUS.
She's not typing anything else in the chat. Maybe I offended her. I don't want her to be embarrassed if she doesn't make a lot of money doing whatever it is she does in theater. I truly was curious.
Just to be sure, I apologize. *Sorry. I didn't mean to bring up your salary. As long as you're doing something you love and it pays, that's all that matters. Right?*
Right. Definitely. So, turnabout's fair play. What do you do, Wordivore?
I stare at the screen. Her answer of *something in the wide world of theater* was obviously not a full disclosure, so I'll meet her with the same level of revelation. It's not that I don't want her to know I'm a Marine Biologist. I just want to hold my cards close so I have bargaining chips too. If she learns all about me, I'll have no enticing secrets to barter when I want to learn more about her.
I type: *I'm on-call.*
Like a doctor?
Something like that. I borrow her phrase and return it to her.
We aren't being honest, are we? As if she has to ask.
We're carefully peeling back a layer, I say. *At our pace.*

131

Agreed.

I promise not to judge you if you tell me the truth, I assure her.

Maybe one day.

Same here.

⌁

How did I let Ben talk me into yet another gathering where I'm the ninth wheel? I already know the answer to that question: Ben. He's as persuasive as a puppy dragging his own leash to the door and then looking up at you with those pleading eyes. It's a brand of charm I'll never acquire, and also, apparently, one I'll always succumb to.

This time the barbecue is at Ben and Summer's. I offered to bring a side dish, so I come bearing my mom's famous potato salad. I made the salad this afternoon after taking a group of marine biology interns out on *Catching Wishes*. We trawled the waters and, not surprisingly, everyone held the sea cucumber on that tour. I partner with the UC schools to offer hands-on opportunities several times a semester. It's a nice break from everything else I do with my degree and experience.

"Hey! Hey! Hey!" Ben answers the door with his arms open wide. "Look who's here! He didn't shy away, babe!"

Summer steps up behind Ben, extending her hands for the bowl of potato salad.

She looks at her man-child of a husband and says, "I told you he would be here."

Then she looks at me. "Stevens, I told Ben you're a man of your word. If you say you'll be somewhere, you show up."

"Thank you."

"Come in. Come in," Ben says, stepping aside. "Everyone's in the back yard. Also there's a friend of Summer's here."

I barely process Ben's comment. And then it occurs to me what he just said.

Noooo. They aren't trying to fix me up, are they?

"Don't worry, man. I'm not on a matchmaking mission. Not exactly. She's cool and we thought you'd like to meet her. No pressure."

He follows this promise with a wink at his wife which he probably does with the intention of making me feel assured. It has the opposite effect of the one he's going for. I feel set up. I'm not big into surprises—especially not when I'm out of my element already. I have half a mind to tell Ben I forgot to turn off the stove, or I'm possibly coming down with an ocean-borne bacterial infection. I think I hear my mom calling me.

No. She'd one-hundred percent be behind Ben on this one.

I give Ben and Summer a forced smile that I hope looks more natural than it feels. Then I take a deep breath and walk through their house and out the back door.

Nothing could have prepared me for what I see when my feet hit the back porch. I should have known. An examination of facts would have helped me narrow down an accurate conclusion. Whether I would have been prepared is another question entirely. I wouldn't. Nothing ever really prepares me for seeing her.

Alana Graves is standing next to one of the two outdoor tables in Ben and Summer's back yard. She's leaning a hip casually against the tabletop, holding a drink and chatting with Kalaine. Her blond curls perfectly frame her face and fall past her shoulders. Her bright eyes sparkle. She's a magnet—the sun, drawing everything into her orbit, but keeping us at just the right distance, because who could handle the overwhelming reality of getting too close to her?

On Joel's boat, I learned to tone down my responses. She started to feel like someone I knew, just another woman—a gorgeous, captivating woman with not only a beautiful face and body, but a sharp wit and clever mind. I saw her vulnerability and it made her human. Then I ran into her at the cove—my cove. And I had an unexpected moment of complete calm, the after-effect of being underwater in my favorite environment. I mustered confidence and even landed a joke.

But this? Her here, in the midst of my friends? She's shining brighter than the crepuscular rays from the sol at the center of our universe. No wonder they call celebrities stars.

"Stevens!" Bodhi shouts over to me.

I'm glued to the back porch, unable to move.

"Are you just going to stand there gaping, or are you going to help us grill over here?"

"Uh. Yeah. Grilling. I'll grill."

Bodhi chuckles, obviously aware of the source of my bumbling words.

I'm grateful to have a grill and the guys clustered around it. Cooking meat will give me something to do besides worrying about how to act around Alana. We aren't supposed to know one another. I'm pretty sure I'm carrying that part off without even trying. I haven't appeared at all familiar or comfortable with her yet.

I think I'm in the clear, but Ben exits his house right behind me.

"Stevens! I want you to meet someone." His voice booms across the back yard.

Everyone present turns to stare at us. Probably people around the neighborhood would stare if they could see over the fence surrounding the yard.

Subtlety is not in Ben's wheelhouse.

"Kalaine, I hate to interrupt," Ben says as he ushers me close to the two women and barges into their conversation with all the finesse of a timeshare salesman.

"You do not hate to interrupt," Kalaine says with an adoring smile at Ben.

"Took the words right out of my mouth," I mumble.

Alana's eyes hook on mine and I can tell she's waiting to see what I'll say and how I'll act. I can't look away. Whether I had met her before or not, I would not be able to turn away from her at this proximity. Solar magnetism. A pull twice as strong as the earth's.

Alana giggles lightly at my comment. I'm so focused on her, the rest of the crowd and even the details of the back yard fade into a blur like peripheral objects in portrait mode.

"Alana, this is my friend, Stevens. He's a nerd, but a cool one. He does marine biology stuff." Ben claps me on the back. "Stevens, this is Alana Graves, as you know."

I send up a private thanks that Ben didn't blurt out what a big fan I am.

"He's such a massive fan of yours."

Premature gratitude.

I'm pretty certain I'm blushing.

"So, you're a fan, huh?" Alana says. Her eyes are playful.

"I admit it. I am."

"What's your favorite movie of mine?" she asks.

"You're going to make me pick?"

She beams.

"I loved you in *Twisted* ... Your performance. I loved your performance."

"We're all eagerly awaiting the release of *Blasted*," Kalaine says.

Alana's still holding my gaze when she thanks Kalaine and then asks me, "*Twisted*, huh?"

"You play a great spy. And those martial arts moves? Wow. Impressive."

I question myself, but apparently all the chill I ever had has exited the premises. "Is that actually you? Or do you have a stunt double?"

Alana smiles widely, dips her head, and then she looks me in the eye again. "That's all me. I do have a stunt double. She fills in for certain scenes, but I do all my own stunts."

"Just like the T-shirt!" Ben says with a laugh at his own joke.

"Yeah. Maybe I should get one of those," Alana says to him.

"You totally should!"

Summer calls Ben's name to help carry bowls out from the kitchen.

Bodhi walks over and asks, "Hey, guys. Mind if I borrow my wife for a minute? I'm thinking she needs to put her feet up."

Kalaine rolls her eyes at Bodhi, but she follows him across the yard to a chair he's pulled out for her with a footrest in front of it.

Alana and I are left alone together.

"Thank you," she nearly whispers to me.

"For loving you in *Twisted*?" I manage to tease her comfortably now that we're alone.

She smiles softly at me. "For acting like we never met."

If only she knew most of my reaction wasn't acting.

"You're welcome. You know you can trust me."

She studies me for a beat and then she says something I'll never forget for the rest of my life. "Yeah. I can."

SIXTEEN

Alana

I'm done being scared.
I'm done living in a world
where I don't get to be who I am.
I deserve a great love story.
~ Love, Simon

A nd so it begins.

Blasted will be released in theaters worldwide in seven weeks. My life is about to speed up like a German motor car entering the Autobahn. Press junkets. Talk shows. Media interviews. Special industry events. The premier. More photo shoots. Public appearances. I'll live at my condo in Hollywood several days a week now. I take a deep breath, grab the garment bag from the hook on the back of my door and walk out to meet the driver who will take me to the docks.

Not in a car. No. This is Marbella. This driver will be taking me in a golf cart at the mach speed of ten miles per hour. I could walk faster.

Stevens is waiting on Joel's boat. This will be our last day together. Joel comes back tomorrow after a delayed flight that kept him two extra days in Minnesota, or Wisconsin, or one of those states with great lakes and a lot of cheese.

"Good morning." Stevens greets me with a soft smile and an extended hand to grab my garment bag from me.

He leaves his other hand out to help me board and our eyes connect as I step onto the boat.

"Good morning. Thank you for doing this. I know it's beyond what you agreed to do for me."

"I'm here. I may as well help out when I can." We walk together to the helm and take our seats. Stevens raises one eyebrow at me. "Unless you have a bevy of men with pre-signed NDAs littered around the island awaiting your beck and call."

I laugh out loud. "Actually, you'd be surprised how many NDA-carrying men and women I have connections to on this island."

"I bet I would. Give me a ballpark."

Stevens twists the key and we back out into the ocean. The cool morning breeze sends a refreshing shiver through me. I'd far rather spend a day out on the water than sit in a stuffy hotel room answering the same questions hour after hour all day.

"Well ..." I consider downplaying the number of people it takes to sustain my day-to-day existence. Oddly, I want him to know. "There's Aria."

"The yoga instructor that works for Alicante?"

"You know her?"

"Ben wanted to fix me up with her."

"Hmmm. I could see that. You'd be the bedrock and she'd be the cloud."

"So you think I should let him?"

"No. Not really."

Why not? I don't know.

I like the idea of Stevens being single, like me. I shake that thought off. He's my water taxi driver for the week, I don't get to vote on his relationship status.

He definitely made me feel comfortable and safe during some very hard days this week. And he's easy on the eyes, as Mother would say. Easy, or hard? It's almost difficult to look at him, he's so rugged and yet, tender. He has the kind of face that keeps pulling your eyes toward him. There's this severity to the lines of his bone structure, but then a contrasting softness to his eyes and lips. I glance away toward the shoreline ahead, where the mainland has not yet come into view.

"Okay, so. There's Aria," I say, veering from the subject of Stevens' dating life. "Three drivers—two locals who work at Alicante, and the son of the owner of the Corner Market. There's Marta. She prepares some meals for me weekly. I have a cleaning team. They all signed NDAs. A landscaping team of, I think it's four guys, who takes care of keeping my land cleared for fire compliance. Harry had to sign one to teach me a single weekend of painting class. My hairdresser. You. Joel. I know I'm forgetting a few. Everywhere I go regularly for services, and anyone who steps foot onto my property has to sign one."

I look over at Stevens. His brows are raised in either shock, awe, or judgment. I can't tell which yet.

"Wow." He shakes his head. "That's ... amazing."

"Amazing good? Or amazing, what a spoiled brat?"

"I've never used the word amazing to describe a spoiled brat before," he smiles that warm, assuring smile in my direction.

"Well, there's a first time for everything."

"Yes. There is."

His eyes scan the horizon. Then he looks over at me. "I mean, wow, it takes a lot to keep your life in motion. And having to have an NDA from all those people ... is a lot. But you still came to the party at Summer's. None of us signed anything. And ... I think this was obvious, but I was completely caught off guard by you being there. I didn't know you were coming. No one told me."

"I was equally blindsided. But you pulled it off. No one would have guessed you'd already been seeing me all week long. Have you considered acting?"

He laughs, more than a little bit. "No."

"No?"

"Definitely not. The spotlight is not my comfort zone."

"I'm not sure it's mine either," I say more to myself than him.

He glances over at me. His lips form a thin line and his brows are drawn together.

"Don't pity me," I force a laugh to lighten the mood. "I'm reaping more than I'm sowing over here. I've got a good life."

He nods.

"So, what are you reading these days?" I ask.

"*The Fault in Our Stars*."

He seems to brace himself for my reaction.

"You have the reading habits of a nerdy high school girl. Do you know that?"

"I'm well aware. I also read biographies and memoirs. And at night, before I go to sleep, I'm currently reading *The Soul of an Octopus*."

I smile, picturing Stevens in bed, with some seriously sexy black-rimmed professor glasses, a white T-shirt and plaid pajama pants, a cup of tea on his bedside table, the lamp shedding the only light in the room. He's leaned back on his fluffed up pillows, reading about Octopuses. Octopi? Octopuu?

"Do you wear glasses?"

"What?" He glances over, confused.

"Do you wear glasses?"

"For reading?"

I nearly retract my question. It suddenly feels invasive and inappropriate in light of my Stevens-reading-in-bed fantasy.

"I do. I have a pair in my top bedside drawer I only use for reading." He looks over at me and, if I'm right, a blush creeps up his neck. "Are you a sorceress? How did you know I wear glasses?"

"Just a wild guess."

"Hmmm." He hums. "What are you reading?"

"*The Glass Castle*."

"Jeannette Walls?" he asks.

"Yes. What a poignant story."

"I read it on audiobook," he says, surprising me once again. "Her voice added even more depth and grit to the story. There's something about hearing a memoir or biography in the person's own voice."

I study him, this marine biologist who set aside days of his life to tote me around—granted, he's being compensated—who emerges from the water like a god after a snorkeling session, who keeps my confidences, and who reads such an interesting array of books. He's kind, thoughtful, funny. Why is he single?

All too soon, we're at the dock. Ken's not working today, so another abnormally large and muscular Viking-esque man who works for our family is at the gate.

Stevens looks down the finger of boat slips at Henry, then back at me. "You know that guy?"

"If I didn't? Are you ready to defend my honor?"

"I'm ready to haul you back into this boat and hit the gas. I'm a runner not a fighter."

I laugh. "I think that's supposed to be a *lover*. You're a lover, not a fighter."

"Maybe that's some other guys' story. Not me. I'm a runner." He winks. "If you're ever in danger, I'll drive the getaway car—or boat."

We both laugh.

Stevens hands my garment bag over the edge of the boat to me. He's driving back to Marbella and returning to take me home late tonight. It will be a very long day for me here in LA.

"Thanks again for acting like you didn't know me the other night at Summer's barbecue," I tell him. "She practically begged me to come—for you, as it turns out."

Am I stalling? Maaaybe. Still. I do appreciate his discretion, among many things I've come to appreciate over this short week we've known one another.

"Well, I appreciate you coming to a barbecue to meet a fan," he says with that soft smile where only half his mouth turns up and two deep dimples appear in that left cheek. "Sorry it turned out to be me."

"I'm relieved it was you. I love meeting fans. But it's also nice when I don't have to be *on*. Summer talked me into it by saying one of my superfans would be there, and she added that I needed to get out more. She's not wrong. It's just ... complicated. But I trust her to screen whomever will be around when I come over. And, I'm glad you're a superfan." I smile coyly at him, knowing full well Stevens does not love that term. "Joel couldn't care less what I do ... So, yeah. Anyway, thank you."

I'm not just thanking him for keeping my privacy intact, and I get the feeling he understands every aspect of what I'm thanking him for.

"Anytime," he says. "I'm around if you ever need a sub for Joel."

"I'll keep that in mind. I'll see you tonight."

"I'll be here. I'll be the guy kicked back on the stern of a boat reading a John Green novel."

~

When I arrive at the London West Hollywood, I'm ushered through the hotel's private access entrance and up into one of the rooms on the floor they have designated for press junkets. The members of the press are in the screening room watching the movie before they'll meet with me and Rex and other cast members. All I have to do all day is sit in the same hotel room while person after person files through asking me many of the same questions the previous interviewer asked. Then Rex and I will be herded into a conference room and the press will have their chance at interviewing the two of us together.

I change into the outfit I brought with me. My hair and makeup are done in a casual style that says, leading actress. And then we're off. Reporter after reporter, along with a few social media influencers and other members of the media come through my room in a blur.

Most of them ask about my role, my feelings about the film, my plans for what's next, the traditional questions. Every last one of them asks about me and Rex. I take the fifth, or whatever the term is for, "No comment," in this business.

My publicist called me yesterday to apprise me of the protocol. Thankfully, she knows me. I had no interest in pulling this charade. She advised me, "Sometimes less is more. The media will fill in the gaps you leave wide open. Say things like, 'I'm not comfortable talking about that yet,' or 'We're glad to be getting to see one another again after the hiatus of not being on set daily with one another.' The media will assume a lot. Everyone will be in a frenzy over you two."

Frenzy doesn't begin to describe what the media are like by the time Rex and I are together at the end of the day. I've only eaten two bites of a bagel with smoked salmon and cream cheese, a few nibbles of salad, and a protein shake. I think I got to the restroom twice, and my vision may be beginning to blur.

We sit at the front of a large room with both our publicists present. Rex and I are side by side in padded chairs. The press goes nuts. Initially, questions are asked politely. Some are about our on-screen chemistry—those are only intended to prime the pump.

Within five minutes of the start of the press conference, reporters are raising their hands like kids trying to get into Wonka's factory. The rapid-fire questions reveal their hunger for more of the story that "leaked" when Mother set up our lunch date.

Rex fields one. "I adore Alana. And I admire her. I mean, look at her. She's talented and beautiful." He winks at me and I smile back at him, grateful he's better at this than I am.

A reporter in the back gets his opportunity. "But are you two an item again?"

"We are exploring a reunification," Rex answers.

I sit mutely beside him, pasting a smile on my face and trying my best to remember that this is what publicity looks like. It's feeding an insatiable beast in hopes that the beast will benevolently feed you in return.

"Was your lunch at The Henry last week professional or personal?" A woman up front shouts without being called on.

"Our lunch was an opportunity to catch up and reconnect," Rex says.

Rex for president. Honestly, his capacity for diplomacy is staggering.

"Alana! Alana!" Another reporter calls my name.

Caroline, my publicist, points to him. "Yes?"

"We've heard from Rex. What will you tell us? Throw us a bone."

I glance toward the back of the room. My mother entered the building midday. She's been around the periphery ever since.

"I'll say that Rex and I feel strongly for one another. And this season is one where we're planning to spend a lot of time together."

I look over at Rex and he smiles warmly at me. I hold his gaze —mostly because it feels much better than looking out into a sea of rabid reporters.

Then I look back at them and say, "And that's all we want to say about our relationship for now. I'm sure you'll understand our desire for privacy while we reconnect."

When I look back at Mother, she's beaming. I didn't lie, but I spun the truth in a way that implied things that couldn't be further from reality.

SEVENTEEN

Stevens

We are like islands on the sea,
separate on the surface, but connected in the deep.
~ William James

I t's late when I get home from bringing Alana back from Los
Angeles. She looked exhausted. I had brought her a sandwich
on instinct after she described what kind of day she expected to
have. She ate that thing with the gusto of a linebacker after a
rough game. I loved watching her devour it.

It's the most peculiar feeling, knowing Alana as I do after this
week, and then trying to pair that knowledge with the movie star
she definitely is. She feels like two different people. But they're
both her. And my reactions to her swing on a pendulum from
wanting to give her a haven from all she obviously deals with, to
feeling like I can't form a sentence in the presence of her beauty
and fame. What's even stranger are the times I find myself relating
to her more comfortably than I ever have with a woman who isn't
my sister or mom.

I get ready for bed and prop a few of my pillows behind my

back. I'm at a good point in the octopus book and I want to read a bit to settle my brain. When I open my drawer to pull out my glasses, I smile. How on earth did Alana know I wear reading glasses? Perceptive. That's what she is. I guess that's what makes her such an incredible actress. She observes small details many of us might pass by.

I'm only a few paragraphs into this section of my book when my phone pings with a notification on my bedside table. Despite how tired I felt only moments ago, I'm re-energized thinking of a *Play on Words* match with SaturdayIslandGirl.

The board opens and she plays VISCOUS with the V on the double letter square. Then she types. *What a day. I'm wiped out.*

I feel my brow furrow in concern. *Do you want to sleep? I don't even know what time it is where you live. But it's late here. We can pick this up tomorrow.*

No. I need the distraction. I'm the kind of exhausted that means I shouldn't operate heavy machinery, but also, I'm wired, if that makes sense. It's nearly midnight here.

I chuckle. And, then it dawns on me. She must be so tired she didn't realize she just gave away her time zone. I look at my clock. 11:25. Nearly midnight. She does not live in Bora Bora or the Caribbean. She's in the Pacific Time Zone with me. She's a car ride or short plane flight away. All this time, she's been here on the west coast. I keep her revelation to myself for now.

So, do you regularly drive heavy machinery? Will this limitation affect your nightly routine of forklift operation?

Ha! No. I can't even drive a car.

You're joking, right?

I am not. It's a long story. But I do not drive.

She must live in a city with fabulous public transportation, like San Francisco or possibly Seattle.

I am imagining your city has great public transportation, then.

Should I say this next thought? Yeah. Why not?

I had pictured you on Bora Bora or somewhere in the Caribbean. But then you said you lived in America, so I checked.

There are over one hundred and fifty inhabited islands which are officially a part of America. I'm assuming you're on an island from your gamer tag.

Are you stalking me, Wordivore?

I am not. I am doing research.

Hmmm. Sounds like stalking to me. She adds a winking emoji and my mouth pulls into a smile.

Friends don't stalk friends.

If you say so. So now you picture me on one of the many islands in America.

What about San Juan Island in Washington? I take a stab, hoping she'll divulge at least a clue.

Angh Angh Angh.

What does that mean?

It's supposed to be the sound of a buzzer when you get an answer wrong.

I laugh out loud and the sound fills my bedroom. I haven't even played my tiles, and neither of us seem eager for me to do so.

I think buzzers usually go something like, bzzzz.

Not ones that tell you you're so very wrong.

I chuckle. *So, not Washington then?*

She doesn't answer right away. But then her cursor blinks and the three dots appear, telling me she's typing. *I do not live in Washington.*

But you do live on an island? I know I'm pressing my luck. But what is luck if not something you can press?

She pauses again. Then she types: *I do live on an island, but that's not the whole reason for my gamer tag.*

You don't want to share with the class, do you?

You always make me laugh. Do you know that?

Only when you tell me I do, since I can't hear you.

Neither of us types anything. My statement implies a barrier we both dance around. We'll never puncture it, even if she does live in the same time zone. Who meets a complete stranger on a gaming app and ends up meeting them later in real life? No one, that's who.

Well, I'm laughing now, she types.

I'm glad.

And, I won't tell you why I made that gamer tag. You now know I live on an American island.

I type: *I do too.*

What? You live on an island? Are you messing with me right now?

No. I'm not messing with you. I want her to know. Whether she ever tells me where she really is or not, I want her to know where I am. *I'm on an island off the coast of California. It's called Marbella.*

The screen sits quiet. Her cursor doesn't move. The dots don't appear. I wait.

Are you still there? I ask. Maybe she had to leave her phone to go do something.

I lay down SCABBARD, making use of her C. Sixteen points. Still nothing from her.

I read back through our chat, checking if I said anything that might have sounded different in print than it did in my head. Tone can be tricky when people are texting. Everything looks neutral.

SaturdayIslandGirl's cursor blinks to life. The three dots start and stop a few times. Then the most incredible words appear on my screen.

I live on Marbella Island too.

I've always heard of people's jaws actually dropping. Mostly, it's a figure of speech. Right now, I have to remind myself to shut my mouth because it is gaping open as I read and reread her sentence.

You live on Marbella? I ask, even though her statement speaks for itself.

I do.

I'm sitting up, away from my pillows now. She's here, right on this island. My body hums with the urge to leave my room, my home, my neighborhood. What if she's across the street, or one block over? She's here. Right here. All along, she's been here.

You're here. On Marbella.

I am.

Is your mind as blown as mine right now?

Hard to say. I don't know how blown your mind is. But this is insanely coincidental. What's the likelihood?

I'm a man of statistics and I still couldn't tell you the likelihood. It's got to be in the billions in probability. Well, no. Billions, based on the earth's population. Although, probability isn't a direct correlation to the exact number of one-to-one options. Anyway ... I can't believe this is real.

And yet, here we are.

Here we are, I echo, my mind still reeling in awe and disbelief. She's here. On my island.

I don't dare ask her where on the island she is. Not tonight. Instinctively, I know I've pushed her far enough. She'd tell me if she wanted to. But from now on, every stranger, every person who isn't attached to someone, will be a potential SaturdayIslandGirl to me. I'll walk around with an invisible antenna, asking myself, *Is that her? Could that be her?*

What a coincidence, I type. *Amazing.*

It is.

She lays down BEATIFY off the B in SCABBARD. Between her mostly two-word answers since we discovered our proximity and the fact that she picked up the game instead of typing more about us both living here on Marbella, I get the feeling we've tiptoed—or bulldozed—right up to the edge of her comfort zone.

More than anything, I want to assure her we're good—that I'm a good man and a safe person, not *actually* some stalker. Not that she thinks I am one, but I need to assure her.

Are you okay? I ask.

Still tired. Actually, my exhaustion is catching up with me. I think I'm going to call it a night. You can play your turn and I'll pick up the game from my end when I'm free tomorrow.

I'm not going to try to figure out where you live—here on Marbella. I just want you to know that.

She types immediately and I settle back into my pillows when I read her response.

This may sound weird, but I trust you.

I smile. *Good. That's good. I wish I could provide you some tangible assurance, but you'll just have to take my word for it. Go get some rest. We can play more tomorrow.*

Goodnight, Marbella Man.

My grin breaks across my face to the point where I feel my cheeks tighten.

Goodnight, SaturdayMarbellaIslandGirl.

～

I'm back from a morning snorkeling the coves near the Alicante with a group using underwater scooters. It's nearly lunchtime and Ben, Kai and Bodhi are working the shack.

"So, let me get this straight," Ben says. "You've been playing your nerdy word games with this woman, chatting her up—which, by the way, is awesome and far beyond what I'd expect from you—and you find out she's here? On Marbella?"

"Yep." I nod, questioning the sanity of having spilled my dilemma to these three guys.

Kai, I'd trust with my life. He's solid. Bodhi's pretty mature too. But Ben is this perpetual puppy. He means well, but he might just knock your coffee off the side table with one exuberant wag of his tail.

"Man," Bodhi says. "That's so wild."

"Tell me about it," I agree. "If that group this morning had any local women in it, I would have been fixated on trying to guess if it's her. I feel like I'm on a quest to find her now. But I don't want to overstep."

"Overstep?" Ben asks. "What is this *overstep?*" He chuckles. "Man, you are going to be the most single guy on the island forever if you think like that. Pursuit. That's what we're wired for. You're the scientist. Tell me if I'm wrong. What do the males of every species do? I'll tell you. They pursue. I pursued the heck out of Summer."

"He did," Bodhi echoes. "It borderlined on pathetic at times."

"Pathetic?" Ben postures. "So pathetic that she's carrying our child right now? I think not. Pursuit, man. That's the name of the game for males from the kangaroo rat to the dolphin. Haven't you ever watched Animal Planet?" He turns his attention from Bodhi to me. "Don't go all mamby-pamby on me now, bro. Man up, Stevens. You are in pursuit of this gamer girl."

I chuckle. "Actually, in nature, most males strut to garner a female's attention, or they set up an amazing display for her, like building a dwelling to impress her or providing an enticing meal. She does the choosing. For example, the male elephant seal stays along the central coast and waits for the females to migrate as far north as the Gulf of Alaska and the Aleutian Islands and then return a year later to mate. No pursuit there. Not a bit. You've seen them. The males stay on one beach. No pursuit, just patiently waiting for the female."

"Well," Ben says, completely undeterred by logic. "You, my handsome friend, are not an elephant seal. I mean, have you seen them?"

He takes his hand and makes a flap of it and dangles it from his nose and then he starts barking and braying. And then he flops around the shop, rearing his head up like male sea elephants do when they are battling another male. He continues to make loud aaarrh, pllbbtt, and snorting sounds. It's so over the top that the three of us are cracking up at him.

Ben wobbles over to Bodhi. "Come on, Bodhi, let's rumble like the ugly elephant seals."

Bodhi chuckles, but he says, "Stay away from me, Ben."

"You're afraid of me? You can't take me in all my elephant seal awesomeness?"

Kai looks at me and shakes his head. "This. This is where you come for relationship advice?"

I laugh and shrug. Where else am I supposed to go? Besides, this is the most entertainment I've had in a while.

Ben's about to say something else in his rant about pursuing a woman when my phone rings. I look at the caller and hold up a finger. "I have to take this."

I step outside, making sure I'm out of earshot and then I answer the call from Joel.

"Hey, Joel. What's up?"

"Hey." His voice sounds raspy and he's congested. "I got sick. Airplanes, man. And sleeping in that airport. You're breathing everyone else's air. The germs travel from all over and we just share them in the airplane. It's a wonder all travelers don't get sick more often."

"I'm sorry to hear it. Can I bring you anything?"

"Nah. I'm good. But I do need something from you."

"I'm free for the rest of the day. What do you need?"

"Layna gets a routine Trader Joe's order. I run to Ventura to pick it up for her once a week."

"You do her shopping?"

"Once a week. Trader Joe's. If she needs something else, I get that too. She has a lot of stuff shipped here, but some things she can only find on the mainland. I bring all those things to her in a weekly delivery."

"You want me to go shopping for her?"

"Yeah, man. If you can." He moves his mouth away from the phone and coughs.

"Sure. I'm glad to."

"Great. Brigitte will send you the list."

"You sure you don't need anything? Mom would make her bone broth chicken noodle soup in a heartbeat if I asked."

"That doesn't sound bad, actually. But I hate to impose."

"She lives to be the mother hen to as many island guys as she can. You know that. Let her do this for you."

"Okay, man. I will. Thanks for pitching in. I'll text Brigitte and she'll get you what you need."

I think Joel's going to hang up, but then he asks. "How'd it go, anyway?"

"Driving the woman we call Layna?"

"Yeah."

"Good. It was good."

"She's special, huh? Surprisingly normal for a woman of her status."

"Yeah. She is. All that."

I take off from the shack, clean up and take Joel's boat to Ventura after Brigitte sends me a list. She also sends me Alana's private address on the island, along with a stern reminder that I'm not to ever tell a soul where this house is, or that I've been there. I would never, but I appreciate the fierceness of Brigitte's loyalty and protection of Alana.

Five hours after I left the shack, I'm driving a golf cart up into the remote hills on the North Shore. The properties here are spread out. Many of the residences are tucked back so you can't even see the primary dwelling from the road. The trees grow thicker here, providing shade and privacy. At the peak of a winding road, I see the address I'm looking for. A wrought iron gate with a call box outside it blocks the driveway. I punch in the code Brigitte sent me. The gate swings open and I drive the rest of the way up to the house.

The home appears to be one level on the front, a small stoop leading to an extra-tall door with panes of glass going from top to bottom. Around the side of the house, there's a deck which is built on stilts supported on the hill that runs down that side of the property. There's a lower level below the deck which I don't explore, since it's obviously not my place to scope out her home.

I grab two of the three paper bags full of groceries out of the back of the cart and walk to the front door. Alana's already opening the door before my finger hits the doorbell.

She smiles at me. "Security alert on my phone."

"Ah. Makes sense."

"Thank you for running this errand for me. I hate to put you out."

"No problem. I had a free day. I'm going to be off island for the next four days for a job, but you caught me on a day when I had nothing planned for the afternoon."

She smiles and extends her hands for the bags.

I walk past her, "Tell me where to set these."

I realize my error only a beat later. "Sorry. I shouldn't assume I can just walk into your house."

"No. No. It's fine. I'll just grab the last of the stuff from the cart. Straight through to the kitchen."

I let out a surprisingly shaky breath. What was I thinking, just walking past her like that? It's what I would do if I were bringing groceries to anyone else. But she's not just anyone else.

Her home is spacious and clean, with windows everywhere making it feel like the outdoors is a part of the home. The views to the east lead out her deck, over treetops and toward the ocean. The rest of the home has a private woods surrounding it.

Her kitchen is stunning. All high-end appliances. I chuckle when I remember her saying someone else cooks most of her meals for her. This space begs to be used by someone who knows how to prepare cuisine. I set the bags on the island and start to remove items and set them on the granite countertops.

"Oh! Thank you. Wow. Joel is going to have to step up his delivery game. He usually just hands me the bags at the door and heads off."

"Oh. Sorry. I didn't mean to intrude. I can just ..." I abandon my unpacking and take a step toward the living room I just passed through.

"No. No. Stay. I'm about to eat anyway. Want to join me?"

"To eat?"

"That is what I had in mind." She laughs lightly, that melodic laugh of hers. "After all, you fed me a sandwich yesterday."

"Was that only yesterday?"

"I know. It feels like a lifetime. What a day. But that's over and we're here in my haven. Have you eaten?"

I have to admit the truth. "I haven't."

"Then stay. I'll feed you and then you can get back to whatever you were going to do with your evening."

"Reading about octopi."

She smiles. It's not a condescending smile. Just warm. And I'm back to seeing her as simply another woman, not Alana Graves, world-renowned actress.

EIGHTEEN

Alana

*And sometimes you love a person
just because they feel like home.*
~ *Bridget Jones's Baby*

Stevens gets back to unpacking my groceries. It should feel odd or intrusive, but he's moving through the kitchen with such unassuming ease I nearly forget he's never been here before. That is until he asks his next question.

"Where does this go?" He holds up a large container of plain Greek yogurt.

I laugh lightly. "The fridge. Where do you keep your yogurt?"

"I guess I meant to ask where your fridge is. All I see are cabinets."

I laugh out loud. Not at him. Then I walk past him and open the refrigerator, which does have a cabinetry front to make the aesthetic of the kitchen more streamlined.

"Ahh. Camouflage. I'm a fan of cloaking in nature. Not so sure how I feel about it in kitchens. At least your stove is out in the open, not hiding in plain sight." He smiles at me.

I smile back. We're closer than we even are in the helm of Joel's boat. And those times have been out on the ocean. I've never caught the way Stevens smells, but it hits me unexpectedly now. He's like the ocean breeze, salt and crisp, but with something soothing like a cup of tea or a bedside candle in the undertones.

I walk back to the last paper bag on the counter and grab out a box of frozen brown rice.

"Heads up," I say, tossing the box in Stevens' direction. He reaches out and catches it, reads the label and sets the box into my freezer.

Unpacking groceries usually serves as a reminder that my week is about to take flight. Tonight feels like an extension of a much-needed vacation.

We work side by side, unloading the rest of the items into my cabinets, fridge and walk-in pantry.

"This place is as big as my entire living room," Stevens says, emerging after setting some raw nut butter and rice cakes on the shelf in my pantry.

His tone is so neutral, I don't feel self-conscious in the least.

I attempt to diffuse the disparity between us by saying, "Well, in my Hollywood apartment, I don't even have a pantry."

Somehow, mentioning that I have an entire separate residence doesn't level the playing field in the least. But Stevens takes it in stride.

"Well, my other dwelling doesn't have a pantry either."

"You have a second home?"

He smiles a smile that should be on billboards, only it's so homey and directed only at me, his new friend—at least I think we might be friends now.

"My other home: the ocean."

"Ahhh." I laugh a little. "I forgot you're a merman."

"How did you find out?" He chuckles good-naturedly.

"Brigitte dubbed you that the day we bumped into you in the cove."

He smiles. I imagine he's secretly entertaining the thought of being a merman. Something nearly boyish crosses his face for a moment. It's a nuance of an expression actors work years to master.

"You being a merman would explain how you stay underwater so long," I add with a wink.

"You're on to me. Promise me you'll keep my scaly secret."

"Cross my heart." I make the X motion on my chest, then I walk to the fridge and open the door.

"Let's see. We have ..." I read the labels Marta put on each container. "Chicken breast with green beans and a balsamic glazed couscous, halibut filet with citrus salsa and asparagus, or a mixed green salad with slivers of lean strip steak and roasted sweet potatoes."

"No pizza?" His face is serious, but I can see the mirth in his eyes.

"Pizza is a rarity."

"Any of that sounds good. But I don't want to take one of the meals you already had planned to eat this week."

"It's fine. I can get more where this came from. And I can always resort to soup. Besides, I'll more than likely be in Hollywood a few nights this week."

"You could always feast on that bucket of plain Greek yogurt."

I laugh. "That will last me a week of breakfasts."

"Surprise me," he says, tipping his chin toward the fridge.

He's certainly surprising me. I watch as he plops onto one of the barstools, pivoting and extending his long legs out to the side.

"Should I help cook?" he offers.

I point to the microwave-convection oven and smile. "I'll do the honors."

I pour each of us a glass of sparkling water, and when both meals are warmed, I lead Stevens out to the deck.

"I'm assuming you're fine with eating outside," I say.

"This is great. I usually eat in my kitchen at a small table.

Once a week I have a meal with my parents, and then one other night I try to bring business to my sister by popping in on her."

I take a seat in one of the oversized wicker chairs in front of the outdoor coffee table at the end of my porch where we'll have the best views of the ocean. Stevens takes the seat next to mine. Our backs are to the wall, treetops, rooftops and the wide expanse of the ocean spread out in front of us.

"Your sister?" I ask, trying to reconcile the idea of Stevens having a family.

He seems so self-contained—so content in his own skin. I don't know what I imagined about him before. My thoughts were usually spiraling around getting to LA or unwinding from being there. But now, I see him as a whole person, with a life apart from substituting as my water taxi pilot. Maybe I saw pieces of him in that light before, but not like I am right now.

"My sister owns Mitzi's Tacos. Her name is Mitzi ... of course ... which would be why her place is called Mitzi's Tacos. You don't meet a lot of Mexicans named Mitzi, I don't think. I never have, anyway. But she loves tacos and food in general, so she went to culinary school in LA and worked at taquerias there while she was taking courses. She's always known she wanted a restaurant."

I hide my smile at the awkwardness that made Stevens rattle on more than usual. These bouts of nerves seem to surge occasionally, like he remembers my life outside the boat or this house and has to work his way back to being at ease around me. I'd do anything to alleviate that for him, but I think I'd only make matters worse, so I let him work it out.

"So, are her tacos any good? Or do you just eat there to support her?"

"They are excellent. Local Mexicans eat there and tell her they think her food is authentic. She always comes to family dinner bragging about anytime someone Hispanic compliments her food."

"I'd love to try her tacos sometime."

"I think I know a guy who could make that happen."

I smile over at him. "You'd have to bring them here."

"Or you could wear those huge sunglasses and maybe a wig and a trenchcoat," he suggests.

I can't tell if he's teasing or being serious.

"Yeah. That getup wouldn't stand out at all," I joke.

"Not a bit. People come to Mitzi's in trench coats and shades all the time. She's got a real *Singing in the Rain* vibe going on."

I snort-laugh and then immediately bring the back of my hand up to my nose as if I can suck back the fact that I just sounded like a pig learning how to breathe.

"Classy." He smirks at me.

"I can't believe you made me snort."

"Oh, I made you? I think you managed that on your own."

"I did, didn't I?"

He nods. I try to remember the last time I had this much fun or truly relaxed with someone. Brigitte. But with a man? Maybe never.

∼

The next day, I'm sitting on my porch in the same chair I sat in for my unexpected dinner with Stevens last night. I'm reading Sally Field's memoir, *In Pieces,* when the phone rings. I set my book aside and answer Phyllis' call.

Phyllis doesn't even say hello. She starts in with, "The guests just checked out at Mila's Place an hour ago and she doesn't have any reservations tonight. I'm joining Mila for lunch and you are too."

Despite her warm and humorous demeanor, Phyllis can be as commanding as my mother. When she summons you to lunch, you clean up and go.

"What if I'm busy?"

"Cancel. You're on the island. You answered your phone. That means you're free. Don't play games with me, Alana. We are overdue for lunch together."

"I'll be there in a half hour."

"Don't make me drive up there and get you, because you know I will."

"Believe me, the last thing I want is for you to drive up this hill. I'll be down in a bit."

We hang up. I set my book aside, slip into the pair of sandals I keep near the door and take a leisurely walk down the hill past the other larger properties surrounding mine. I know who most of my neighbors are. A few of them may know it's me who lives in my home, but we don't really interact outside the occasional wave when we collect our mail or see one another out on the street.

In the neighborhoods below ours, darling beach bungalows and a few larger homes dot properties. Picket fences frame the small front yards. No one needs much of a yard when the beach is only a few blocks away. I pass the Corner Market and turn toward Mila's Place, a bed & breakfast owned by Phyllis' niece.

Phyllis is on the porch swing waiting for me.

"There she is! There she is." Phyllis comes down the porch steps and pulls me into a hug. "Oh the beauty! If Hollywood hadn't already snatched you up, they would do it today. Tell me how you are, Alana. Is it junket time for that next picture of yours?"

"We just got through that this week."

"Through it? No. No. We both know that's only the drop of the flag at the races. You're in the thick of it for a few months now, aren't you?"

"Yes. And my next film starts production only a few weeks after the release of *Blasted*."

"Oh, this business. They'll eat you alive if you let them."

"You didn't let them," I smile over at her.

"Nearly, dear. Nearly. But, I made it out by the skin of my teeth. And here I am—a testament that you can survive fame and live to tell about it. Of course, I wasn't famous like you. Never a household word. Not where there was a feeding frenzy whenever I showed my face in public. No. I didn't have to mess with all that nonsense."

"Nonsense, huh?"

"Give me a better word for it, and I'll use it."

"I can't find one off the top of my head."

"And that's coming from you, the wordsmith."

"I'm not a wordsmith. I just like playing word games."

I think of Wordivore. There's a real possibility he's right here —on this block, as we speak, or even next door for all I know. The idea thrills and overwhelms me in equal parts.

Mila steps out onto the porch. There's a glow to her these days—something peaceful and magnetic. She's always been sweet and welcoming, careful about keeping my anonymity and privacy. And she never overstepped the fact that her aunt and I are close. I respect her for that.

"I made chicken salad," she announces. "It's my recipe with grapes and celery, not the savory one."

"I like them all," Phyllis says with a flourish of her hands. "And this one needs to eat." She wraps an arm around my shoulder and gives me a squeeze before leading us up the steps to the inn.

I smile at Phyllis. Always trying to feed me.

"How about we eat out on the back terrace?" Mila suggests.

"Perfection! Perfection!" Phyllis says, not waiting for me to chime in with an opinion.

"So, dear, tell us what's new," she says to me as we all pull out seats at a pre-set table. The sandwiches are on a tea tray in the middle with bowls of fruit salad and a green salad flanking the stand.

"Wow. This looks amazing. You didn't have to go to all this trouble."

"She did," Phyllis glances at me with a faux warning. "Her favorite aunt is here for lunch. Don't dissuade her, dear. I love being pampered."

Mila and I laugh.

"You sure you don't want to get back into acting?" I offer.

"Are you kidding me? No, thank you, and that's that. I adored my time in the biz. Most of it. Even took a husband from the experience as a parting gift. Lost him just as quickly, as Hollywood romances go. You know."

Mila and I share a look. This is the most Phyllis has ever spoken of her love life—to me anyway.

But, as quickly as she opens the can, she seals the lid back up.

"So, how about you? I see the tabloids." Phyllis takes a sip of her iced tea and raises one eyebrow as if she knows better than to believe what she reads.

"Well ..." I start in.

"Is this your mother's idea of a promotion for the film?"

"I'm not at liberty to say."

"Just as I thought. Well, give me something juicy then."

"I don't have anything too juicy."

"Oooh." Phyllis rubs her hands together. "Not too juicy means it is juicy."

A few veins show through the silky skin, one of the only signs she's old enough to be my grandmother.

"There's this guy online," I admit.

"Online dating?" Mila asks with a softness to her eyes. "Isn't that a bit tricky for someone as high-profile as you?"

"Dating at all is tricky for someone in my position. But we're not online dating. We're playing a word game. And we chat."

"Much better," Phyllis says before taking a solid bite of the croissant sandwich in her hand. She quickly chews and adds, "A man who plays word games isn't online for only one thing. Plus, he's bound to have a good vocabulary."

Mila chuckles. "I think you get more ridiculous with age."

"I get more honest," Phyllis corrects her. "Now tell us about this man."

"Well ..." I trust them. I may as well say it. "It turns out he lives here."

"On Marbella?" Mila's face is giddy with excitement.

"Yes. Can you believe it?"

"What are the odds?" Phyllis says.

"I know. I'd almost wonder if he arranged it all, you know? Like maybe he found out where I lived somehow and then figured out who I am on the game. But there's really no way he could have. Maybe someone could discover I'm here. But no one knows my gamer tag. It's a bonafide coincidence. We've been playing forever, chatting more and more over time. Our discussion about where we live came out of left field this week."

"You just found out?" Mila's usually calm demeanor is tinged with a contagious spark of interest. "I wonder who he is!"

"Me too. Believe me. It's not like I can just go roaming around trying to find him, carrying a sign that says, *Wordivore, is that you?* I'll just have to see what happens. A part of me wants to meet him. But the other part ... he doesn't know who I am. It's ... refreshing being just another woman. Everything could change when he sees I'm Alana Graves."

"But you have a history with him on this game?" Mila asks.

"Yes."

"Then he already knows you apart from your fame. That's a gift. If he wants to meet you without knowing who you are, that means he's attracted to you for you."

Mila's phone pings with a message notification.

"Oh, excuse me. I should check that in case it's Noah's school."

She pulls her phone out of her pocket, reads the message, and says, "It's nothing. Just Kai telling me he'll be late. He's going out with Stevens, taking a group out on a night snorkel."

"Stevens?" I ask without thinking.

"Yes. The guy you met at Ben and Summer's barbecue," Mila says.

"Ah. Yes. I remember him."

NINETEEN

Alana

In its purest form, dating is auditioning.
(And auditioning means
we may or may not get the part.)
~ Joy Browne

"So, it's Kelly Clarkson, Jimmy Fallon, and Jimmy Kimmel. Two tomorrow and the second Jimmy the next day. Got it?" Brigitte asks. She sounds out of breath.

"What are you doing? Running from someone?"

"Oh, yes. You know me. I'm being chased down by hordes of hot men. I have to outrun them because, goodness knows, if they caught up to me, I'd have to date. And then I'd have to pick amongst them all ..." she trails off. Then she shouts, "Hey! Watch it! Pedestrian right of way, dingus! That's why I'm in a crosswalk! See me, the girl walking with a garment bag? Pedestrian!"

She returns her attention to me. "Where was I? I swear. These drivers. Oh. Yes. I was talking about men chasing me. As if."

"Men would chase you, Bridge. You're adorable, sharp, funny, and quirky in a way that makes you special."

"Special has sooo many meanings."

"Special has one meaning when it comes to you. You're one of a kind."

She's breathless, obviously rushing wherever she is. "Again, that could be good or bad. One of a kind, rare, or one of a kind as in God broke the mold because He knew the world could only take one of me."

"All the good. Now, stop fishing for compliments. What's got you out of breath?"

"I am running errands for the Queen of Hearts."

"She's got you running errands?"

"For you. Errands for you. It's my job, you know? You have three talk show appearances over the next two days. You need the consummate outfits, pressed and ready. And a whole slew of other things. Things you don't need to fret about. Trust me. And, yes. I have five minutes to get my car out of a space that is metered so I avoid a ticket."

"I'll pay the ticket. Slow down."

Brigitte may not even hear me. She's on one of her rolls, which are entertaining as long as she's not actually suffering.

"Why do they have meters in Los Angeles? Also, why do some meters only allow parking until six p.m.? If you're going to charge me, let me park here round-the-clock. It's insanity. Meters are of the devil." She pauses. Her voice turns cheery. "Hi!" Another pause. "Yes! It's beautiful out." Her voice goes up an octave. "Isn't he a little cutie? Aren't you cute? Awww. You're the cutie patootie cutie badootie wootie. Yes, you are." Her voice drops back to normal. "Have a nice day."

Brigitte seamlessly returns her attention to me. "Sweet old lady out walking the absolutely cutest little Frenchie. Those dogs are the cutest. Anyway, I was saying, it could take me those precious five minutes left on my meter to stand in line at the dry cleaner on a busy day. Then what? I'd have to pay because some suit from West LA got in line before me and felt the need to complain about the level of starch in his shirt. It's ludicrous, I tell you."

She's breathless, but doesn't pause to take a breath. "Yet, we have to feed these insipid parking machines. Besides, isn't living here costly enough? Not that I'm griping. I'm not. We have the best climate in the country. And the men are delicious to look at, though, too many of them know it. And you pay me plenty. Don't you fret."

"I don't. But you can ask for a raise, you know."

"What did I tell you about that? When I feel I've earned one, I'll ask. I already make more than so many assistants in the business."

She's worth it. Note to self, give her a big, fat bonus this week for all these errands.

"It's just a crime against humanity to have these parking meters everywhere. There's like one open spot available for every hundred cars. It's a design flaw, I tell you. If I were in charge, the first thing I'd do is have them rip out all these meters. We could melt the metal down and make something useful—like another parking garage!" She laughs at her own brilliance. "Whatever happened to survival of the fittest? We should be allowed to vie for parking spaces, and may the best man—or woman—win. Don't you think?"

"Yes. Of course."

"Says the agreeable movie star who never drove a day in her life." Brigitte pauses. "New mission. We are getting you a driver's license."

"Because you make driving seem oh so appealing," I joke.

"Driving is amazing. Except for traffic. It's the parking that kills me. Anyway, I've got to get going. I have three more stops and my stomach is growling. You've got the itinerary? Rex is joining you on Kelly's show. Not that I get to call her Kelly, though I have the feeling she'd be down for that. Anyway, he's with you for Kelly. The other two are just you. We'll prep potential questions and answers when you're here. I'll see you tomorrow. I'm riding along with that beast of a bodyguard of yours and Miguel to come pick you up. Got all that?"

"Got it." I smile. She is adorable. And I'm so lucky to have her. "And, Bridge?"

"Yeah."

"Go eat. We'll figure the rest out later. Don't run yourself ragged on my behalf."

"Okay. Yeah. I see a smoothie place. I'll drop these clothes in my car, pay for more time—grrrrr—and stop to grab a smoothie. You're right. And you? You better eat and then go get your beauty sleep."

I smile.

I hear the opening of her car door. "Sweet dreams. Don't let the bedbugs bite." She seems to be done, but then she says, "Do they even have bedbugs on that beautiful island of yours? I bet they don't."

I chuckle. "Go eat. You're getting hangry."

"Yeah. Yeah. I'm going. I'm going. Love you, boss. See you tomorrow."

I eat a salad, wash my bowl, and spend a half hour doing yoga. Then I brew a cup of tea and head to bed early. Tomorrow will be a whirlwind, starting with the boat ride to Los Angeles, then a few days of talk show appearances. I pick my phone up off the bedside table. I didn't play the word game last night because Stevens was here past dinner. I read a little after he left and then went to sleep.

Wordivore might not even be online tonight, but I always secretly hope he will be. Knowing he's here on the island makes me wonder so many things. Where is he right now? Does he live on the north shore near me, or in Descanso near the resort? What does he actually do for work? He said he's on call. Is he an island doctor? His words were, *Something like that*, when I asked. A veterinarian? A nurse? EMT?

When I pull up the game on my phone, a board has already been started by Wordivore with an invite to join. I click, *Accept*, and when the screen comes to life with my tiles fanning out at the bottom, I nearly hold my breath waiting to see if he's here or if he just played a word and signed out.

Hey there, he types. *I was about to log off. Didn't know if you were going to show up tonight.*

I'm here. What an answer. Of course I'm here. Nothing like stating the obvious.

I see that. He pauses, and then he types, *And, I'm glad.*

What is this feeling in my belly? Nerves? Giddiness? Excitement? I feel like a high school girl with a crush. I try to talk sense to myself, but this small—no, not so small—part of me is feeling off-kilter over Wordivore. It's pleasant and simultaneously disorienting.

I look at the board. MUZZLE with a Z on a double letter is already there.

Nice start, I say.

Some days you get all one-point vowels. Some days are double Zs.

You outdid yourself with thirty-six points.

It's sheer skill. Not an ounce of luck involved.

Just as I always say.

Speaking of saying things …

He stops typing and I wait on pins and needles. I haven't felt this nervous since my early days as an actress auditioning for a role I needed to land.

Okay. Let me start that over, he types. *Speaking of saying things, what would you say to coming out to dinner with me?*

I reread the sentence twice. Didn't I want him to ask just that? But now that he's said it, I'm faced with the reality. If we meet, he'll know who I am. No more hiding behind SaturdayIslandGirl.

I chicken out and lay down F-U-T and then E-D around his Z to make FUTZED. Ironic, since I'm futzing around not answering him.

Let's pretend I didn't just ask that, he says.

Ugh.

No. No. It's okay. I just have to think about it a minute.

Can I be totally honest with you? he asks.

I would hope so.

I've been thinking about you a lot since I found out you're here on Marbella. Wondering if you're someone I know or have seen. It's distracting. So, I talked to a few friends—close friends, only a few of them—and they said I should go for it and ask you. So, this is what I get for listening to my guy friends. I wasn't sure. Two of them are far bolder than I am. One is a bit more reserved, but even he thought I ought to ask. Please know there's no pressure. I don't want to make you uncomfortable.

You don't. Can I have a few minutes? I'll be right back.

Man. I really blew it, didn't I?

No. Not at all. I just need to think this through.

Going to call a friend?

I laugh. *Basically, yes.*

Go for it. I'll be here. And ... one more thing.

Yeah?

Call the friend that will tell you to say yes.

I can't help but smile. *I'll take that under advisement.*

I swipe my phone so the app lifts and my keypad is on the screen. Then I press Brigitte's contact.

She answers on the first ring. "Yes. Yes. I had a smoothie, Mom. I feel much better, thank you."

I chuckle. "I'm not calling to ask if you had the smoothie. I figured you would."

"What are you calling for? Wait ..." There's a ruffling sound, then she says, "It's eight thirty. You usually text if it's this late. Are you sick? Do you need me to rally some remedies and have them shipped to you by drone drop? Did someone unearth your location? Is your mom flipping out about yet another detail for these interviews? No. No. She'd call me if she were. Ummm ..."

"If you give me a minute, I'll actually tell you so you don't have to guess."

"Good. Great. That's a good idea. So?"

"So ... that guy on the word game?"

"The one you found out lives on your island?"

"Yes."

"Yeah?"

"He wants to take me to dinner."

"Um. Yes!"

"Wait. You don't even know who he is. Shouldn't I ask for a photo or something? Have him sign an NDA? Get him screened?"

"Are you planning on going to his house?"

"Definitely not."

"You'll meet him in public?"

"Yes. A restaurant, I guess."

"On Marbella?"

"Yeah. I think so. Definitely. We're both here. Yes."

"Then, what's the problem? Isn't there like exactly no crime there? And if you're at a restaurant you'll have eyes on you. Want me to call your goon squad and have him show up there to keep an eye out?"

"Tank?"

"Yeah. That mountain of a man. He'd come over there for you if you need it. You've just never needed it."

"No. I don't need Tank. You're right. Marbella is safe. It's more the idea that Wordivore will know who I am after this."

"I hear you, Alana." Brigitte's quiet for a beat. "Let me ask you something?"

"Sure."

"Do you want to end up in a relationship? No. Skip that. Forget about a relationship. That's so next-level right now. Would you like to go to dinner with this guy—the guy you've been telling me about forever. The one you feel like you can trust and share things with. Would you like to go to dinner with him?"

"Yeah. I would."

"There's your answer. Now get off the phone, go tell him yes, and get your butt to bed. You have interviews tomorrow and Maleficent will have my finger poked with a spinning wheel needle that puts me to sleep for years if I don't get you there without bags under your eyes. But, then again, maybe I'd meet my Prince Phillip if I went through all that."

I laugh. "Okay. I'll tell him yes and I'll get to sleep."

"Good. And, admit it. You're just a teensie weensie bit excited now, aren't you? Butterflies flitting around? A perma-smile?"

"Stop spying on me."

"I knew it! You deserve this. Go be a normal girl on a dinner date. Love you, boss."

"Love you too, goofball."

"That's one-of-a-kind goofball to you."

We hang up and I tap to reopen the app. Sure enough, Wordivore is there, waiting ... for me.

Hey, I type.

Hey, he answers. *So, let me down slowly.*

I'm not going to. I smile big, and then I type. *It's a yes.*

I rarely dance, but picture me doing a happy dance. Scratch that if it sounded creepy. I'm just glad you said yes.

I smile and decide to tell him so. *I'm smiling.*

Me too.

A text comes through from Brigitte. I pause to read it.

Brigitte: Don't give him your private cell number. New cell phone acquired one minute ago. It will be with me when we pick you up in Ventura tomorrow. Here's the phone number ...

She types the number and I sit there marveling at her mad skills.

Alana: I don't pay you enough.
Brigitte: Okay, pay me more since you keep insinuating you want to.
Alana: Okay. I will.
Brigitte: Okay, then. Now get to bed.

I chuckle.

Alana: Night, Bridge. You're the best.
Brigitte: So are you. Seriously. Now go get some rest.

I click over to the game.
Wordivore: *Did I lose you?*
Nope. Just getting a phone number for you.
It took you that long to get your phone number?
It's complicated. You'll understand when we meet.
So you ARE a spy. I knew it!
Lol. Not a spy. Well ... not exactly.
Hmmm. So, when should we have this dinner? I'm off the island for a few more days and then I'm back by Saturday.
Saturday is good for me. I tell him, smiling again while my nerve endings buzz with a cocktail of so many emotions I can't even identify them all.

So, here's my number. He types it in the chat and I enter it in my phone for safe keeping. *And I have a few questions. Are you ready?*
That depends.
They're harmless, I promise. Just some pre-date prep. Do you want something super-casual, moderately casual, or pretty swanky?
Wow. Swanky? I haven't heard that word in a while.
There are a lot more words where that came from.
Promises, promises.

My grin could split my face. This is flirting, right? I'm so out of practice. Aside from scripted romance scenes with Rex, I haven't flirted in real life in ages. I may not know how to do this. Then again, I just managed a pretty decent response.

I definitely don't want something "swanky" on a first date. *I'd say casual to moderate.*

Great. That helps. Now, picnic on the beach, pizza and pasta place, tacos, or Thai?

Stevens said his sister owns a taco place. What if we accidentally pick a night that he's there? *I'm going to go with pizza/pasta.*

Perfect. I know just the place. I'm assuming you want to meet there.

Definitely. Did that sound abrupt? *What I mean is ... first date, we've never met ...*

Date? Is this a date?

Is it not a date? I'm sorry. I assumed.

I'm kidding. It's whatever you want it to be. It's dinner. We'll meet and we'll share a meal. My treat because I asked you. If you don't want to flee after an hour or two over bolognese and drinks, we'll decide if we have been on a date or a friendly meal with someone we've finally met in person.

It's very much a date. I know it deep, deep down. Otherwise, I wouldn't be going to these lengths to actually meet him. And I wouldn't feel like I'm not going to be able to sleep until I actually see him in person. This is definitely the weirdest situation I've ever been in. And I've been in some weird situations—like fake-dating my co-star.

That sounds just right, I tell Wordivore. It does sound just right.

Okay, great. Saturday at six? Let's meet at Cucina Descanso. I'll grab a table when I get there.

Perfect.

I yawn. Then, I type, *I'm sorry. Please don't take this personally, but I have a huge day at work tomorrow and I'm yawning. Can we pick this game up later?*

You sure this isn't because I'm already seven points ahead of you and obviously going to win this match? He adds a winking emoji.

I'm certain. Because, for one thing, I'm only seven points behind you, and I'm the dark horse in this game.

Okay. Well, sweet dreams, dark horse.

You too, Wordivore.

TWENTY

Stevens

I wanted it to be you.
I wanted it to be you so badly.
~ You've Got Mail

"Y ou did it! Man, I'm so proud of you." Ben's gushing, loudly. So loudly.

I'm just glad there are no customers in the shack right now. I'm pretty sure the presence of other people would not deter his celebration. He already pumped his fist in the air as if his favorite team won the final match of the season.

"Pursuit, baby. That's where it's at. You made an example of those elephant seals. No sitting on a beach looking like a washed up, overgrown otter with a deformed nose for you. No, sir. You pursued her."

He shakes his head with a big smile on his face and claps me on the back.

"If there were an off switch, I'd hit it for you," Kai says with a sympathetic look in my direction.

"Off switch?" Ben practically rolls his eyes at Kai. "You need an on switch. This guy asked his online crush out to dinner. Get a little excited, bro. It wouldn't kill you."

"I'm happy for him," Kai says.

"Happy for who?" Bodhi walks in.

"Happy for Stevens. He's got a date tonight."

"Not sure it's a date." I pull my lips into a thin line and make eye contact with Ben.

"How do you not know if it's a date?" Ben's face scrunches up.

"I told her we'd decide if it's a date after we've eaten. I wanted to take the pressure off."

"Smooth," Bodhi smiles at me. "See, Ben? He doesn't need your Animal Planet documentaries on mating habits. He's got this."

"It's my speech that gave him the impetus to pursue." Ben crosses his arms and stares Bodhi down. "Wasn't it, Stevens?"

"I'm sure it helped."

"I'm *sure* it did." Bodhi's voice drips with playful sarcasm. He chuckles. "Ben here is the relationship guru."

"Darn right, I am."

"Okay, Guru, go get ready for your surf lesson. They'll be here any minute," Kai says. He turns to me. "I'm happy for you. Can't wait to hear how this goes."

I swallow the newly formed lump in my throat. I've never been so nervous for a date in my life. So much feels like it's riding on this encounter. We've got rapport and ease between us online. Will that carry over into real life? And if things flop in person, will we stop playing Play on Words together?

As if he can read my mind, Kai adds, "Don't be nervous. She already likes you. When she sees you, she's going to think she hit the jackpot. You're a good man. Go have a night with a woman you've been getting to know. It's not complicated unless you make it that way."

"Right. Thanks."

I smile at Kai and then I leave for the afternoon. I've only got two hours until our date, or not-date, or whatever it is.

I arrive at Cucina Descanso at five forty-five. The hostess tells me to pick any booth or table. I opt for a bistro table for two near the window. Cucina is nestled within a row of shops facing the beach just south of the resort. The sun isn't setting yet, but we'll have a good view of the water from our table.

"Can I get you something while you wait? Bread basket? A drink?" the waiter asks.

"I'm fine with water for now. I'm expecting someone. I'll wait for her."

"Let me know if you change your mind."

I watch tourists and locals cycle and walk by outside the window. The waves break in the distance. Beneath the waves, an entire universe exists where no one waits nervously for their anonymous crush to arrive for pizza. No wonder I feel more at home underwater. It's a far more straightforward world down there.

Five minutes pass. Then ten. Fifteen. It's only six. She'll be on time if she walks through the door right now. I have a good view of the entry and hostess stand, but I've been staring out at the beach, so I glance around to be sure I didn't miss her. Why didn't we exchange names or at least give one another descriptions of what we look like?

I know why I didn't. It felt more mysterious at the time—like some movie my sister and mom would force me to sit through where the guy's at a table and in walks the love of his life and they know instantly when their eyes meet: *that's the one.*

I glance at the door and am beyond surprised when I see Alana walk in. She's wearing those large sunglasses—the ones only she could carry off while still looking beautiful—and her hair is held back by a multi-colored scarf that's tied at the nape of her neck, curls recklessly falling behind the scarf past her shoulders. It's so obviously her, but maybe only to me. I'm torn as to whether to wave, or stand and greet her, or leave her alone. I'm so shocked to see her out on this side of the island, and at a restaurant where anyone could spot her.

I stay seated. She may want to feel invisible. I don't want to intrude on her night.

She looks around as if she's searching for someone. My eyes are on her. How can they not be? She's in a simple pair of dark jeans that flare at the bottom. Heels. A crisp white oxford-style shirt with wide lapels. She looks like Jackie Onassis, only with blond curly hair. Elegant, stately, effortlessly gorgeous. And, also confused. Is the person she's meeting not here?

I glance around the room, silently assisting her search. No one. I'm the only man here alone. The rest of the room is filled with couples and a few four-tops of friends. It's not busy yet, but it will be bustling within the hour.

It's obvious the moment she sees me. Her face softens with a smile.

She says something to the hostess and then approaches my table.

When she's near enough, I stand.

Her face appears partially relieved but she also looks a little concerned. "Stevens, what are you doing here?"

"Oh. I'm meeting a friend."

"Oh." Alana looks around again.

"The bigger question is: what are you doing here? I didn't think you'd be out in public like this without being under duress." I smile at her, hoping to ease the part of her that definitely is riddled with nerves. "*Are* you under duress? Blink twice if you are."

She laughs. Oh, that laugh. It's fleeting, but still as sweet as ever.

"I'm ... uh ... meeting a friend too."

From the way her cheeks pinken just the slightest, I get the feeling this is a man-friend.

"Is he running late?" I ask, my eyes sweeping the room again.

"Apparently. And, your friend? Is she running late?"

"You assume it's a woman."

"And you assumed it's a man."

"Fair enough. Well, do you want to wait together?"

She deliberates. Looks around again. "Um ... maybe I should get a table? Or ..."

"Yeah. That makes sense. We don't want to start our dates with them walking in to see us with someone else. That would be ..."

"Awkward," she finishes for me. "Well, it was good seeing you."

"You too. Have a nice dinner."

"You too."

Alana smiles and I remain standing until she's halfway across the room. I watch as she approaches the hostess, who waves her arm toward the room and tells Alana to pick any open table or booth. Definitely not swanky.

My brow creases as I consider the facts. We're both here to meet a friend at six p.m. for dinner. Those friends aren't here. She's here, on a part of the island that is not near her home. She's out in public when she'd likely rather be sequestered and unseeable.

No. Nah.

Sometimes all the facts seem to line up, but the scientist has what we call bias. Wouldn't it be amazing if my online crush were Alana Graves? I chuckle to myself. It's odd enough that Saturday-IslandGirl lives on Marbella. The likelihood of that particular overlap already broke the statistical record books. There's no chance my island woman is Alana Graves.

Dream on, Stevens. And, also, stop wishing it were Alana on a night you are about to meet SaturdayIslandGirl. That's just wrong.

And since when do I have lengthy inner monologues?

Dating. It's not for the faint of heart.

I glance over at Alana intermittently. Her date hasn't shown yet either. She catches me looking over at her a few times and smiles an uncharacteristically shy smile. She's still wearing those sunglasses, as if the sun can hide from the rest of the solar system. Even in a booth near the kitchen, she shines like the star she is. Eyes drift in her direction regularly—not just my eyes.

At one point, a group of young women approach Alana in her booth.

It's six twenty. I'm getting restless and toying with the idea of texting the woman I'm waiting for. I don't want to appear needy. Maybe she changed her mind. Something could have come up. It's only twenty minutes. I'll wait. She's got my number. If she needs to cancel or she's got something to tell me, she'll call or text.

I watch the scene unfold at Alana's booth, feeling suddenly protective of her and her privacy. The group of women is being respectful. Alana takes a piece of paper and pen from one of them and signs it. She smiles up at them, says something. Then she removes her glasses and stands. The women flank her in a group and take selfies. There's giggling and a round of thanks, and they leave her. Other customers watch, but they turn back to their meals after the group of women leave. Alana's not the only celebrity or famous person on the island, though she's definitely the biggest name by far. The resort draws a wealthy crowd. I'm grateful no one makes a scene.

I stand and walk over to Alana's table.

"Are you okay?"

She smiles up at me, returning her glasses to her face. "Why wouldn't I be?"

"You just got spotted."

"They were fine. I love my fans. If I can make their night with an autograph and a selfie, I'm glad to do it."

I smile down at her. "Mind if I sit? It's getting a little ..."

"Lonely?" she asks, tipping her head toward where I've been sitting alone for over a half hour.

"No. I'm good with solitude. It's just getting a little weird. I guess something happened to my date ... friend."

"Date or friend?" she asks.

"That was going to be determined when she had finished eating with me."

Alana slowly drags her sunglasses down her nose in that way she did on my boat. The way she did on the big screen that one time. She studies my face. Her mouth tips up in a half-smile.

"Everything okay?" I ask.

She's silent for a few beats, and then with the perfect timing of a seasoned actress, she delivers the line that I will remember until the day I die.

"After bolognese and drinks?"

I'm nearly dizzy. My chest feels simultaneously hollow and full. I stare into her glistening gray-blue eyes. "That's what I told her before she bailed on the game we were playing."

"I didn't bail. I had to sleep. I had back to back days of talk show interviews."

"You?" I say, still needing someone to put a defibrillator to my chest. An oxygen mask would be helpful too. *My online crush is Alana Graves?*

I all but collapse into the booth across from her.

"Wordivore?" she asks, her previous pulled together facade slipping just the slightest.

"SaturdayIslandGirl." It's not a question, but I'm still in shock.

TWENTY-ONE

Alana

What if someone you never met,
someone you never saw,
someone you never knew
was the only someone for you?
~ Sleepless in Seattle

I'm in shock.

"*You're* Wordivore?"

He laughs this low, mellow laugh and it fills me like helium.

"Statistical probability? ... One in infinity," he says with a look of awe that I'm sure mirrors my own.

"On call?" I ask.

His face forms a mask of confusion for a moment. Then his eyes light up with the memory of our online conversation.

"My remote work as a marine biology consultant. I work on call. I forget if I explained the structure of my job when you asked me that day on Joel's boat. I leave the island for a few days a week, sometimes longer. It's unpredictable, but steady. I consult to various organizations, and the government at times. And, when

I'm free, I also tote celebrities back and forth to and from the mainland ... among other odd jobs." He winks.

I smile. I can't stop smiling. "Celebrities? Like who?"

"Oh, I'm not at liberty to say. I signed an NDA. Keeping my word to her is extremely important to me."

"I'm sure she appreciates that more than she can say."

"And you?" He asks as if we're actually on a first date where we need to get to know one another. "You're sort of like a spy?" His one brow lifts.

Neither of us have stopped smiling. My glasses sit off to the side, abandoned now that I know who he is.

"In my recent trilogy of movies."

He chuckles. "Ah, yes. Anya Blackman. The Red Falcon."

I smile. I forgot he was a fan. He hides it well.

The waiter approaches our table. "Are you ready to order now?"

He's carrying two menus, but I answer him before he even sets them down.

"Yes. We're ready."

I turn my eyes toward Stevens.

It's still surreal. He's Wordivore. The man who made me feel so at ease on Joel's boat. The one who brought me a sandwich when he knew I'd be hungry. The same man I invited to dinner at my home. The one who reads *Gone With the Wind,* and some book about octopi at night, in bed, wearing sexy reading glasses. He's the one who helped me muster the courage to set a boundary with my mother. This man I've been flirting with online ... is Stevens. Wordivore is Stevens.

Without taking my eyes off Stevens, I tip my mouth into a coy smirk. Then I ask the waiter, "Do you have anything with bolognese?"

Stevens beams. He's so transparent and unpretentious. Comfortable. We're both a little nervous, or maybe we're simply adjusting to the jaw-dropping reality of all these overlaps between us. If I believed in luck or serendipity, I'd say this was destiny. Right now, I don't know what to call it. Uncanny, for sure.

"We have a house-made bolognese that is our customers' favorite," The waiter explains. "You can choose the pasta you'd like it on. We make it fresh every morning and then allow it to cook all day so the flavors are rich and married like a couple in the beautiful Emilia-Romagna region of Italy."

"I've been there," I tell the waiter. "It's lovely."

"I'm from Dozza."

"Dozza? With the painted wall?"

"Sì, bella donna."

I smile at him and glance back at Stevens. His eyes scan my face, flitting from feature to feature. A soft smile turns his mouth up when our eyes meet.

"The sauce, it can go on the tagliatelle pasta," the waiter tells me. "Or your choice, bella."

I'm still staring at Stevens when I answer. "Le tagliatelle, per favore. E un'insalata."

"And she speaks Italian," Stevens says in a low voice, nearly to himself.

I smile over at him—the same smile that's been pulling at my cheeks since I discovered his identity. "And French."

His smile breaks open like the sun through clouds. We're old friends who never met. It's the oddest sensation, melding the layers together into one cohesive reality. We even have private jokes.

"And for you, sir?" the waiter asks.

"Same. Bolognese. On the pasta."

"The tagliatelle."

"Sure. Yes." He doesn't take his eyes off mine. "Whatever she's having."

"So, also the salad?"

"Right. Yes. The salad, please."

We're a sight, I'm sure. Two people, locked onto one another so steadily that the rest of the world could blow up and we'd miss it.

"Molto bene. Very good," the waiter says.

He offers us a selection of beverages and we make our choices, only glancing at him momentarily and then back at one another.

It's as if looking away for too long might break the spell. Would Stevens disappear? Is he even real?

I reach out without thinking, my hand landing on Stevens' forearm.

He slowly glances down where my fingertips touch his skin and then back up at me.

"Just checking," I say.

"If I'm a mirage?"

"A dream, a mirage, a fugue state ... you know. The usual."

"Yeah. I get that all the time," he jokes.

"I bet you do."

He's truly gorgeous. I admired him before on occasion, but he was my temporary employee. It didn't feel appropriate to fully acknowledge his appeal then.

He raises an eyebrow.

"What? You have to know you're attractive."

He shakes his head, dropping his eyes toward the table as though I've embarrassed him. It's adorable.

"I'm aware that I garner attention. Sometimes it's less welcome than others."

"Hmmm. And when is it welcome?"

I sit back, crossing my arms over my chest, grateful that our capacity for banter is alive and well. I had wondered whether seeing Wordivore in person would squash the way we so freely verbally spar with one another.

"When I find a woman desirable. Then, I don't mind if she finds me attractive."

He's different in this moment. Commanding. Masculine. I've seen this side of him a few times as Stevens, my taxi pilot, but not so much as Wordivore. And now, it's a heady thing, sitting across from him while he owns his attraction and calls mine out in equal measure.

If this were a real first date and the guy were being this unabashedly invested in me, I'd be sneaking to the restroom to text Brigitte for an escape plan. Stevens and I are being intimate and forward. In reality, we're not strangers. We know one another. This date feels like a culmination, a benchmark, and a rite of passage in a relationship that has been brewing for over six months.

The air is thick between us. I lick my lips and Stevens watches me. He takes a sip of his water and then smoothly shifts the conversation away from the crackle of our mutual attraction to something more neutral and appropriate for the setting.

"So, you had a few days of interviews?"

"You really don't follow Hollywood buzz much, do you?"

"If by not much you mean not at all, then yes. That's true."

I can't explain why this delights me like it does.

"Well, I was on The Kelly Clarkson Show—with my co-star."

"Rex Fordham?"

"Yes."

I stuff down the memories of that interview. Kelly was delightful, but the obvious insinuation that Rex and I are together was established and never refuted. She was gracious enough to only tease us about what a beautiful couple Rex and I make. She didn't focus on us and our relationship for longer than was needed. She's so down to earth. I loved chatting with her if you set aside the fact that our interview probably solidified a lot of rumors.

"Do you know who Kelly Clarkson is?" I ask.

"I do. My brother sings country, so I get familiar with a lot of artists through him and his passion for that genre. Kelly was married to a country singer for a while."

"Your brother sings country? Professionally?"

"He does paid gigs around the island and over in LA. He's moving to Tennessee."

"Ahhh. Nashville. Pursuing his dreams to be a big country star?"

"No. Not exactly. He's actually moving to join a station—a fire station—in a small town between Nashville and Knoxville. He's a fireman."

"Does he look like you?"

"A little, but he's more muscular and built like a brick house, why?"

"I'm just indulging in a little fantasy. Give me a minute."

He laughs. "Not your type. I assure you."

"Oh?"

"Yeah. I think you'd be better suited with a ... I don't know ... a nerdy marine biologist who knows his way around the local kelp beds."

"Oh, yeah?"

"Mm hmm."

We both laugh. And then I remember. "Wait! Your brother. The one leaving the island. Only I didn't know it was an island at the time. He's moving away and ... I'm sorry. It's all piecing together now."

"That's the one. You really helped me that night. I was blind-sided. But you're right. I can visit him, and he'll be back for visits here too."

"It's not the same as living on the same island, for sure. So, you actually have family suppers?"

"Once a week. And I do go to Mitzi's Tacos weekly too."

"Isn't this weird?" I look into Stevens' deep brown eyes. "Every time I remember a piece of a conversation we had, or the night you showed up at Summer's barbecue ... the boat rides ... you in the cove when Brigitte was visiting. I have to lay it down in the puzzle so it attaches to the rest of who you are to me. You've been more than one person in my mind for so long. I'm trying to stitch them all together."

"Yes. It's unusual. But, not ... unfortunate."

"Not at all," I agree. "More like Christmas morning, when

you thought you'd opened all the gifts, but then you find that last one hidden under the tree."

He smiles at me. "And that one turns out to be the very thing you wanted all along."

"Smooth, Stevens. Really smooth."

"Trust me." He smiles that half smile where the dimples form these nearly-edible lines on one side of his face. "I'm not smooth. I'm pretty ... unsmooth, actually."

"I don't know. You've come up with some snappy one-liners over the time I've known you."

"Online. I don't do that in person."

"Not even with me?"

"Maybe with you, now? But I'll reluctantly remind you of the day we met on Joel's boat."

I laugh lightly. "You had your moment."

"Not smooth." His eyebrows lift and drop. It's sexier than it should be.

Our salads arrive and we eat. Stevens asks me about my other interviews with the two Jimmies as Brigitte has dubbed them. I ask him about his work—my motive in asking now is so different than it had been. Before, I was curious. Now, I'm interested.

He looks at me over our plates of pasta, about halfway through the meal. "I've got a project I've been working on. It's sort of a secret."

"Ooooh. I love secrets."

"I'll have to show you sometime."

"Is this like where a guy asks a girl to his flat to see his sketches?"

He chuckles. "Something like that. Only, you'll be snorkeling —or diving."

"I'd love that."

"I thought you might."

We finish dinner, and Stevens insists we share a tiramisu. I generally don't eat dessert, but I can't break that fact to him when he looks at me instead of the waiter and says, "She needs to try your tiramisu."

When the waiter asks, "Two servings?" Stevens holds my gaze and says, "We'll share one."

The waiter leaves and arrives with the dessert. We stare at one another and smile the goofiest grins.

"So?" he asks cryptically before taking a bite of tiramisu and placing it in his mouth.

"So, what?"

"What's the verdict?"

I'm so satisfied between the effects of the delicious pasta and the decadent dessert, my half-glass of wine, and the way Stevens keeps looking at me, I don't even know if I can process his question.

"The verdict?"

He sits up and crosses his arms across his chest. "Was this a date? Or was it two friends finally connecting after months of cultivating an online relationship?"

I don't hesitate. I'm not coy. I've waited too long for him already. "This was definitely a date."

"Good to know." His smile is soft and promising.

Stevens pays the bill and we walk out, side by side, into the cool evening air. His hand brushes my lower back. The sun has set and the sound of the waves hitting the shore provides the perfect soundtrack.

"How did you get here tonight?" he asks.

"I had one of my drivers bring me."

"Ah, yes. Your drivers."

"Are you mocking me?"

His face grows serious. "Not at all. You've earned all the drivers and cooks and cleaners and brick walls who protect you from rabid fans."

"That's what Brigitte says."

"She's right."

"She's also the one who told me to say yes to a date with you."

"She's very right."

The confidence oozing off him right now feels like a drug. He may think he's awkward. And I have experienced that side of him, but he's also incredibly strong and self-assured at times. Never cocky or arrogant. It's a rarity. Usually when I meet men like him, they're so full of themselves there isn't room for another person in their self-focused universe. Not that I've ever met a man like Stevens. I'm quite sure I haven't.

"What else did Brigitte tell you to do?" he asks.

"Hmmm? Oh. Nothing, besides to get my sleep when I had a big day ahead."

He chuckles. "So, no advice on the goodnight kiss?"

"None. But I think we both knew I could make that call on my own."

He reaches out and brushes my curls away from my face. They spring back when his fingers move away.

"Let's grab a cart from the resort," he suggests. "I'll drive you home."

My brow lifts.

"And leave you at the front door," he adds with a wink. "No use having a driver come out when I can take you myself."

"Where do you live?" I ask. "You've been inside my home. It's only fair I know where you live."

"Want to see it?" he offers.

"Your house?"

"It's not much to speak of, but it's only a few blocks from here."

"Actually, yes. I'd love to see your house."

He smiles at me. And with the fluidity and tenderness of a man with far more prowess than he claims to possess, he reaches down and captures my hand in his. He intertwines our fingers and begins walking down the street, past the row of shops next to Cucina.

"Let's take the sand," he suggests, looking down into my eyes. "Can you? In those?"

He points down toward my sandals. I'm wearing heels.

"I can take these off and carry them," I say. "I'd love to walk on the beach."

Stevens surprises me when we've reached the small strip of sidewalk running right along the sand. He drops to one knee.

"You're proposing?" I smile down at him. "It's a little early for that. Don't ya think?"

"I'm taking your heels off for you."

"Oh." My teasing tone is blown away on an ocean breeze. "Okay."

Stevens taps the back of my ankle, coaxing me to lift my foot onto his thigh. I don't know how I don't wobble and fall over. He's focused and gentle, sweetly caring for me in a way I'd never imagined a man could or should.

I've been dated, pursued, stalked ... yes, even stalked. I don't think a man has ever done anything so thoughtful and romantic before.

Stevens carefully puckers the strap of the sandal so it pops from the clasp. His fingers graze my ankle. His eyes look up to mine, but then back to his self-appointed task. He slips my sandal off my foot and hands it up to me. Then he wordlessly removes my other shoe with the same tender reverence before he stands and intertwines our fingers again. I loop the sandals over my finger on the opposite hand and we step onto the beach together.

The night is cool but not chilly. The light of the stars and moon reflect off the water. Couples dot the sand in loosely scattered silhouettes.

"Want to walk along the shore pound?" Stevens asks me.

"Won't your legs turn into a tail if you touch the water?"

"I guess you'll have to just wait and see."

TWENTY-TWO

Stevens

You should be kissed and often,
and by someone who knows how.
~ Gone With the Wind

Alana Graves.

I'm holding hands with Alana Graves. Only, not really. She's not Alana Graves right now. She's just Alana, my Saturday-IslandGirl. I can't allow my mind to think of her image when her face is the size of four men standing on one another's shoulders, shown on big screens across the nation to paying crowds of moviegoers. I can't drift into thoughts of anything but this moment. She can't be a famous celebrity when it's just the two of us.

I give her hand a gentle squeeze. Everything between us is simultaneously new and familiar. I know her. And yet I'm only just meeting her. I've touched her, but only to help her on or off a boat. We've flirted, but only from the safety we found behind our screens. And yet, not holding her hand right now would feel unnatural.

We walk to the water's edge, I toe off my shoes and we wade in, ankle deep. Alana cuffs her pants and rolls them high enough so that she can go deeper. I follow suit. I'd go under, fully clothed, just to be with her wherever she's leading right now.

Alana spins in a circle, her arms outstretched and head upturned. She returns to my side, wrapping one arm around my waist. I loop my arm behind her back and we stand there, staring out into the sea.

"What made you want to be a marine biologist?" she asks softly.

"It's kind of embarrassing."

"Oh?" Alana gives my side a tug. "Now you have to tell me."

"The most basic answer is that I love the ocean. Always have. I never tire of exploring it."

Her fingers draw lazy patterns on my side and I feel like Bodhi's dog, ready to lay on my back so she knows not to stop.

"In elementary school, this guy came in to tell us about the ocean and all the animals in our local waters. He talked about conservation. But, the clincher was when he talked about the green sea turtles in our Channel Islands—how they're endangered. All through his presentation, I thought ..." I pause. "Here comes the embarrassing part."

She smiles. "Thanks for the warning. Now I'm prepared to properly tease you."

"Good. Just wanted to make sure you were paying attention."

Her hand stills and she looks up at me. The light of the moon and stars reflects in her eyes with the same sparkle as the ocean.

"You have my attention, Stevens. All of it."

Whew. There's this feeling underwater when you're free-diving. Gravity ceases to exist. You're one with the beauty surrounding you—unrestricted. The experience is intimidating at first, and wholly overwhelming. This. She's my free dive.

"Well," I glance out at the ocean. "I decided I was going to save the sea turtles." I look down at her. "You know, all of them."

"All of them." She smiles.

"Yeah. All of them." I laugh. "Needless to say, I had to modify my mission statement over the years. But I still feel strongly about protecting the ocean."

"You really are Poseidon."

"Minus the rage issues, yeah. Maybe a little."

Alana pivots, turning her back toward the incoming tide. Her face tilts upward, her intention is clearer than the night sky.

I run my hand along her cheek. She leans into my palm and I cup her beautiful face.

Alana loops a hand behind my neck and runs her fingernails across the sensitive skin there.

I sigh or maybe make a noise. Hopefully nothing too crazy. I can't tell. My eyes drift shut and shivers race along the skin on my neck.

Have I kissed women before? Maybe. I can't remember any of them. She's all that exists—her, and this unexpected moment between us.

I lean down a fraction of an inch, uncertainty threatening to rob me of our connection.

Alana's hand tugs at my neck, gently urging me toward her.

The waves continue to gently caress our ankles, but all I see is her face and the invitation written across her features. I bend the rest of the way, and she raises on her tiptoes until our mouths brush together like a whisper. My hand is looped behind her head, woven into her soft curls. Our kiss is nearly reverent—her lips soft and pliant. I feel this kiss everywhere even though we've barely allowed ourselves any contact. I pull back. I want to preserve this feeling. It would be too easy to shift gears, like a motor boat once it clears the channel markers. Not tonight. I run my knuckles down her cheek, settling my hand on her shoulder.

She smiles up at me. "You don't push the limits, do you, Stevens?"

"Depends on which limits you're talking about."

Her hand comes up and cups my jaw. She drags her thumb across my stubble.

"Sweet man," she mutters nearly under her breath. "You're the sweetest man I've ever met."

I know I'm blushing. I'm grateful for the dusky light. No one has ever called me sweet—not the way she is right now.

I draw her into my arms and hold her to me. She leans into me, and we're comfortably quiet in one another's arms. Just Alana, me, and the ebb and flow of the water beneath us.

"Did you still want to see my house?" I murmur the question into her hair.

"I definitely want to see your house."

"It's ... okay. I want you to see it too. Are you ready?"

"Yes."

We retrieve our shoes from the sand, and Alana extends her hand to me. We're quiet for most of the walk, stealing glances at one another and smiling softly when we do.

Is this what contentment feels like? Adrenaline burned off into a sedate, floaty sensation where there's nowhere to be, nothing to do, and a pervasive sense that all's right in the world? Or is this just her?

It's her. All her.

We step off the sand and I lead Alana to a bench.

"I can take sandals off," I tell her. "But you're on your own when it comes to putting those back on."

"I think I can manage. Though, I may want a repeat of the sandal removal again in the future."

"You know where to find me."

"I will in a few minutes. Once you show me where you live."

"So, you're saying you might just show up randomly at my door, asking me to take your sandals off for you?"

"Would that be a problem?"

"Not from where I'm standing. I don't see a thing wrong with that at all."

"Good to know." She smiles and stands, her heels securely strapped to her feet.

We walk to my house, hand in hand.

We're turning up my street when Alana asks, "Did you grow up on this side of the island?"

"I did not."

"Where did you grow up then?"

"On the North Shore. Not far from your place, actually. But down in the neighborhoods at the bottom of the hills. If you know where Marbella Elementary is, we were a block downhill from there. Still are, actually. My parents have lived in that house since my mom was pregnant with me."

"You've always lived on the island. Wow."

"You haven't?"

"No. We vacationed here. But I grew up in LA. My parents sold our vacation house when I was twelve. We didn't have the luxury of spending time here when they were so focused on cultivating my career."

"At age twelve?"

"Yeah."

There's a sadness to her voice, even though she's masking it.

"Well, I feel like a total slacker. I only started pursuing my career in earnest in my twenties."

She laughs, light and sweet. And I feel like I won the Nobel Prize.

"I love your laugh," I tell her.

"Do you, now?"

"I actually do."

I take my keys out of my pocket and turn up the walkway to my home. "This is me."

She drops my hand so I can unlock the door, and then she steps into my house ahead of me, with my hand gently grazing her back to guide her.

"When you would tell me I made you laugh during one of our matches on *Play on Words*, I always tried to imagine what your laugh sounded like. And then I made you laugh a few times when I was taxiing you to and from LA."

She pauses and looks up at me.

"Knowing I made you laugh and hearing what it sounds like … feels like a gift."

"Do you always say things like that?" she asks.

"Like what?"

"Kind, thoughtful, amazing things that make a woman feel special?"

"I'm not really in the habit of talking to too many women besides my mother and my sister. And the women who go out on tours with me. But, mostly then I'm explaining how to operate a tank, or describing the life of a sea cucumber."

She laughs so hard she snorts. "There you go, making me snort again."

"I'm still pretty sure you managed that without me."

"I never snort. My mother would be horrified."

"What's she like?"

"My mother?"

"Yeah." I walk through my small living room into the kitchen. "Can I get you anything? Water? Tea? Something to eat?"

"I'm fine. And my mother is … unique. A force. Someone I hope you never meet … well, for a long time. She's … selective and … difficult. Let's just put it this way, Brigitte calls her Mother Gothel."

I pour myself a glass of water and walk back in the living room. "From Tangled?"

"You've seen the movie?"

"I've seen many movies that most men would deny watching, thanks to my mom and sister. Tangled is one of my favorites, though. You've gotta love Flynn Ryder." I contort my face into an exaggerated smolder.

"Oh my gosh! You even smolder. What have I gotten myself into? That's wholly irresistible."

"Is it?" I laugh. "Want a tour? It's really lengthy. I'm not sure you've got the amount of free time it will take to peruse my luxurious abode."

"… to peruse your luxurious abode?" She chuckles.

"Here," I wave my hand around the living room. "We have the living room, family room, sitting room, entry, and parlor. Also, the library." I point to my bookcase. "No rolling ladders, which is why Belle left me for the Beast."

"Understandable," Alana says, her smile filling her face. "A girl needs her rolling ladder, after all."

"And talking dinnerware. That's another thing I'm short on."

She's looking pretty entertained, so I keep going.

"And in here, just through the house, in the north wing, we have the kitchen, the butler's pantry, and the ..." I smile. "Yeah. That's all I can think of for this space."

I look around my ten by ten kitchen. It serves me, and I'm not ashamed of it. I like living simply. I don't begrudge people who live more affluent lives. I've just never had a need for anything beyond this small bungalow.

Alana's still beaming. "And down that hall?"

"Ah, yes. The hallway, passageway, corridor, portico ..." I chuckle.

"You're just showing off now."

"You think?"

She smiles. "So, down the corridor?"

"That is the master's quarters and the powder room, dressing room, spa facilities, and gentleman's wardrobe."

She busts out laughing. And I'm joining her, even though I'm not that funny. There's this contagious lightness between us and it's ballooning the longer we're together.

Joy. Maybe this is joy.

"May I see where you keep your glasses?"

"My ... glasses?"

She nods shyly.

"What is it with you and my glasses?" I smile at her warmly for no other reason than the fact that she makes me smile.

"I imagined you wearing them."

"Ahhh. Well, far be it from me to keep you from realizing a fantasy. Besides," I say, as I turn on the hall light and walk the three steps it takes to get to my bedroom door. "I have to outshine these inaccurate fantasies you have about my younger brother. Firemen. Pfft. What's so hot about that?"

I open my bedroom door and she follows me, lingering in the doorway.

"Probably nothing," she says with a taunt in her voice. "Firemen. Totally not hot."

"Exactly. Trust me. Biologists are where it's at."

"Do you want a T-shirt?"

"I have one."

"Really?" She's slack jawed.

"Yeah. My *Biologists Are The Hottest* shirt? It's right through here." I move toward my closet, then I stop, turn toward her and smile. "No. I don't own that shirt. That would be ridiculous. And troublesome. Women would ... Yeah. No."

"Women would what?"

"They don't need a billboard, or a T-shirt."

"I bet." She smiles and her gaze grows appreciative.

It may be the first time I've ever wanted anyone to look at me the way she's looking at me right now. I walk to the side table, pull open the drawer and extract my glasses from the place where I store them.

"Is that the octopus book?" she asks from her spot in my doorway. She's leaning against the jamb now.

"It is." I hold it up.

There's this nearly imperceptible lift of her brows. Her eyes soften.

Oh, why not? I've gone this far, I may as well ...

"So, every night ..."

I pick two pillows up and stack them along my headboard.

"I climb onto my bed." I do just that, extending my legs out on the mattress.

"And I grab this book." I hold it up like an exhibit.

"And these incredibly-sexier-than-any-fireman glasses." I wink over at her.

She laughs. It's a few soft chuckles, but they are nearly as sweet as her full laughter.

"And then I place these on my very rugged, marine-biologist face." I do that and her cheeks pull up into a grin. "And then I open the book and read."

I open the book and look at the page where I left off. Then I look up at her and she's staring at me through her lashes.

"Yep," she announces. "Hotter than a fireman."

I laugh as I take my glasses off, put them back in the drawer and shut the book.

"Well," I walk toward her. "That's the tour of my mansion."

Her voice is soft when she says, "It's lovely, Stevens. Just right."

"It serves the purpose. Oh. I also have a back yard, but it's too dark out to show you on this particular tour. You'll have to do the daytime one to see everything properly."

"I'll have to make arrangements for that, then."

I have nothing witty to say. We're less than a foot apart. I'm caged into my room and she's blocking the doorway, smiling up at me. I lean in and place a soft kiss on her forehead. Then I turn us both so we're heading back down the hallway.

We walk out of the house together and I drive Alana to her home.

She's quiet on the drive. We're on the hill going up from the resort toward the other side of the island when she reaches over and takes my hand in hers. I smile over at her and then return my attention to the road.

"Tonight was ... unexpected," she says as we near her home. "And ... wonderful."

"Wonderful." I echo. "If you don't mind leaving a Yelp review? And also, mention the whole biologists rule, firemen drool thing ..."

"You're just making me want to meet your brother. You know that, right?"

"Me telling you he drools makes you want to meet him?"

She laughs again. Then her voice softens. "Thank you."

"For?"

"For dinner. This evening. For making me laugh. For the walk on the beach. Definitely for the house tour and indulging my hot biologist in dark-rimmed glasses fantasy."

I smile over at her. "It was my pleasure. Thank you."

Alana's beauty nearly knocks the wind out of my lungs. For a while, I forgot. I acted like a complete goofball. And now, we're here at her hilltop acreage with ocean views.

Alana Graves. A voice deep within me chants her name, tempting me to elevate her above the woman who joined me for dinner and a pretty awesome date.

"This was the most fun I've had in a while," she says when I park the golf cart in front of her gate.

"Me too."

Alana opens the gate with a code and I step out of the cart to walk her to her door. It's far later than I'd imagined it would be when this date ended. And I'm nowhere near ready to let her go, even though we both need our sleep.

Alana turns to me on the porch. I draw her into a hug. She tucks into me and nestles her head under my chin. I feel her release a sigh. When she pulls back, I place a kiss on her lips. It's soft and quick. Leaving me wanting so much more. Hopefully leaving her feeling the same way.

"I'm entering a busy season of my work life," she says, apologetically.

"So ... don't expect you to return my calls?"

She stares up at me. "I'll return your calls anytime I can. Just know I won't be around as much. The six to eight weeks before a release tend to be like a freight train without brakes."

"So, you do want a second date?" I can't help smiling.

I have no chill. I'm literally the male elephant seal, lolling around in a floppy mass, waiting for her return. Pursuit is not in my wheelhouse. Waiting for her definitely is.

"I'm already thinking of a fifth date." She surprises me, and I feel my eyes go wide.

"Too forward?" she asks.

"No. Not at all. I'm just ... adjusting."

"Me too. But I want to adjust together. With a heads up that I won't be here as much for the foreseeable future. But when I am, I'll let you know." She pauses. "Because, I'd like to see you."

I barely register her last sentence. I'm hit again with the reality of who she is and what she does for a living—the chasm between our lives and lifestyles couldn't be greater.

"There's no pressure to let me know when you're here," I say. "I'm sure you need time away from people."

"From people. Yes. I don't think I'll need time away from you for a while."

"On that note, I'm going to back away slowly. Before you change your mind."

She giggles. It's different from her usual laugh. This one is more girlish. I picture her as a little girl, curls bouncing around her shoulders as she runs in and out of the surf. Like a girl I played with when I was a boy.

"Oh no you don't," she says, reaching for me. "Not without a proper goodnight."

I pull her into me, holding her to my chest and she wraps her arms tightly around me for another hug. We stand there, embracing one another, delaying the inevitable change that will begin when I drive back down that hill.

I kiss the top of her head. "Goodnight, Saturday Island Girl."

"Goodnight, Marbella Island Man."

She pulls back, leans in for one more quick hug, kisses me on the cheek and then turns to walk into her home.

TWENTY-THREE

Alana

I fell in love with him the way you fall asleep.
Slowly, and then all at once.
~ The Fault in Our Stars

I'm not even finished pouring my coffee when I press Brigitte's contact on my cell. I didn't call her last night because it was late, and also, I needed time to let everything coalesce in my own mind. This morning I woke up with a smile on my face. If that has happened before, which it must have, I can't remember it feeling like this. I'm floating. There's not another word for it. Floating on the memories of last night, on the reality that Wordivore is Stevens. That man is the whole package.

"Hello? What's up?" Brigitte answers.

"Good morning. You're not going to believe this." Even I hear the song in my voice.

"Oooh. I love when I don't believe things. What is it? You quit show biz? You told your mom you ordered a whole pizza and ate it? You've bought us tickets to Taylor Swift and they include backstage passes and a private meet and greet with Travis?" She pauses, but not long enough. "Oh my gosh! I *wouldn't* believe that. But I'd love it. Just sayin'. It's a little early for Christmas, but that's the kind of gift you need to get on early. So, chop chop if you haven't already!"

I'm laughing. "None of the above."

"Awww. That's a shame. You should eat more pizza, honestly. In front of your mom. Or ... you know, just post a pic of you taking a big ol' bite on your socials."

"I don't post on my own socials. You do."

"So, I'll get us pizza. You eat. I'll document the event with a photo. I'll post. Your mom will go viral!"

"Isn't it viral when a post spreads like wildfire?"

"Your mom will be the wildfire. She'd be so hot and livid. It would be fun, don't ya think?"

"Do you possibly want to know what I called for?"

"Oooh. Yes! I nearly forgot, what with Travis and TayTay and pizza and you quitting."

I laugh again. "Okay. Here goes." I pause for effect. "It's him."

As soon as I say the words a warmth spreads through me. My smile takes over my face. I feel that smile in my toes and the tips of my hair. I walk out onto my balcony porch and take a sip of coffee while Brigitte reacts. I've got time. I'm going to tell her. Her reaction is half the fun.

"Who's him? Okay, cryptic girl. Him. Him. Him. Wait! It is Travis! No. You said it wasn't Travis. Zac Efron? Chris Hemsworth? Any of the Ryans? Who is he? And what are we talking about here?"

I'm laughing into my coffee mug, afraid to take a sip because I'll choke or spit it out.

"The guy. My word-game friend. He's Stevens."

There's a longish silence and then Brigitte asks, "Stevens? The merman?"

"Yes! The merman." I smile thinking about how we joked about him being a merman, and then I sigh. He wants to save all the sea turtles. What a man.

"Wait. Wait, wait, wait. The merman is your word-friend?"

She's catching up. She always does if given time to spiral and reel herself back in.

"Yes. The man Joel asked to sub for him. The one who has been taxiing me to LA when Joel was in the midwest—is Wisconsin the midwest? Anyway, the one who ate dinner with me when he dropped off my groceries. Him. Stevens. He's the one."

"Hold the phone! You had dinner with him? At your house?"

"He brought groceries in. I asked if he was hungry. We ate a meal together. He had fish. I had chicken. That's not important."

"That's not important? Alana? You never have anyone in that house. It's like the freaking Bat Cave. Only Alfred, that's me, and Batman, that's you, and Robin ... that's not your mom. I don't know who Robin is. Maybe I'm Robin. No. No. I'm definitely Alfred. Anyway, my point is, no one enters the Bat Cave. It's your private lair. And you let Stevens in?"

"He brought the groceries in. It just seemed polite to invite him to stay."

"Mmm hmmm. So polite. I'd like to be so polite. That man is a snack."

"Watch it."

"Right?! That's what I mean. You're different with him— with Stevens. And now this? He's your word-guy. Oh, hello. Hello, hello, hellllooo."

"Should I even have called you?"

"Um. Is that even a question? Yes. You should call me. This is massive. So. Are you going to see him again? What happened? Did you kiss?"

"No, we didn't kiss," I lie. "Of course we didn't kiss."

I'm not sure why I hide our kiss from Brigitte. I tell her everything. My kiss with Stevens feels like something sacred and private. I still need time to process the way he touched my cheek, looked into my eyes and then gently brushed his lips across mine. How something so small and subtle as the kiss we shared could rock my world to the core ... Yeah. I need time to process that, alone.

And now my mind is drifting to thoughts of Stevens, our kiss, and our night together. The way he played out my Stevens-in-bed-with-dark-rimmed-glasses fantasy. Gah. She's right. He is a snack. And, he's so careful with me. Respectful. He leaves me yearning. No man has ever made me yearn for him. And here he is, this unassuming man, affecting me like no one ever has before—and I'm quite sure no one else ever will.

"Why didn't you kiss?" Brigitte asks. "That man is so very kissable. I mean, seriously. Some men are. Some definitely are not. You know those men you look at and you just want to send them to the dentist, give them a loofa, and buy them complimentary Listerine?" She pauses, but not long enough for me to get a word in. "Ewww. Just no. And then there are the guys who would label themselves kissable. Like they probably practice on a mirror. Also gross. But Stevens? Oh, yes. Kissable. Massively kissable."

"You are making this so awkward."

"Why? Because I appreciate a gorgeous man when I see one? I'm not attracted to him. I mean, I wouldn't turn down dinner ..."

"What! You aren't going to dinner with him!"

"Mm hmm. You're right I'm not. And why is that? Because he's yours. As he should be. I'm just saying befoooore. Before he was yours, when he was emerging from the watery depths with rivulets of water sluicing down his perfect pectorals ... and that smile ... and those eyes ... and that voice. Yes. I would have gone to dinner with him. But now, he's like a brother to me. A hot, sexy, very much my boss' boyfriend brother."

"He's not my boyfriend!" I don't shout, but my voice is raised and adamant.

"Not yet. I get it. You need the build, the slow burn, the development of ground rules, the testing of the chemistry. All that. But you know him, Alana. You know him from all those millions of chats through the game, and you know him in real life. And he's not into you for your fame. This is perfect. Think about it. The man likes you because of your mind. No girl gets that. We always get to be assessed for our looks alongside everything else. You've been given a gift. Take that gift and run with it."

My voice is quiet. "I think I just might."

"Atta girl! So ... tell me everything else. All about the night. Was it amazing? Did you feel like a normal woman on a date? Or did you feel all, *I'm Alana Graves*?"

"Definitely a woman on a date. I don't know how he does it, but I never feel like anything but me when I'm with him."

"Well, in truth, both parts of you are you—the public and the private, the actress and the reclusive, witty, smart, sometimes stubborn woman with a heart of gold. You're both. And I think he's actually the man to handle all that. I mean, he's not afraid of diving deep underwater. He can handle you."

"Handle me?" I laugh.

"You heard me. Don't make me repeat myself." She laughs a little. "And, Alana?"

"Yeah."

"Let yourself have this. Don't let the Wicked Witch of the West steal your Toto."

I'm laughing too hard to answer Brigitte. But once her words sink in, my warm fuzzy feelings head straight into an ice bath.

My mother can never ever meet Stevens. That's for certain.

TWENTY-FOUR

Stevens

Being with you is the only way
I could have a full and happy life.
You're the girl of my dreams and apparently,
I'm the man of yours.
~ 50 First Dates

"How was the big date?" Ben's question catches me off guard when I approach the guys for a morning surf session.

I set my board on the sand next to their three and stare out at the waves. It's a good day for surfing. None of us have lessons or tours this morning, so we decided to meet up to hit the waves. I don't always join them.

Today, I could use the distraction from thoughts of Alana, our kiss, our night, the way she smiled and laughed. And, most torturous of all, whether I should call her, text her, or give her space. I'm so rusty when it comes to dating, and I've never dated someone where the stakes felt so high. I don't want to mess this relationship up before it's even gotten sea legs.

I keep reminding myself she's SaturdayIslandGirl. She knows me. We have more hours logged making a connection than many couples spend together over years of dating. That does help. For a minute or two. Then the nerves creep back in, along with this unfamiliar warmth. Just thinking of her makes my face break into a smile.

"Uh, Kai? Looks like we've got a diver down over here." Ben chuckles. "Man. You got it bad, Stevens. Must have gone well."

"Yeah. It did. I think."

"You think?" Ben asks.

Bodhi and Kai give him twin looks of warning.

"What are you basing your assessment on?" Ben asks. "What tells you it went well?"

"We laughed. She came to my house. I drove her home ..."

"She came to your house?" Ben asks.

"Just to see where I live."

"Yeah. That's why women come to a guy's house after a date. To check out the architecture, the floor plan ... to see if the load-bearing walls are holding up." He laughs.

Did I blow it? Was my goofy tour a misfire?

"What did you do when she was at your house?" Ben wags his eyebrows.

Bodhi shuts him down. "Not your business, bro."

"I uh ... gave her the tour?"

"Oh! No! No, you didn't!" Ben is cackling.

Bodhi looks at Ben with a scolding expression a father would give his child.

"I did, actually."

I thought she liked it. Did I misread her?

"What exactly is included in the tour?" Bodhi asks, with a soft look to his face. "I mean ... your house is like a 20 second tour tops. No offense."

"None taken."

I don't answer right away because I'm busy overthinking Alana's expressions and what I did and said. I'd rather be buried alive six feet under this beach than tell them about the *hot biologist in glasses.*

"Are you blushing?" Ben asks.

Kai turns on Ben. "Look. It wasn't too long ago you were nearly crying in my lap about Summer, so you need to take it down at least ten notches."

"It's okay," I assure Kai.

I don't know if I've ever heard Kai so upset. He's as steady as the waves on a flat day. Kai's not yelling, but he's slightly red at the neck and his face says he means serious business.

Ben raises his hands. "Sorry." Then he looks at me. "I'm sorry, Stevens. I didn't mean any harm. You know how we all are. We rib one another. It's what we do. So, tell us about the tour. If you want."

I do. I want their perspective. Minus the glasses part. That's between me and Alana.

Alana.

I smile again.

"We had dinner at Cucina."

"Good. Good," Bodhi encourages me.

"And it was good. The food, our conversation ..." The fact that she's *ALANA GRAVES.*

I don't say that, of course. These guys actually know her. They've all hung out with her in person far more than I have at this point. Summer and Alana are both in the movies. Mila is Phyllis' niece. And Phyllis and Summer are close. Kai is connected that way.

But I just met her. And kissed her. Another smile ... I don't think I've smiled this much in the cumulative past five years. Not like this. Not the kinds of smiles that won't quit.

"Yep. Dinner was good. Look at that smile." Ben grins at me.

"It was. Then we walked to the beach. I uh ..." Took off her sandals. Not saying that either. But I think she liked it when I did that. "Held her hand."

"She let you?" Ben's voice is like a doctor checking for symptoms so he can give a diagnosis.

"Yeah. She laced her fingers in mine."

"Lacing of the fingers! This is good," Ben says in that same tone. "That's next-level hand holding. A good sign."

Kai sighs heavily.

"Some dogs don't potty train," Bodhi mutters to Kai. "What can you do?"

"I heard that!" Ben shouts.

"And she wanted to see my house."

Because I've seen hers, and it's only fair. They would freak out if they knew.

Plus she joked about showing up unannounced. At least, I think that was a joke.

"So we walked to my place, and I gave her the tour."

"Which included?" Bodhi's waxing his board now, glancing up at me casually.

"I told her in advance how practical and small my house was. It's just a place to live. Nothing fancy."

"It's clean and ... Mila called it cute." Kai shrugs.

"Yeah. I keep it clean. Match the decor. Whatever. It's just a place to eat and sleep and hang out when the weather keeps me from being on my boats."

"Or underwater," Bodhi adds with a smile.

"Exactly. So, anyway, I made it fun. I was like, here's the living room, family room, great room, entryway, and the library ... You know, pointing around at that small front room and my bookcase."

"That's actually funny," Ben smiles. "Good on ya."

"What are you, Australian now?" Bodhi asks Ben.

"I'm a surfer, dude. I can speak Aussie or any beach language."

"Aussie isn't a language," Kai corrects.

"What do you call, good on ya?"

"A saying." Kai crosses his arms over his chest.

"In ... Aussie. Which ... is a language." Ben crosses his arms over his chest.

"You were saying?" Bodhi asks me.

"Yeah. So I did that kind of exaggerating intro with each room of the house."

"What did she say? What was her reaction?" Ben asks.

"She smiled and laughed. I think she liked it."

"That's great! Ya' little ripper!" Ben affects an Australian accent, and he doesn't even do it well.

"Ben! Cut it with the Aussie talk," Kai says.

Ben just smirks at Kai. I'm laughing. Ben's funny, and I need the laugh.

I also need to wrap this up before I leak that my date was actually with Alana. "So, anyway, we finished up the tour and I drove her home in the golf cart."

"Where does she live?" Ben asks.

It's a reasonable question.

"North Shore. So ... everyone up for some waves?"

"Nice try, apple pie," Ben smiles. "First, your grade."

"My grade?"

"On your date."

I have nothing to say. At least he's dropped trying to narrow down where Alana lives.

"I give you a B plus. No. No. A minus. You definitely passed. You brought in humor. You got the interlaced fingers. You drove her home. Did you get a kiss worked in sometime during this tour?"

During the tour? No. Not unless you count the kiss I gently brushed across Alana's forehead when we were walking out my bedroom doorway. Which I'm also not sharing.

"No."

"Well, B plus, then. I think you get to ask for a second date."

"I get to ask?"

Bodhi chimes in. "That's how it works. I mean, sometimes the woman asks the guy these days, but usually it's still the guy."

"Purrrr-soooooot!!" Ben shouts, garnering the attention of a few other surfers who are zipping up their wetsuits down the beach from us.

Bodhi shakes his head, his shoulder length hair swinging with the motion. "Sorry about him. You know how he is. But, unfortunately, this time he's not wrong. Ball's in your court, man. Call her. Or text. Send her something. Let her know you're thinking of her and you had a good time and you'd like to see her again."

Kai nods silently in agreement.

"What did I tell you?" Ben asks.

"Pursuit," I say like a dutiful elementary student.

"That's what I'm talking about. Pursuit. Go get 'er, Tiger."

"Let's go get these waves," Kai suggests.

Surfing does the trick. I'm focused on the salt air, the feel of my board beneath me, and the familiar scenery of Descanso across the beach from where we're riding. We surf for a few hours and then say our goodbyes. I store my board in the shed at the side of my house and pull my cell out.

Bodhi's words echo in my mind. It's up to me to reach out. Maybe I should send her something. But what? Flowers seem so overdone and unimaginative.

I get an idea and make a call before I even have a chance to chicken out or question myself.

"Brigitte here! Is this the illustrious Stevens?"

"Doesn't your phone have caller ID?"

"I'm kidding! What can I do for you mister merman, sir?"

I chuckle, and I think I'm blushing a little. Alana said Brigitte was the one to dub me a merman. I'm not complaining. It's just a tad awkward hearing it from her.

"I want to send something to Alana."

"Oooh. What? I'm all over this like white on rice, like spots on a cheetah, like salt on a margarita glass, like petals on a flower ... Wait. Is it flowers?"

"No. Not flowers. They seem too ..."

"Boring. You are so right. I mean, if a man sends me flowers, you will not hear me complaining. But they are boring. Unimaginative."

"That's what I thought."

"So? What's your plan?"

I have no idea if Brigitte knows I went out with Alana last night, but something in her tone of voice tells me she knows.

"I want to send her ..." Is this crazy? It may be. But it's the best I've got. "Tacos."

"Oh. My. Gosh! You want to send her tacos!"

"It's bad? Right? It's bad. Okay. Okay. Not tacos."

"Nooo! It's flipping *AWESOME*! Where did you come from, you taco-sending merman? Are there others in your species? This is incredible. It's creative. It's fresh. It's so never-been-done. And, Alana loves tacos. I mean, she never eats them unless they're like tofu tacos with microgreens on some sort of oat-based, grain-free tortilla that was hand-fashioned by Tibetan monks in the hills of the Himalayas or something. But she neeeeeds tacos. And she does love them. And if you send them, believe me, she'll eat them."

"Okay." I'm relatively stunned into silence.

"So, what's the plan?" I can almost hear Brigitte rubbing her hands together.

"Well, my sister owns a taco place here on Marbella. I thought I'd order tacos to be delivered, but then ..."

"You realized she can't have any deliveries."

"Right. And I really want them to arrive like a flower delivery, brought by someone else ... otherwise I'd take them to her."

"Okay. I've got you, boo. I can get one of her guys who regularly drives for her to drop them off at her place. And, lucky for you, she's home. After this, she's outta Dodge for a few days. She's got this premier thing."

My stomach feels like someone blew up a balloon in it and then popped it. Premier. Because she's a movie star. And I'm sending her tacos. What am I thinking?

"You got awfully quiet over there, merman. I think you might be freaking out. Please don't. She likes you. Keep it simple. Alana.

She's just a woman. And you're a man. And she likes you. That's all. Keep all the other stuff an ocean away, because trust me, when you get close to it, the glamour dies off real quick."

"Thanks."

"No problemo. Now. Tell me where you're getting this order. Better yet, call the order in. I'll text you the name of the guy who's going to pick it up and we're golden. You just tell the taco place his name. Alana's going to freaking love this. I'm serious. Also serious about whether you know other taco-bearing mermen."

She laughs, so I can't tell if she's really serious.

"No. I think I may be the only one."

"That's what I was afraid of. Well, good for Alana. She needs a good man in her life."

She does? And I'm it. Wow.

TWENTY-FIVE

Alana

All you need is love ... and tacos.
~ Unknown

"You sent me tacos!" I take each one out of the styrofoam container, placing them on a tray on my island. "And chips and guac! I feel so spoiled."

"Do you like them?"

"Are you kidding me? Who doesn't like tacos? Are these from Mitzi's?"

"They are. I got you one of each of my favorites."

This man. I stare at the tacos as if they arrived in an iconic forget-me-not blue box from Tiffany's. They're better than a two-carat diamond. They're perfect. He's perfect.

"There's just one problem," I tell him.

"What's that?"

"You're not here to eat them with me."

"I ... well."

He pauses, and I almost say something.

Then he says, "I didn't know how soon we should see one another after last night. I didn't want to assume anything."

"I told you, Stevens. I want to see you. And my life is about to be a sideshow at the circus—no. Forget the side show. I'm the full three rings."

I sigh, then I ask him. "Are you busy today?"

"I actually just got in from surfing and took a shower. I didn't have anything else planned. No tours. No jobs. Just me and the octopus book."

"Well, bring your book and yourself and come up here. I leave early tomorrow morning to head to LA. That is ... if you want to come over."

"I do. Definitely. I'll be there in less than a half hour. I'll stop for more tacos."

"I can share."

"I don't want you to. I got those for you. Start eating while they're warm."

"I'll just put them in my warming oven on a very low temp. They'll be fine. I'll wait for you."

"Okay. Thanks."

"And Stevens?"

"Yeah?"

"I'm looking forward to seeing you."

"Me too."

My stomach flutters with nerves when I hang up. He's coming here. It's not like he hasn't been here before. But then, I had no idea. And now ... now he's ... him.

I putter through the house. There's nothing to tidy. Nothing to clean. I'm a ball of energy with nowhere to release this buzz in my veins.

My phone rings and I literally jump.

Mother.

I'm tempted to let her go to voicemail, but with the premier and party tomorrow, I need to take this.

"Hello."

"Well, don't sound so happy to hear from me, darling."

"Hello, Mother. It's great to hear from you."

"Alana. Please."

"I'm kidding. How are you?"

"I'm great. And I had your dress taken to your condo. Everything is set up there. Hair and makeup will arrive at three tomorrow. Do you have everything you need?"

"I always do."

"True. True. That Brigitte is an asset, isn't she?"

"She's a wonderful person. And she's funny and amazing. I gave her a raise this week."

"Good. Good. You want to keep the good ones, Alana."

"Anything else you wanted to tell me?"

"Do I need an agenda to call my own daughter?"

"No, but you usually have one. Right?"

"Touché. No. I have no agenda, but to tell you I saw your interviews and they were fabulous. You and Rex look perfect together. The ideal Hollywood couple. He's a nice man, you know. You could do much worse."

"We aren't in love, Mother. He's a friend. A colleague. We respect one another. We're not actually dating. We never were. You know that."

"I think he'd be glad to come to an agreement, darling. A union between the two of you could be like Hepburn and Tracy."

"They never married, you know."

"Yes. But they were a force. Nine films together and a twenty-six year affair. That's common-law marriage nowadays. You and Rex could be like that. Iconic. And powerful. It's so good to have an ally in this business, Alana. It softens the blows, gives you someone on your side of the fence. And you like Rex. Feelings can grow."

"Not happening. I appreciate your concern. It's just ... not happening. Please drop it. I already told you he and I are only doing this until our premier. Then it's over."

"Maybe you'll reconsider." She hums. "I'll back off. I'm patient and I can wait."

There's a knock at the door—Stevens.

"Mother, I have to go. We'll talk when I'm there, okay?"

"What's your rush, dear?"

"My ... uh ... yoga instructor just arrived."

I open the door and smile at Stevens. Then I step back so he can come in. He's carrying his octopus book and a paper bag identical to the one my tacos came in. His hair is a little windblown. He smells clean, and he looks amazing in a white T-shirt with a surf logo and khaki shorts.

And he's wearing his glasses. Good night. This man will be the death of me in those glasses. And we both know he only wears them for reading, so he's wearing them just to taunt me now. And I am here.for.it.

He slowly removes them down his nose and then, as if he didn't just tease me, he says, "Hey, should I put these in the kitchen?"

"That's your yoga instructor? I thought she was a woman," Mother says from the other side of the phone.

"Yeah ... She ... No ... He ... It's a man. Okay. See you tomorrow! Bye." I click my phone.

It rings immediately and I turn off the ringer.

Stevens stands there with an amused half-smile on his face as though seeing me stammer through my goodbye to my mother was the best part of his week.

"My mother."

"Ahhh."

"Come in. Come in," I say, somewhat flustered by the phone call.

It feels like she's here, lurking in my home—invading this private moment that should be just me and Stevens.

Instead of walking toward my kitchen, Stevens takes a step in my direction. He runs his palm down my cheek.

"You seem a little rattled. Everything okay?"

"Yes." I look up into his calm brown eyes. "No ... Sort of."
I blow out a breath.

He sets the bag of tacos on my entry table and pulls me into a hug.

"What's got you unsettled?"

I lean into him, wrapping my arms around his waist and sinking into the comfort he's offering.

"My mother. She's ... pushy, demanding, overbearing ..." I look up at him.

His eyes are so tender. Concern is etched across his forehead, like he'd absorb anything for me, stand between me and whatever distresses me. If only he could. I won't let him. What I face regularly is not something I want anywhere near him. He's too good.

"I'm making her sound horrible. She's not, you know."

"I believe you." His voice is soft and compassionate.

He runs the back of his hand down my face and tips my chin up toward him. I think he's going to kiss me—I want him to. But he just smiles softly.

"Let's eat tacos," he says. "I've found tacos solve many problems. And the ones they don't solve, well ... they don't hurt."

"Is that so?"

He steps back, retrieves his bag and walks toward the kitchen.

"You don't think so?" he asks, setting the bag on the counter and opening it.

"I don't know. I haven't ever tested that theory."

"Yeah. That's what Brigitte said."

"What did she say?"

"She said you don't eat tacos unless they have tofu. Something like that. Is it true?" He's got a teasing look to him when he glances at me. "Do you eat tofu tacos?"

"I have."

"Are they any good?"

"Compared to what?"

"Carne asada, shrimp or mahi mahi?"

"I don't know."

"You ... you've never eaten those kinds of tacos?"

"Um ... no?"

He stares at me like I'm joking.

"My diet's pretty strict. It's part of my job."

He nods. "Well, let's dig in then. Get ready to be utterly corrupted." He wags his eyebrows and rubs his hands together mischievously.

He moves through my kitchen, pulling down plates after opening a few cabinets to find them, pulling open the warming oven after finding it on the first try, and placing the tacos on plates alongside chips and guacamole. I grab down glasses and pour us some sparkling water.

"Eat outside?" he asks like he's been here a hundred times.

"Sure. I'd love that."

He carries our plates and I follow him out onto my deck.

There's this contagious ease to him, like nothing can shake the foundation he's standing on. He oozes quiet confidence without saying a word. Even in the moments when he's slightly awkward, the strength of something deeper permeates the atmosphere around him.

My mother's looming presence has been properly relocated to LA, just like that. All it took was one solid hug from Stevens and she vanished like a specter being chased by an exorcist.

He takes his place in the same chair he sat in when we shared our dinner here the other night. All that time, he was Wordivore, and I didn't have a clue.

I take my seat next to him. A breeze blows in from the water, rustling through the treetops, cooling the air while the sun shines down to warm us.

I bite into a taco—the one with carne asada. It's so good I actually moan. And, I guess I close my eyes because when I open them, Stevens is staring at me with a full smile on his face and a glint in his eye.

"I wish Mitzi could have seen that. She would have gone nuts."

"She likes it when people enjoy her tacos, huh?"

"She would love it if Alana Graves moaned while eating one of her tacos."

I smile. It doesn't bother me to be Alana Graves when he puts it that way.

"I'd love to meet her," I say, knowing full well the complications that would invite into our lives—his especially.

"You will. One day. I hope."

He takes a bite of his own taco, exaggeratedly lets his eyes flutter shut and lets out a moan that's a little too enthusiastic. Then he cracks open one eye and peeks at me.

"Am I being mocked for my taco love?"

"Never." He winks at me, then his smile spreads across his whole impish face.

I want to kiss him, really kiss him. And I want to spend the rest of my life on this porch eating tacos and making him smile just like that.

"You'll meet Mitzi," he says. "But for now, I want to keep you to myself. I'm selfish like that. It's one of my many flaws. You'll discover them all in due time."

"I think I'm selfish too."

"Yeah?"

"I want to keep you to myself too."

TWENTY-SIX

Stevens

So it's not gonna be easy. It's gonna be really hard;
we're gonna have to work at this every day,
but I wanna do that because I want you.
I want all of you, forever, every day.
You and me. Every day.
~ The Notebook

W e clear our dishes together.

Alana leans her forearms on the island counter. "So, do you want to grab your book and read out on the patio with me?"

"Are you trying to get me to put on my reading glasses?" I ask. "Who me?"

I walk around the island and pull her into my arms. I'm pushing my luck, but also too keenly aware we'll be apart for the next few days and then it sounds like we'll be borrowing time with her upcoming hectic work schedule. And who knows if my job will conflict with her free days.

"Yes, you," I tug her in toward me.

"I can't help myself. You in those glasses. It's like my kryptonite."

I close my eyes and shake my head. In what universe am I Alana Graves' kryptonite?

When I open my eyes, she's smiling up at me, still caged in my embrace.

"Are you going to kiss me, Stevens? Or do I have to do all the heavy lifting around here?"

I chuckle. "What the lady wants ..."

I raise one of my hands and run my fingertips along the curls resting on her forehead and down her cheek.

"I love when you do that," she nearly purrs.

"Do this?" I run my hand along her curls again.

"Mm hmm." Her head tilts up and our eyes meet.

I bend down and brush my lips over hers. She grips the back of my shirt and kisses me like I've never been kissed before. I lean back on the island, pulling her in toward me. She runs her fingers through my hair. I'm dizzy from the connection. Weightless. Suspended. Her hands move over my back and then grip my biceps. I lace my fingers through her hair and hold her to me. Her lips go soft and she smiles into our kiss. I pull back and place one last kiss on her mouth. She drops her hands, running them down my arm one inch at a time as if she's practicing topography, mapping out the dips and rises of my muscles. When she reaches my hands she grasps them, looks up at me, and smiles.

She lets out a contented sigh. We stand there gazing at one another. How did we get here? Alana's such an unexpected development in my life. I wasn't even looking for her—and to think, I had her all along. It's mind boggling.

"What are you thinking?" she asks in a sated voice.

"I'm thinking how amazing it is ... you and me."

"I still feel like I'm imagining you," she says.

She reaches up and runs her hand down my jawline. I bend my head and kiss her palm.

"You're imagining me? How is that even possible? You're ..."

"Alana Graves. I know." She sounds slightly deflated.

I take her chin between my thumb and pointer and tip her face up toward mine. "When I'm kissing you ... When I'm sitting out on a balcony eating tacos with you ... When you make me laugh? You're just Alana. My SaturdayIslandGirl. I'm not here because of Alana Graves."

She smiles softly at me. "I know. That's what's so amazing. You really aren't. And it means the world to me."

I drop my hand, trailing my knuckles along her cheek, collarbone, shoulder, arm.

I need to be open with her—I sense how much she needs my candor.

"Sometimes it hits me—your fame. And then I have to recalibrate. It's not like I don't get overwhelmed by your status. I do. But that's not who you are to me. It's only a fraction, and it's the least important of all the pieces. Plus, I'm still adjusting to the fact that you're my SaturdayIslandGirl, and you're Alana who needed a water taxi, and ... you're a household name."

"So is Clorox."

I chuckle. "I'll take you over Clorox any day."

"And I'm *your* SaturdayIslandGirl? Yours?"

I smile down at her. "Mm hmm. You are."

"I like that a lot," she tells me. "I like being your SaturdayIslandGirl."

"Does it feel odd to you too, putting all the pieces of me together into one person?" I ask.

"A little. But I have a solution." She pushes away from me.

"What's that?" I follow after her like a shameless puppy.

"I had something delivered up here this morning."

"You and your deliveries," I tease her.

She looks at me over her shoulder. "Hey. I'd go shopping if I could."

Then she bends down and opens a cabinet under the big screen and pulls out a board game.

Scrabble.

"I thought this would help us consolidate all the pieces of ourselves into two whole people if we played in person."

"I love that. Just so long as you don't mind losing in person."

"Oh, I have no intention of losing in person. So, as long as you don't mind being humiliated while I watch you go down in flames, we're good." She smirks at me as she hands the box over.

"What about a wager?" I ask.

"Depends. What are we betting?"

"If I lose, I have to kiss you."

She smiles. "Done. And if I lose—which I will not ...?"

"You have to kiss me."

She laughs. "Those are some stakes. You drive a hard bargain for a merman. And, you've got a deal. Here's to one of us losing!"

We're smiling like two people who have nothing better to do with their afternoon than sit out in the treetops on an island, playing a board game together while they fall deeper into something that feels pretty promising.

We set up the board out on the coffee table on the deck.

"So, the guys asked me about our date last night," I tell her.

Alana lays down LAXER with the X on double. Eighteen Points.

"Oh? What did you tell them?"

I lay down FELSIC.

'Is that a word?" she asks. "Or was that the boss of young Ebenezer Scrooge?"

"Ebenezer's boss was Fezziwig. Felsic is a word in geology."

"No fair using scientific terms." She smiles over at me.

"I'm playing to lose here, don't distract me."

"You're playing to lose now?" Alana asks.

"Think of what I get if I lose ..."

She just grins and I smile back.

"We're obnoxious," I tell her. "It's good we don't have any witnesses."

"I don't think I've ever been obnoxious like this before."

"I know I haven't."

She's the only woman who's ever drawn out this side of me to this degree. I reach across the board and lift her hand to kiss her knuckles. Just because I can.

"Now look at who's being distracting," she teases, and then she lays down DIETERS on my I.

"I told the guys about my epic home tour," I wink over at her.

She giggles. "One of my favorite parts of the night."

"One of your favorite parts? There was more than one?"

"It was a great night."

"Unbelievable," I agree.

I fill her in on the guys and their ridiculous questions and the way Ben taunted me this morning. She laughs all the way through my story.

"I didn't tell them it was you. They just knew I was finally meeting SaturdayIslandGirl."

"You didn't tell them it was me?"

"I didn't know if you would want me to. And, I guess I don't want the complication. They already know you better than I do. They'll have a lot to say when they find out—aspects of our relationship I don't want to have their input on yet, if ever. If I want it, I'll ask for it. Usually Kai's the one I go to if I want to have a man to man. And more often than not, Ben jumps in uninvited. Ben's not always a jokester. He's got a huge heart. But at times he teases when I need things to be more serious. Anyway, that's why. I just want the two of us to establish what we're doing here before we invite the rest of the world in to spectate and make commentary."

"I agree. And," she pauses and looks over at me. Then she places her hand over mine. "There is a complication. It's temporary, but you need to know about it."

I'm quiet, waiting for whatever changed her mood to something more serious.

"I have a co-star, Rex."

"Rex Fordham."

"Yes." She rubs her thumb across my hand. "Rex Fordham."
She sighs.

"Weren't you two dating in the past?"

"We were not." Her voice has a finality to it. "I hope you don't think less of me when I tell you this."

"Pretty sure that's not possible," I assure her.

"Well, he and I pretended to be in a relationship. It was a publicity thing our people worked up. It made fans happy and boosted interest in our movies."

I nod. I only barely knew about the purported romance between Alana and Rex because of my mother's obsession with movies, Hollywood, and all things Alana Graves. I don't track with the media and who's who. If they pulled off a fake romance, I'm sure that's par for the course in the industry.

She's got a look in her eyes that tells me there's obviously more she needs to say.

"Well, this time around, with *Blasted* coming out in less than two months, my Mother and my publicist cooked up a reunion of sorts—to make it seem like we're back together."

Her eyes plead with me, so I flip our hands over and cup hers in mine, brushing my thumb back and forth in what I hope is a gesture of assurance.

"Thanks to you, I told my mother I won't pull off any charade with Rex past the premier of *Blasted*. But that means nearly seven weeks of me appearing to be Rex's girlfriend again."

"Thanks to me?"

"You encouraged me to set boundaries. When we were chatting on *Play on Words*."

I smile, remembering that chat. The longstanding connection we've shared matters. It made a mark on both of us. It's why we're so familiar even though being together is also brand new.

"I'm sorry, Stevens. I wish this weren't going on right when we started seeing one another."

"Why would you need to apologize? For one thing, you and I weren't doing whatever we're doing now when you set up this recent publicity stunt. I don't know much about Hollywood, but I'm guessing this sort of thing happens a lot."

She nods. "It does. Fake news. Twisting the truth to help sell something. It's all part of the business."

"The bottom line is that your relationship with him is not real. It's a part of your job. A publicity stunt. We all have things we have to do for our jobs that we don't like, or that test our morals and convictions."

"My morals have been tested, and I failed. I'm lying to my fans —again."

"And it eats at you. Which shows your true character. We grow forward, not in reverse. You don't like faking, don't do it again in the future—if that's an option. I don't mean to overstep."

"I won't have to fake. I'll have you."

Her declaration sounds like a foregone conclusion, as if it's not a question as to whether we'll be together. I'm not a passing fancy or temporary diversion. She wants to see where this will go as much as I do. And I want her to know I'm right there with her.

"You will."

It should feel odd to be declaring something so permanent when we only shared our first kiss last night, but that kiss was months in the making.

She stares into my eyes and squeezes my hand. "I don't want the press near you."

"I'm pretty sure we won't be able to eliminate the inevitable. If I'm with you long term, they'll find out. And when they do, they'll want to know about me. And that could get a bit hairy for a while. But we can ride it out. If that's what you want."

"I do. I want this—to give us a chance."

"I do too."

Her tone shifts back to something more relaxed. "What have you ever had to do that tested your morals?"

"You say that as if you don't think I have."

"Sorry. I just can't imagine how saving sea turtles challenges your morals. You are true to who you are. I admire that about you."

"In most things, I am able to maintain my integrity. But I work for industries and the government. They constantly want to encroach on the ocean. Is that beneficial for humans? They sometimes think so. Profit-driven companies don't care. But in the long run, the ocean is part of a whole series of interconnected ecosystems. And when we damage the ocean or demand too much from it, we throw off the balance of nature. The ocean suffers first, but we will suffer next. So, I delay or mitigate that impact by keeping big business from killing off endangered species. But I don't stop them from depleting resources. I actually help industries expand. It's not what I wanted to do with my degree, but it pays the bills. And it allows me to do what I want to do."

"Saving sea turtles," she giggles as if she's remembering ten-year-old me and my idealistic dreams.

"Among other things. Come with me the next time you have a whole day free and I'll show you."

TWENTY-SEVEN

Alana

There's nothing more beautiful
than the way the ocean refuses
to stop kissing the shoreline,
no matter how many times it's sent away.
~ Sarah Kay

I wake feeling groggy, but a smile blooms across my face before I even toss back the covers. I leave for LA in an hour. And I'll be there for two days because of this premier event—the one I'm attending with Rex. None of that is the reason for the private smile that's like the sun shining through clouds.

Stevens stayed for dinner and left when Brigitte called to tell me to get into bed. She heard Stevens in the background and literally squealed so loud I had to hold the phone away from my ear. Of course, he found this utterly amusing. Then Brigitte started shouting, "Let me talk to him!" So I reluctantly put him on the phone. It's not like they haven't spoken before. She arranged all the details when he taxied me or ran for my groceries. This was different. I have no idea what she said, but Stevens smiled and laughed the whole minute I allowed them to chat before I grabbed my phone back and sent him packing for the night.

And, I lost at Scrabble. So I got to kiss him. And I did. Kissing Stevens is like nothing I've ever experienced. He's so careful and passionate. Maybe it's different because of all the emotions he brings up in me. Whatever it is, I feel like I never really kissed a man until I kissed him.

I shower, dress, drink my probiotic green drink and grab the garment bag and duffle I'm taking to LA with me. Then I meet my driver out front to be taxied to Joel's boat. I consider texting Stevens, but the sun is just rising. He may be asleep. I'll call him later.

The golf cart slows to a stop at the dock and I hop out, taking my bags from the young man who drove me. I make my way down the dock, and squint at the boat as I approach.

Is that ... ? I blink. He steps out onto the dock and stands there looking at me with an impish grin on his gorgeous face and I break into a shameless run.

"What are you doing here?"

"I traded with Joel. I figured, he's got an NDA, he can't tell anyone. I didn't say why. I just told him I needed to go to LA anyway so I'd relieve him. He's happily getting paid to sleep in today."

I drop my bags and throw my arms around Stevens' neck.

"You're amazing!" I breathe the words into his shirt and then inhale the now-familiar scent of him.

"I'm really not, but let's keep that illusion going for a while ... possibly indefinitely."

"You are amazing. And I'm glad you don't know it."

I press a soft kiss to his lips and he tugs me to himself. The misty morning air surrounds us, seagulls and shorebirds call out across the water. The waves slosh under the pier. Stevens runs his hands down my back until they rest on my hips. He kisses me like a man welcoming his girlfriend home at the airport. It's one of those kisses that says *I missed you*. And even though we've only been separated for a night, I get it. I've missed him forever. And we'll be in forced separation regularly for the foreseeable future. This is the kiss of two people desperate for more of one another than they are allowed. We're grabbing at crumbs, savoring the small samples of time we get and trying to make a meal out of them.

When we separate, he gently pushes my curls back from my face.

He stares into my eyes and murmurs. "I brought you a breakfast burrito."

"I think that might be the hottest thing a man has ever said to me."

He chuckles. "You need to get out more."

"Maybe I just need to get out with you."

"Definitely that."

He releases me and bends to pick up my bags for me. "We'd better get going. You're on a schedule, or so Joel informed me."

"Yeah. I am." I inhale a sweet breath of ocean air. "Tonight's the premier with Rex—not our film, obviously. This other one."

"Well, let's get you to LA, then." Stevens boards the boat and turns toward me to extend his hand. I take it—whether I need it or not, I just want to touch him.

He takes the helm and I sit next to him. Maybe if Joel were driving, I'd be in the back of the boat today, letting the breeze off the water still my nerves about pretending with Rex.

We're about five minutes out when Stevens says, "Want to drive?"

"Drive the boat?"

He makes a show of looking around. "The boat seems to be the only thing you can drive out here."

"Smarty. You know I don't drive."

"And that was the story of every single driver up until the day they learned."

"I really can't afford to wreck Joel's boat."

"I think you actually can afford to wreck his boat." He winks at me. "But I won't let you. I'll be right beside you. Come here. Let's see what you've got."

I stand, assuming Stevens is going to take the seat I was in. He slows the engine so it's nearly idling. He steps back and gestures for me to step in front of him. I do. And then he's surrounding me, his arms coming around mine, my back flush against him.

"Oh, I like driving," I coo.

He chuckles and I feel the rumble spread through me.

"Is this how you teach all the girls?" I tease, glancing over my shoulder at him.

His face is serious—kind, but intense. "Only you, Alana."

That thrills me more than he could know. I'm aware he takes groups of women out regularly for lessons and tours of all sorts. But the way he says, *Only you*, feels possessive, proprietary.

Stevens' tone turns all instructional while he reaches around, looping his arm past my waist to point to gauges, the key for the ignition, and the throttle. He runs through the basics while we sit idle. Then he tells me to turn the key since the engine is already dropped.

I turn the key and the engine starts, but we're in neutral, so we don't move.

"Grab the throttle, Alana."

This is entirely too much fun already. My nerves are buzzing. Every inch of me is aware of Stevens.

"I hope you know what you're doing," I warn.

Then I grab the throttle and push it up to accelerate, keeping one hand on the wheel. Stevens places his warm palm over the back of my hand and presses lightly on the throttle. His other hand covers mine to help me steer.

I push the throttle up and we take off.

I squeal.

If Stevens' hand weren't over mine on the steering wheel, I'd have surely veered us all over.

"You've got this," he says, bending over so his words and warm breath hit my ear.

"Not if you keep that up, I don't!" I shout over the sound of the engine and water.

"Easy, easy," he guides me to back off the throttle.

He steps back just a little, lifting the hand that's covering mine on the throttle. I look at him and then back at the water, as if I'm about to hit something when we're in the middle of the open ocean.

"You've got this," he says, lifting his other hand off mine.

He's standing just behind me, but we're not touching anymore.

I steer like that for a few minutes. Then I see something in the water. A shadow or a lump. I jerk the steering wheel hard to the left to veer around whatever it is.

The boat responds. Oh my gosh, it does!

We jerk hard, Stevens staggering and tipping behind me and then grabbing for the wheel as I stumble into his arm and nearly pitch overboard. Stevens has me pinned between his arms in no time, both of his hands on the wheel as he maneuvers it to right the boat.

I'm breathing fast, my heart near my throat, beating so hard I can feel it.

"Oh my gosh!" I shout once Stevens has the throttle lowered and we're back on a straight course at a moderate speed.

"Hey." His voice is calm and his eyes are soft when I do a one-eighty to face him. "You gave a whole new meaning to learning curve."

He's trying not to laugh, I can tell.

I bust into laughter, half-fueled by nerves, and he joins me.

"I could have killed us!" I shake my head.

"Not on my watch. You're fine. Now, turn around so you can have another go at it."

"What?" I look into his eyes. He's smiling down at me with a combination of amusement and affection. That expression is my new favorite cocktail. "Are you out of your mind? You want me to drive *again*?"

"I definitely want you to drive again. What made you jerk the wheel?"

"I saw a thing."

He chuckles. "A thing?"

"Yeah. A shadowy blackish thing."

"In the ocean?"

"Yes. In the ocean." I pop my hands on my hips.

"Alana, you know there are dark shadowy things all over down there: sea otters, sea lions, dolphins, whales even. We have octopi, giant squid, and all types of fish."

"See! And I didn't want to hit it."

His grin is so big it pops both his dimples and scrunches up those adorable lines next to his eyes.

"These animals navigate in the water. They will swim around you."

"Are you sure?"

"I'm sure. You won't hit one. Not unless it's already so sick it's dying."

"It would have been nice if you had told me before placing me behind a wheel."

"Point taken." He smiles again.

My belly literally flutters, like little happy fairies waking up and flitting around. They're the Stevens fan club of fairies and there must be hundreds of them.

"Okay, so ..." He gestures toward the steering wheel.

"Okay. Let's do this," I agree.

The second time behind the wheel, I do much better. Stevens lets me drive for a good fifteen or twenty minutes, and then he takes over.

"Joel has never had me in a life jacket because his boat is over twenty feet long," I tell him as we switch places so he can drive.

"I never saw the need before today." He winks again. Cheeky man.

We ride along in silence for a little while as the shoreline comes into view, breaking the spell. Only, unlike Cinderella, I apparently prefer my life of pumpkins, mice, and simple living. I'm in no hurry to resume princess status.

I look over at Stevens, he's got this peaceful resting face, scanning the horizon, one hand loosely controlling the steering wheel. He catches me staring and smiles over at me.

"What's on your mind?" he asks.

"I hate that you have to keep our relationship a secret."

"I don't know," he glances at the water and then back at me. "I think there are perks to this arrangement."

"Such as?"

"Stand up and I'll show you."

I make a show of deliberating, but then I'm at his side in less than two beats. He pulls me into an unexpected kiss, glances back at the water and then bends so his mouth is right up against my neck. "I get to date you."

I giggle when his morning stubble grazes my skin. "And I get to date you."

He pulls back and fixes his attention on the water ahead of us. "I'm pretty sure you drew the short stick on that one."

"I am completely sure you're wrong. And I love that you don't know it."

I stand next to him the rest of the ride into the harbor, stepping back when the dock is in view. We don't kiss goodbye. This harbor is far busier than the private one on Marbella where there were plenty of boats, but we were nearly the only two people moving around at sunrise.

I step off the boat, only glancing back once to commit the image of Stevens standing there watching me to memory. Then I make my way down the dock to Tank who has a weirdly knowing look in his eyes despite the fact that his face is essentially as neutral as ever.

Two days.

I'll be in LA for two whole days and then I can see Stevens again. In the meantime, I have to fake being in a relationship with Rex.

What is my life?

TWENTY-EIGHT

Alana

And there's only one person t
hat makes me feel like I can fly ... That's you.
~ Hitch

A hairstylist and makeup artist show up to my condo in the mid-afternoon. I'm dressed and ready by six when Rex arrives in his limo, or at least the one he's rented for the night. The driver rings my bell and I take the elevator down three flights to the lobby and walk out onto the street. No one makes too much of a fuss about me in this neighborhood, but occasionally paps are around in hopes of catching me taking out the trash or something equally mundane and uninteresting.

Yes. I've had my share of tabloid photos dubbed, *Yikes! Is Alana Graves Letting Herself Go?* Or *You Won't Believe What Alana Graves Looks Like After Her Breakup!* Needless to say, I've learned to brush my hair, wash my face, and put on at least a few swipes of mascara before descending to the first story of my condo here in Hollywood.

The driver opens my door to the limo and I step in.

"You look beautiful," Rex says from the seat next to me. He's scrolling on his phone when he looks up at me, smiles and then returns to whatever he's doing.

"So do you."

He flashes me one of those grins he's famous for. It's star-quality, that's for sure. But my fairy brigade doesn't even make a rustle. Nope. It's Stevens for me. My mind drifts back to this morning's boat ride which seems like it was weeks ago in a world far away.

Rex and I make small talk along the drive about our upcoming projects and a few things we're scheduled to do together before our movie releases.

When we arrive at the premier, Rex steps out of the car ahead of me to screams of his name and shouts from photographers. He pauses to wave at the crowd and then extends me his hand. When I emerge, the screaming amplifies. Shouts of "Alana!" ripple through the crowd. I turn my head to try to connect with as many eyes as I can, and then I focus on stepping forward with Rex. We walk the red carpet together, stopping at the points designated to answer questions from reporters representing all the major media outlets.

Most of the questions center around me and Rex and whether we are back together.

We stop in front of a reporter I recognize.

"Hello, Rex and Alana." Her microphone extends between us. "Are you two back together officially?"

I look to Rex. Somehow it feels like less of a lie if he answers for me, even though I'm still complicit.

"We're seeing how things go," Rex smiles down at me and I smile back up at him.

Cameras flash incessantly.

"Alana, what made you give Rex another chance?"

This one is directed right at me, I can't deflect. I answer as ambiguously and truthfully as I can. "Rex is a great man. Working together brings a closeness you don't have when you're on separate projects."

We walk through the gauntlet, giving open-ended, vague answers all along the way. The media prefers those kinds of statements anyway. It leaves them more room to speculate and drum up drama. We take our turn in front of the step-and-repeat backdrop, stopping every ten feet or so for a new set of photos to be taken and more questions to be asked as we pose.

Finally, we're in the theater and we're ushered to seats off to the left, only eight rows back. I glance around and see my mother and father a few rows ahead in the center section. People greet one another in the typical Hollywood fashion, and then the movie begins, providing over two hours of distraction and relief before we move on to the rooftop party.

The transition from Grauman's Theater to the Waldorf Astoria involves returning to our limos after the showing. Fans are out in droves, seated across the street on temporary bleachers and standing around the edges of the ropes surrounding the red carpet.

They're shouting our names, yelling out questions, screaming, "Alana and Rex! We love you!"

We wave and smile all the way to the limo. Once we're inside, I collapse into the leather seat.

"Are you okay?" Rex asks, sincerely concerned for me.

"I'm seeing someone. It's new. But he's someone I've known for a while. It makes all of this so different, knowing he's at home while I'm on your arm."

"I know." Rex's face is somber.

I study him. He does know.

"I'm sorry. I never realized how hard it must have been on you and Ingrid that whole year."

"It wasn't all bad. We were able to have a relationship off the radar. That's kind of rare, as you know. It was good for us at the time."

"Off the radar," I repeat.

"Yeah. Keep this guy off the radar too, if you can."

"That's the plan."

∿

The following evening, I'm back on Marbella. Joel came to pick me up at the dock, and I tried to cloak my disappointment for his sake.

I'm comfortably hanging out in my favorite burgundy velour pair of Lululemon leggings and matching track jacket when Stevens knocks at my door.

I had texted him from the boat, saying, *I'm not sad that Joel came to pick me up in Ventura. Nope. Not sad. Didn't want you to be the one I saw when I walked down the dock after two days in LA. Just in case you were wondering.*

My phone rang right after I hit send. Stevens was laughing when I answered, and I instantly felt like someone had given all my little inner fairies a dose of melatonin. Maybe I should be concerned about the impact he has on me and my moods. I don't have it in me to drum up anything but gratitude. I'm riding the bliss for now, trying to keep reality at bay as long as I can.

We chatted for a few minutes, and he told me he was making me dinner. He didn't ask, and I loved him taking charge and caring for me more than I could say.

When I hung up, Joel had a curious look on his face. I didn't tell him what was up, and he didn't ask. Sometimes an NDA comes in handy. Though, Joel would keep my privacy and confidentiality without the paper standing between us.

Stevens is on my porch holding two reusable grocery bags when I open the door. And he looks good enough to eat. I don't know how I missed him so much over only two days' time. I just did.

"Hey," he says with a note of shyness, or maybe it's caution.

"Hey. It's so good to see you." I take the bags from him

without even looking at the contents, set them on my entry table, and turn back to him.

"I'm restraining myself from jumping into your arms right now," I confess. "I want bonus points for that."

"You'll get no such thing," he says with a far more relaxed smile. "Bonus points come for jumping in my arms, not avoiding me. Get the scoring system straight, Graves."

I laugh like a giddy girl with a crush—since I am one. And then I take a flying leap into his arms and he, thankfully, catches me. I'm wrapped around him like a spider monkey and he's grinning up at me like he won the lottery. I lean down and kiss his forehead, his eyelids, his nose, and finally those perfect lips.

He drops me slowly, and I slide down until my feet are on the floor, our kiss continuing until I pull away reluctantly and say, "Come in."

Stevens smiles and wraps his arm around my waist, leading me alongside him and shutting the door behind us.

"How was LA?" he asks.

I started to text Stevens this morning, but Mother was around my condo and I didn't want her getting all nosy, so I was only able to type, *Hi, can't wait to see you after I'm back.* He responded by sending me a photo of a shadow under the surface of the water. No caption. I snort-laughed and my mother raised an eyebrow in my direction. I quickly swiped the message app and said, "Brigitte," to my mother, by way of explanation.

"So, what's on the menu?" I ask Stevens as we stroll toward the kitchen. "I can't keep eating breakfast burritos and tacos all the time. I do have to keep an eye on things. I'm just saying."

"How about I keep an eye on things?" He wags his eyebrows playfully.

"Right back at you," I say. "Now what are we eating, and can I help?"

"No need. I marinated some fish. I'm going to bake the fish in that overpriced oven of yours and I have mashed potatoes I'll warm, and some asparagus I'm going to sauté with garlic and bacon."

"My mouth is watering. Where did you learn to cook?"

"Mom. Dad too. But he's more of the grill master. She's the one who cooked all our meals except on Sundays."

"What happened on Sundays?"

"It was guys' night to provide the meal. Mom and Mitzi would do whatever and we'd fix supper."

"You do realize that's beyond sweet, don't you?"

"I actually do. I may have had some issues with my family growing up, but in hindsight, they're pretty awesome."

Stevens washes his hands and gets to work. I take a spot on a stool at the island and watch him move through my kitchen as if he lives here.

"So? LA?" he asks again.

"We were hounded by paparazzi at the premier. Other than that, it was relatively uneventful. The fans are so sweet. The paps are a whole other story."

"I get it. I relate, actually."

"To being hounded by paparazzi?"

"Oh, yeah. I mean. I'm famous too." He looks over at me as if I should know this about him.

"You ... are famous?"

"In marine biology circles, I had fame of sorts." He smiles that impish grin I love. "I wrote an article on the wonders of the sea hare ..." he pauses, obviously for effect. I'm grinning so fully my cheeks nearly hurt.

"... and it spread through the scientific community—well at least the marine bio branch. I couldn't even walk into work without women staring and men's jaws dropping open as I passed. I was like the Hemsworth of biological oceanography. The Henry Cavill of sea sluggary."

"Sea sluggary?" I snort.

Stevens levels me with a glare. His mouth is upturned in a

smirk and there's this twinkle of mischief in his eye that makes me want to lock him in here so he'll never leave.

"People asked me to lunch." He pauses again. "Lunch, Alana." He shakes his head as if lunch were the equivalent of one hundred cameras clicking incessantly in a chorus of privacy invasion.

"It was ... well, overwhelming ... being in the spotlight like that. I don't have to tell you." He winks and his grin widens slowly. I sigh—audibly. He's so incredibly attractive.

Then he shrugs as he finishes off his story. "It was rough. But I handled it. As one does."

I'm cracking up and he's standing there, chest puffed up proudly because he knows he's got me and he's the one who can make me laugh like this.

"I never realized we had so much in common," I say through my laughter.

"Yeah. Celeb status. It's a cross I bear silently."

I laugh some more.

Being with him is like taking a hot air balloon ride. Everything that usually surrounds me in a looming presence fades into perspective as I drift aimlessly over it all, carried by the wind of whatever it is he makes me feel. I'm light, airy, carefree.

And then, as if she has some crystal ball that tells her when I'm having too good of a time, my mother calls.

I look over at Stevens. His sleeves are rolled up and he's chopping the ends off asparagus like he's in some Williams Sonoma ad featuring hot guys who cook. I'll take ten of those knives and twenty cutting boards, thank you. I'm so sold.

"It's my mother."

"Take it. I'm not finished. We've got about twenty minutes til we eat."

I accept the call. "Hi."

"Alana. Hi."

"We just saw one another less than five hours ago."

"I'm aware, darling. I forgot to remind you of the fundraiser.

Next week. I'll put it on Brigitte's calendar, but I want you to be aware. It's the evening of the day you're here for the photo shoot with Rex." I hear the smile in her voice.

"Still not happening, Mother."

"I know. I know. You are holding fast—for now. Anyway, this will be another opportunity for you to be seen with Rex in public."

"Yippie," I deadpan.

"Alana."

"Okay. Okay. I'm assuming you'll arrange all the details with Brigitte."

"Yes. I will. And have you seen the papers or checked the feeds?"

"No, I have purposely avoided all that. I just got in a few hours ago and I'm about to eat."

"Well, it's all good. So good. The two of you look the part. And the press is having a field day with all the buzz about your reunification. Some of the pictures of the two of you should be printed and framed. Maybe one day."

"Not one day. We're friends."

I look over at Stevens. His brow furrows.

I mouth, *Rex*, to him. And then I roll my eyes so he's certain about where I stand.

"I'm going to eat. Thanks for the update. I'll see you then."

"We could actually have a conversation, Alana."

"I know. And we did have conversations—all morning. I need a little breather tonight. It's been a long few days."

Stevens turns the burner off, rounds the counter and walks right up to me. I'm so nervous he's going to say something loud enough that my mother will overhear and want to know who he is and what's going on. If he did speak, my mother would have to deal with it. But I want to keep him to myself a little longer—a lot longer, actually.

But he doesn't say a thing. He simply steps behind me and wraps his arms around me from behind. And he holds me. I lean back into him, letting him take the weight of everything, knowing he'll gladly absorb it.

"I'll talk with you tomorrow," I tell my mother.

"Okay, darling. We can talk later."

We say our goodbyes and hang up.

I look over my shoulder at Stevens.

He doesn't say anything. Just places a soft kiss on my forehead, and then he walks around the other side of my island and back to the cooktop, where he turns up the burner and finishes cooking the asparagus.

I don't know how long I'll be able to keep him tucked away from the public eye. If forever were an option, I'd take it. But something tells me our clock is running out when it comes to shielding him from the world.

TWENTY-NINE

Stevens

Bottom line is they can't drive the boat.
They're actors.
~ The Truman Show

I pack the picnic basket in the storage compartment in the middle of my sailboat and look around. The sunlight sparkles across the water and there's a breeze in the air making this the perfect day for a sail.

My phone buzzes in my pocket. I pull it out. *Alana*. My face tugs into the smile she always puts there. I'm trying not to over-think our circumstances—especially the fact that she's a huge celebrity. When we're together, everything else fades away, including her status and fame. She brings out a playful side in me I had only let loose on the game before this. If my friends saw how I acted around her, I'd be roasted like a pig in a pit. But I couldn't care less. I'll take anything for her—even being the target of Ben's incessant teasing. I know Alana wants to protect me from being in the splash zone of her fame. I'm a realistic man. She can only keep that tide from spilling over for so long.

We will be drowning in it eventually. Thankfully, I'm a good swimmer.

I check her text.

> **Alana**: I'm running late. Sorry! I had to take a call from Caroline, my publicist. Apparently she thinks she needs to coordinate publicity before this film releases. Rude. ;)
> **Stevens**: The nerve of some people, trying to do their jobs.
> **Alana**: Right?! Doesn't she know I have a hot date with a marine biologist this afternoon?
> **Stevens**: Does she know?
> **Alana**: Of course not. Only Brigitte knows.
> **Stevens**: You're going to be the first person to see what I'm going to show you.
> **Alana**: That sounds way too intriguing. I'll be there asap. My driver is waiting.

Alana had a break from the madness the past two days, and was home on Marbella. Unfortunately, I wasn't free. I got called out to consult on a job in El Segundo. We talked at night while I lay in my hotel bed, the window open so the ocean breeze could filter in. I challenged her to a match in *Play on Words* while we chatted by phone. It's nowhere near the same as seeing her in person. Now that we've been able to actually be together, any time apart feels like a punishment for a crime I didn't commit.

But, today, we both have a free day before she returns to LA tomorrow for an event. I actually have something I have to attend in LA tomorrow too—a costume party fundraiser for a cause that's especially close to my heart. The organization funding a good portion of my secret project is hosting it.

Less than a half hour after her text, Alana is walking down the dock to the slip where I keep my sailboat, *Sea Ya*. She's in a ball cap and those huge sunglasses, a navy tank top and some white shorts. The tie of her swimsuit shows around the back of her neck. She still looks like a star, even dressed down and climbing on my boat as if she's any other woman.

I extend my hand to Alana and she climbs aboard.

"So, what's this grand adventure we're going on?"

Her face is covered by those huge glasses, but her mouth spreads wide in an excited smile.

"It's a surprise," I tell her. "I've got a secret project—sort of a passion project—and I want you to see it. We'll snorkel to it."

"Oooh. Underwater surprises! I wore my suit. I'm ready."

"There's actually a few parts to this date. You told me you didn't have plans, so I took the liberty of planning."

Alana walks over to me, setting her sunglasses on the center compartment in my boat. And then she drapes her arms over my shoulders and stares up into my eyes.

"I'm yours for the day. Completely free until the clock strikes midnight and I turn into a pumpkin ... Actually, make that ten o'clock, or Brigitte will personally come looking for me. I've got a photo shoot tomorrow followed by this event at night."

"I'll have you home by nine thirty." I smile down at her, and then I lean in and kiss her.

It's been over two days since we kissed and I feel the absence even more acutely when our mouths connect. Her kiss comforts me and fuels my desire for more of her. She's unattainable, and yet somehow mine. She kisses me like she's coming home to me. And I lay out the welcome mat. She's soft and vulnerable, and the way she trusts me translates into our kiss. I take charge, telling her without words that I'm here for her, that what we have runs deep enough to weather separations and all that lies ahead, whatever that entails.

Alana cups my jaw. Her hand drifts slowly down my neck until she's gripping my T-shirt at the shoulder and humming softly into our kiss.

"You." She pulls back, looping her arms loosely over my shoulders and looking up at me.

"Me?" My tone is playful as I look to my right and then my left.

"Yes, you. Finding you has been such a pleasant surprise. To think, all this time you were right here."

"I wouldn't change it."

"Why?" Her head rears back. "Wouldn't you rather we had days like this for the past six months, or even longer?"

"I would. But I don't think that would have been the way it would have happened. You needed to get to know me. The timing was perfect. We had six months of progressive flirting and banter. Six months of you getting used to me beating you at board games. It all led us here."

She smirks at my comment about beating her, and then she nods once. "Maybe. I still would have liked being able to kiss you and sit with you over meals, going out in your boat when we could, spending our spare hours together. I would have loved to have all of that a lot sooner than now."

"The past is behind us. We have one another now."

"True." She considers my words. "Well, then take me on an adventure, merman."

I smile at the quasi-nickname.

"You're going to learn to sail today."

"I'm going to sail. Have you seen me drive a motorboat?"

"I saw. And I think you'll get the hang of this too. It's a little more complicated, but we'll be fine."

"Your faith in me is admirable. And also insane. There's a fine line between genius and insanity, you know. And I think you just crossed it."

I chuckle. "I'll be right there with you."

"Do I get to lean into you, like on Joel's boat?"

"If that's what you want. You can even sit in my lap."

"Deal." She smiles at me.

Maybe I am insane. I'd do anything for her. Especially if the reward is a smile like that—one just for me. And it's not because she's Alana Graves. That's the smallest detail to me now. It's her —her laugh, her thoughtfulness, her dry sense of humor, the way she watches me, this innate connection we've had since we started regularly seeking one another out on *Play on Words*. It's like we knew, even then. We knew.

"So this is your boat." She waves her hands around as I lower the engine into the water.

"Yep. One of two. I have this one, *Sea Ya*. And my trawler, *Catching Wishes*."

"Two boats. Impressive. What's the other one like?"

I pull the cord, the engine revs to life and I back us out of the slip.

"She's a trawler. And she smells like fish."

Alana laughs. It's that musical laughter I love.

"She's the one I use for tours."

"She. Why do sailors call their ships women?"

"Because our ships take care of us the way a woman nurtures a boy. And then we care for them the way we care for a woman."

"That's utterly romantic. Is that true?"

"It's one theory—the one I like the best."

"Hmmm."

We sail out a little way under motor power until we're in the open waters. I kill the engine and then we have to set the lines so the sails catch the wind. I'm only going to give her control of the rudder. I'll manage the sails.

"We're headed around the north point of the island to a cove on the edge of the back side shore. We'll anchor there and snorkel. Come over here."

Alana's standing at the rail, her glasses stowed in her bag, her eyes closed and the wind hitting her face. She pivots when I call her and walks toward me.

"Take a turn at the tiller. I'll be right here."

She raises her brows like she's questioning me, but she drops into my lap anyway. I place her hand on the tiller with mine on top.

"Relax and I'll show you how to work this."

She looks down at me and wags her brows.

I chuckle. "Don't distract me." I make an attempt to be serious despite the playful energy bouncing between us. "With a steering wheel, like the one in Joel's boat, you turn left to go left, right to go right. With a tiller it's the opposite. Like riding a horse. Have you ever ridden?"

"Yes. I have ridden a horse. I took lessons most summers. When I was fourteen I rode in a mini-series where I played a girl on a ranch."

I shake my head in wonder at her and then I admit what I know. "*A Slow Ride Home*?"

She turns her head quickly to look straight at me. "You said you weren't a massive fan."

"Maybe I understated that a little bit."

She grips my cheeks with both hands, causing me to hold the tiller alone, and then she plants a kiss on my lips.

"My biggest fan," she says softly against my mouth.

"That, I'm sure I am."

She kisses me again and I have to pull away so I can keep us on course.

"You're going to capsize us if you keep that up."

She giggles and my chest fills with something like laughing gas, only it's soothing and sweet and I want to inhale her forever.

"Okay, I'll be serious." Alana places her hand on the tiller and I cover it with mine.

"Just guide the boat to the left or right, slowly."

I wrap my arm around her waist and hold her on my lap while she pulls the tiller slightly to the right. We veer to the left and I tug the line just the slightest with my free hand.

"Steady," I encourage Alana.

She leans back into me and I can feel when she's needing less of my guidance. But I keep my hand over hers anyway. I explain how to use the compass to guide us.

"We never merely rely on the things we see on the surface—like dark shadowy things, for example."

She elbows me lightly.

"Our eyes may deceive us," I explain. "And there are times, if you are sailing between two land masses where all you'll see is water in every direction. The compass is all you have."

She pulls her head back so she's looking straight in my eyes. "I could use a compass in life."

I tug her toward me, kissing her temple.

I could say so many things in an attempt to assure her I'll be here to help her navigate any storm, or I could tell her I'll never let her capsize. Instead, I hold her. She releases the tiller and leans into me, resting her head on my shoulder. I hold on to her while I take over steering. We remain like that the rest of the sail to the spot where we anchor.

We've played games together, bantered, eaten meals and kissed. Holding her today feels like the most important and intimate time we've shared. Ever since I met Alana in person, and even during our conversations on the game once we started chatting more openly, it's been obvious she needs someone she can truly lean on. Everywhere she turns someone wants a piece of her. She's told what to do and who to be. She doesn't truly belong to herself.

With me, she can be anyone she needs to be. All her moods, her struggles, her silliness, her silence—I'm here for it all. I can give her a place to relax, to fall apart, to be held. I will never take for granted the privilege of being that man for her as long as she allows me to be.

I anchor the boat and drop the sails.

We strip to our swimsuits and I grab snorkels, masks, and diving fins. I drop off the edge of the boat first.

My head surfaces and I shout, "Woooo! It feels great!"

Alana dives in right after me. It shouldn't surprise me how

fearless she is, but I'm still blown away by the way she takes on new experiences, literally jumping in with both feet.

Her head pops up and she has a huge smile on her face.

"Are you good to go under with the snorkel? If not, you can stay at the surface."

"I can go down."

"I'm not surprised. I thought you'd be up for a snorkel."

I pop my snorkel in and she follows suit. Then I dive under, giving a few strong kicks of my fins to propel me toward my nursery.

Alana kicks up beside me and I point. She looks in the direction where a kelp forest sways with the current, our native orange Garibaldi fish swim by in a school, darting around us along with silvery anchovy, and blue-silver mackerel.

But that's not what I want to show her.

We surface and blow the water out of our snorkels. I dive back under and she follows. Then I point to the PVC "trees" scattered and tethered along the reef. Alana nods, her face bunching in confusion. I swim closer. She pops up, then dives back under to rejoin me. When we're both a few feet from my nursery, I point to the clusters of coral sitting on and dangling from each "branch" of my plastic trees. Then I swim up and Alana joins me above the surface of the water. I take my snorkel out and she does too.

"What are those?" she asks.

"It's my coral nursery. I'm helping replenish damaged reefs." I smile over at her with the smile of a proud parent, or probably it's more like the smile of a kid at parent-teacher night, proudly showing off his science project.

"That's amazing, Stevens. So, this is your secret project?"

"It is."

"I want to hear all about it," she says.

"Later. Let's enjoy the water while we're here. I'm dying to see if we can spot some unique marine life while we're down there."

Alana smiles at me, pops her snorkel back in and we both dive back underwater, swimming together in my private section of the island for a few hours.

After we finish swimming and dry off, we take towels up to the bow of my boat. We're laying side-by-side, the sun warming us while the gentle breeze keeps us from overheating. My hand seeks Alana's and she laces our fingers together, rubbing her thumb across my skin. We're silent, sharing the unique brand of contentment that comes from spending time under the ocean's surface.

I shared my passion project with her and she asked questions when we first climbed back on board. I answered all of them—about my funding, the purpose of replenishing coral, why the reefs are endangered. I love that she cared enough to ask.

"I love your coral nursery," she says in a drowsy voice. "It's so amazing that you dedicated your free time to raise funds to build something that will bless people for generations to come. You're saving sea turtles and so much more."

I turn my head and smile over at her. "You make it sound more monumental than it is."

"You don't take enough credit for how amazing you are."

"I guess you'll just have to keep telling me."

I prop myself up on my elbow and lean over her and kiss her. Her lips are warm and soft from the sun and she tastes like salt and sea breeze and sunshine and the best dream I ever woke up remembering.

I pull back and stare down at her. We share a smile.

I bend over her and brush my lips against hers. She clutches the back of my neck and holds me to her. I run my fingertips down her arm and she shivers slightly. Then she pulls away, laughing. I kiss the tip of her nose, her forehead, and then I pepper kisses along the small freckles on the top of her shoulders.

She sighs and hums this sound of contentment. Closing my eyes, I rest my cheek on hers and breathe her in. She smells of sunscreen and saltwater, and there's a scent that's all her, like honey and ginger—invigorating and sweet.

I lift away from her, running my hand down her wild curls and looking into her eyes. "I'm serious about you, Alana."

She smiles up at me. "The feeling is extremely mutual, Stevens. I think I found my person."

I lay back down on my towel, tugging her with me so her head rests on my chest. We lay like that, in contented silence, with only the sound of the waves gently knocking against the side of the boat, the sound of the gulls, and her head just over my heart.

On the boat ride back to the harbor where I dock *Sea Ya*, Alana surprises me.

"I've been thinking."

I'm at the tiller and she's sitting with her back against my arm. She's got her knees bent up and her feet resting out in front of her on the cushioned bench we're sharing. Her curls are wild from our swim. The wind catches them and blows them around her face at times.

"You've been thinking about ... ?" I ask.

"Telling your friends about us."

"Which friends?"

"The guys who were at the barbecue at Summer's. Those are your closest friends, right?"

"On the island, yeah. They are. And my brother. But I don't want to tell him yet. That would force him to keep something from Mom. When we decide she can know, you're going to need a crash helmet and ear plugs."

She chuckles. "Do you trust those guys who work at watersports for the Alicante?" she asks. "So far I've been able to trust them. They've never told anyone when I came to a barbecue or hung out on the beach with them."

"I do trust them."

"Then I think we should tell them."

"So, you're tired of keeping me to yourself?" I lift my free hand and poke just beneath her ribs and she squirms and giggles.

"Stahhhp!" she squeals.

Then she turns and tickles me, making me jiggle the tiller so that the boat swerves and the sails slack. She grasps onto my shoulders as I right the boat and pull the lines to trim the sails.

"Okay. Okay," she says once we're stable. "No tickling the captain." Then she adds. "... while at sea. Tickling on land is fair game."

"Is it now?" I ask.

"For me. Fair game for me. I still get a chance at you today since you started it."

"I'm pretty sure you had your chance just now—as evidenced by our near capsize."

"I love when you talk all science-y."

"What did I say that was science-y?"

I'd love to make notes so I can keep saying exactly whatever it is she loves so much.

She makes her voice deep like mine and affects a scholarly tone.

Then she says, "As evidenced by ..."

She gives me a coy smile. "It's hot when you talk like a scientist."

"I always talk like a scientist," I say. "Technically, since I am one."

"And ..." She kisses my cheek. "You're always hot."

THIRTY

Alana

I felt like we had a secret, just the two of us.
Like that thing where you just
wanna be with one person all the time.
You feel like the two of you get
something no one else gets.
~ American Hustle

I grab my cell on a whim while Stevens drops the motor and turns it on so we can dock. After I've sent two texts, I pocket my cell and walk over to Stevens.

"I have a surprise for you. Do you like surprises?" I ask him.

"Honestly?"

"Of course."

"No. I don't particularly enjoy surprises. But I like you." He kisses me on my nose and tugs me into a hug.

I snuggle into him, soaking up moments like this one before life hits the gas pedal again.

Then it hits me. This harbor isn't private like the one where Joel parks his boat. We're also closer to the resort. I've been so relaxed that I nearly forgot about being Alana Graves for a whole afternoon. Now, I remember.

I fumble around my bag for my ball cap, a hair tie and my Jackie Ohhs. Once I'm in some semblance of a disguise, I walk back over to Stevens who is puttering around locking things and wrapping the lines around the metal thingies on the side of the boat.

"So, you know how I said you could tell the people you trust about us?"

"Yeah. I'd probably only tell Kai. He's the one I trust the most." Stevens glances over at me. "I trust them all, but Kai's the one I go to if I need to talk something out."

I hope I didn't misstep here, but I want people to know. I'm only protecting Stevens from the media hearing about us. As much as I love squirreling Stevens away like my own private stash of happiness, I want to live like a couple, surrounded by people who care about us. I'm tired of my tower. I think of that cartoon movie Brigitte showed me. Just like Rapunzel, I'm finally feeling that this is when my life actually begins—with him.

I put my hand on Stevens' cheek. It's a little scruffy. I look up into his eyes. He thinks I'm going to kiss him. I can tell by the way he glances down at my lips and back up into my eyes. When his eyelids start to shut, I decide I'd better kiss him first. It's not like it's a hardship.

My hand stays on his jaw and he dips his head low, splaying his palm on my back. Our lips meet in a comforting, soft, sweet kiss.

I pull back, Stevens is still holding me to himself.

"I did a thing. I hope you won't mind," I confess.

"What sort of a thing?"

His lips pinch together slightly and his mouth tips up in that adorable half-smile.

"I asked Summer and Ben to see if everyone wanted to join us for a bonfire tonight on the southernmost beach in Descanso."

"You ... asked my friends to a bonfire?"

"Technically, they're my friends too. I just don't see them often enough to really connect with them the way you have. Maybe they can be ... our friends?"

"Our friends." He smiles. "I like that."

He kisses my lips again. "I can't believe you organized a bonfire." His lips trail across my jaw in a series of lazy kisses and then down to my shoulder. His eyes meet mine when he lifts his head. "You do know a bonfire will be held outdoors, in public, where someone could possibly see us."

"Summer said that part of the beach is pretty private. Most people use the pits nearer to the resort. It will be dark out. I just ... want this."

"I want it too. It's basically everything I want." He lifts his hand and starts touching his fingertips one by one as he lists out his wants. "You. I want you. Any way I can get you." He smiles down at me and lets that statement sink in. "And you hanging out with my friends, relaxing. That's basically my whole list." He's holding up two fingers to emphasize his point. "Good surprise, Graves."

I giggle. "I like when you call me Graves. It makes me feel like a ball player or something. No one calls me Graves."

"I'm glad you like it."

Stevens shakes his head and chuckles.

"What's so funny?" I ask.

"Ben. I'm thinking about what he'll say when he sees us together. He's going to give me so much shade."

"He's one of a kind." That guy makes me laugh every time I see him.

"That's one way to put it."

We share a smile and then I look around. I need to make a getaway to wherever we're going next without being seen.

Stevens must sense the shift in my mood.

"I was going to make you dinner—at my place," he tells me.

"But? ..."

"But, nothing. I still want to. I don't know if that's what you want. Afterward, I was going to take a friend's glass bottom kayak out into the water, sort of near where we're going to be hanging with *our* friends."

He emphasizes the word *our*, and I love the sound of it. *Our* friends. I want to share everything with him, friends, my life ... everything except what's on the other side of the ocean from here.

"I wanted to experience the bioluminescence with you." He tugs gently on the mass of untamed curls coming out the back of my ball cap.

"Like the lanterns ..." I say to myself.

"What?"

"Nothing. I'd love to see that sometime with you. Are you okay with the change in plans?"

"I want to do whatever makes you happy." He says it so easily.

I scroll through my brain trying to remember another time anyone who mattered to me has ever said anything like that to me. Brigitte has told me I need to get a life. But she's never said she'd do anything for me and my happiness. Of course, she does things for me every day. But she's on payroll. And yes, a part of her would still have my back if we weren't connected by my career and hers. But she's not driven to make me happy. She wouldn't bend to whatever I like just to see me smile. Stevens will. I think he always will.

"I'd love dinner at your place," I tell him. "And then time with *our* friends on the beach."

Stevens nods and heads toward the side of the boat nearest to the dock. "I've got a cart ready. Just walk alongside me like you paid me to take you out sailing. I'm constantly taking people up and down this dock to my boats. No one will pay a lick of attention to us."

"I hope you're right. Even on Marbella, if I'm near the resort, it tends to be a crapshoot as to whether someone will recognize me."

"But you came to Cucina to meet me—where you could have been recognized by anyone."

"I had to. I wanted to meet you so badly."

Stevens hops out of the boat with the agility of a man who's been living on the ocean his whole life. Then he extends me his hand and helps me onto the dock. I do as he said, walking alongside him like he's just another taxi driver ... which, he was, only weeks ago. It feels like years.

We make it to the cart without any major interference. Stevens drives me to his home where he grills us burgers served with a salad and some sliced fruit. I don't eat everything. I can't. I've got gowns and preselected outfits to fit into over the coming weeks. We eat in his backyard. It's simple and absolutely perfect.

When the meal is over, the sun is only just beginning to set. It's that dusky time of day where everything dims just enough to blend together. The orange glow of the sunset etches into the clouds overhead in hues of pastel pink, lavender and pale yellow.

"We could walk to the beach, if you like," I offer.

"I would like that. Are you sure you're ready to come out as my girlfriend?"

"I'm not trying to hide you for any other reason than I want to keep the media from having a field day with you. Once they find out about us, they'll hunt you down like a wounded gazelle. I don't watch the Nature Channel for a reason."

He chuckles.

"You laugh now. They can be so vicious."

"I'm sorry you've had to be on the other side of that kind of treatment."

"Me? I'm worried about you."

"I'll be fine."

"Said the gazelle." I mutter my words, but my heart clenches at the reality.

It's not a matter of if, but when.

Stevens is strong. He's quiet, but he's got this incredibly solid core inside—like an inner bedrock. Still, he's never been the victim of the paparazzi. I've seen them level even the most confident of stars. I'll do anything to keep him from that kind of abuse.

We walk to the beach holding hands. I know I'm being a little reckless, but I crave connection with Stevens so much, and our time is limited. As much as I'd do anything to protect him, I can't bring myself not to indulge in our time together. Besides, we're walking down sleepy streets in beach neighborhoods and then out onto the sand at a more deserted section of the beach. The fire is already going in the pit when we walk up, and our friends are all here.

During dinner, Summer texted me saying they decided to barbecue on the sand. I told her Stevens was cooking for me and we'd meet them later.

Ben is the first to look up as we approach. I wish I could catch his reaction on camera. He looks at me, then at Stevens, then at our enjoined hands. Back at me. Then to Stevens again.

Ben's jaw literally drops and he stands there with his mouth open for a beat of one ... two ... three ... And then he's shouting, "OH! MY! GOSH! What am I seeing? Wait. Wait. Waiiiiiitt. Okay. Okay. I know what happened. You," he points at Stevens. "You were fixing something at her place. And you used superglue. And somehow you grabbed her hand and you're stuck together. Alana. Sweetheart. Hang in there. Why didn't we ever come up with a safe word? That's such an utter fail! Forget the safe word. You can tell me. Did this man glue himself to you?"

Summer is chuckling lightly. She walks over to Ben while she tells me, "I didn't say anything to him, obviously. I thought you might enjoy his unfiltered reaction." Then she looks at her husband. "Babe. It's okay. They're dating."

"What? No." He looks around at everyone gathered here. "Psych! Okay! Ha! Ha! Guys. But my birthday isn't until next month. So, yeah. You can stop the charade." Then he looks at Stevens. "That was convincing, bro. I almost believed you. But no. You just met her at our barbecue and you lost your marbles when you saw her. There's no way you're dating. Joke's on me. Funny!"

He starts laughing. No one else laughs. I don't drop Stevens' hand.

"Guys." Ben looks around.

Everyone else is smiling. Summer must have told them.

"It's true," I say. "We're dating."

"But ... how? You do know this guy is a biologist, right? I mean. You're Alana Graves. He's a guy who teaches elementary school field trips about the sea hare—which is a nasty little underwater snail that lets out a stink you won't soon forget. Has he shown you a sea hare yet? I'm guessing ... not. Because the day he shows you a sea hare? ..." Ben points to our enjoined hands and then waves his pointer finger between us. "This? This will all be history."

Ben gets this serious expression and looks at Stevens. "I don't know what kind of sorcery you're pulling, man, but please, for the love of Poseidon, don't show her that creepy burgundy snail."

Stevens chuckles. "Good advice as always, Ben. I won't."

"Nawww." Ben shakes his head. "You're still acting like this is real."

Summer places a hand on Ben's shoulder and turns his head toward her. "Maybe I should have given you some warning. This is real. Alana and Stevens are dating. They've been playing word games together for a while. They just discovered one another in real life this month. And they are officially dating."

"Waaaaiiitt!" Ben shouts. He points at me. "You? You're that girl on the game?"

I nod.

"I'm dead. How did we not hear about this sooner?"

Then Ben looks at Stevens. "The day after the date, you're all, *We laughed. She came to my house. I drove her home* ... as if she's any other woman. No offense, Alana. I mean that with respect. But, *DUDE*. You went out with Alana. Freaking. Graves. And you come strolling out to a surf sesh all chill and nonchalant the next morning? I would have been running down the sand waving my hands and doing a double back handspring while I shouted her name."

"Might be why you never dated her," Kai says with a smirk.

"I didn't ever want to date her," Ben says. "I had my eye on Summer. She's the only woman for me."

"And do I inspire you to do gymnastics on the beach?" Summer asks Ben, obviously as an attempt at diversion more than anything.

"Every day, babe. You know that, Monroe. I'd do gymnastics all day for you."

Stevens squeezes my hand. Then he walks me closer to the group where Mila's sitting on a large piece of driftwood, watching the Ben show in comfortable silence. Riley and Cam are in chairs they brought down. Kalaine and Bodhi are on a beach blanket on the other side of the firepit.

"Hey, everyone," Stevens says. "You know Alana, obviously."

Everyone greets us. Not one of them acts like anything's out of the ordinary.

Ben keeps looking at us, shaking his head.

He finally gathers his wits and walks over to us again.

"Sorry, you two. I haven't been this surprised since I found out Riley's dad gifted her a refurbished VW bus for our trip out here from Ohio. It took me a minute to get over my shock. But ..." He shakes his head again as if he needs to dislodge his disbelief. "Okay. Yeah. So you two are dating. Got it. Welp, congratulations. I'm really happy for you. And Alana, for real, besides being a reclusive brainiac who loves slimy underwater creatures, this guy is solid. He's a good man. I'm sure he'll be good to you."

Stevens smiles at Ben. "I will."

"He is," I tell Ben, and then I smile up at Stevens.

"Would you look at that?" Ben says. "You two really do like each other. Man. Okay. Well. I assume this isn't public knowledge yet."

"It's not," I tell Ben.

"Well, you have my word." He runs his pinched fingers in front of his mouth. "My lips are sealed. I'm the vault. Just ask Kai. Right, Kai?" He makes the zip motion again.

"Not that again!" Kai shouts from where he's sitting next to Mila, skewering a marshmallow.

"What?"

"That zipped lip thing."

"Hey. I kept your secret about Mila," Ben protests. "I'm a good secret keeper. You see all this?" Ben waves his hand up and down his torso. "This is a vault. And this ...?" He points to his mouth. "This is the door. And this ...?" He pinches fingers together. "Is the key. Now, watch closely." He twists the "key," turns it, and tosses it. "And that, ladies and gentlemen, is how you keep a secret."

We all laugh. It feels so normal hanging out with this group— being here with Stevens at my side—like a gift.

One I know has an expiration date.

THIRTY-ONE

Stevens

I never saved anything for the swim back.
~ *Gattaca*

I took the main ferry over to Ventura this morning, lugging an oversized garment bag with my costume for tonight's fundraiser. The World Coral Restore Corps is hosting a gala of sorts. Only, instead of tuxes and gowns, I was informed we needed to come up with a costume representing an animal or part of a habitat impacted by coral reef degradation.

I chose the bolbometopon muricatum, or as it is more commonly called, the green humphead parrotfish. These shallow ocean water fish are vulnerable. And ugly. They have a protruding forehead and the appearance of buck teeth, which is really one gigantic tooth attached to their jawbone which they use to chip algae, bacteria and microbes off coral. Mom made me a costume, and it's ... ugly. But in the best of ways.

My costume looks just like the parrotfish with its pinkish tint on the front of the face and a bulbous forehead framed in light chicken wire and filled with light stuffing under the scaly fabric so it remains upright when I put on the costume. The buck teeth on the beak of the fish really are the capstone of the costume.

Thankfully, I'll be surrounded by a bunch of science nerds who will (1) immediately identify what animal I represent, and (2) appreciate why I chose this particular fish. Not only is the parrotfish dependent upon the reefs, but his excessive excrement helps contribute to the regeneration of coral. What a guy!

I spend the day in LA, having lunch with an old colleague—a man I knew during my fame for the sea hare article—and then I take some time driving around Hollywood. I know Alana's here somewhere, and the idea of us being near one another, of me being in her habitat, so to speak, makes me happy. I see billboards, studios and theaters through new eyes today.

Just before dinner, I pull into a low-cost gym that has locations all over California. I have a membership for when I travel. I use their restrooms to change into my costume, and then I walk out through the lobby with my scaly head held high, avoiding eye contact with the abnormally buff guys walking past me as I exit and get back in my car.

To say driving is a challenge would be an understatement. There's a reason fish dwell in the ocean. Fins are not good for gripping steering wheels. Thankfully, the gym is only a few blocks from the event, which is held in the ballroom of a high-end hotel in the middle of West Hollywood on the Sunset Strip.

I park my car with the valet, who gives me a quizzical look that stymies me since he must be seeing all manner of crustaceans and chondrichthyes parking here for the event. I walk through the lobby and heads turn. It must be the costume. Mom knocked it out of the park. Sure, I could have rented a lobster outfit from some Halloween store online, but I wanted to represent an animal pertinent to the cause we're raising funds for tonight.

I was initially asked to be the keynote speaker talking about coral restoration and my specific project, but a PhD from St. Thomas is coming in—an expert in this particular field of marine biology.

I take the elevator up with an elderly couple. The woman scoots to the other side of her husband when I say, "Good evening," to them. She keeps giving me furtive looks, and not the kind a woman gives a man when she's interested. I don't know what danger she fears a man in a fish costume could pose to her, but I keep my fins to myself the whole ride up to the tenth floor.

The ballroom is through a fancy bar area which serves as a foyer and entry to the event. The floor is lined with large black and white checkered tile and the whole room is paneled in dark wood. Very high-end. I waddle past a group of men in tuxedos. Maybe there's another event here. Or they could simply be enjoying a drink at the bar before they go on with their evening. Women's heads turn. Women in stunning gowns. So far no one else is wearing a fish costume—or any costume for that matter.

I walk into the main ballroom.

Not a fish in sight. No crabs. No mollusks. Not even an anemone.

You know those dreams where you show up to school or work buck naked and your feet are superglued to the floor while all eyes turn toward you? No? Only me? Well, I'm living the dream. Not that dream, but the fishy version of it.

How did I misconstrue the dress code as "costume party" attire? I know I saw those words along with the description of what types of costumes might be considered as options. I'll double check the invite later. It really doesn't matter since I'm here in all my scaly glory and everyone else is definitely sporting formal wear.

As if this night couldn't get worse, people are discreetly raising their cells and snapping photos of me. The lone parrotfish in a sea of well-dressed penguins.

And then, I see her.

Alana.

She's wearing a red ball gown. Its form-fitting satin shimmers in the light with her every movement. She's the image of elegant grace. Her hair is up in some sort of twist with a jeweled comb holding all her usually wild curls in place. Only a few tendrils frame her gorgeous face. Her makeup is done more heavily than usual, black lines drawn tastefully above her lashes to accentuate her crystal blue-gray eyes, and lipstick the color of her dress on those lips I kissed less than twenty-four hours ago.

This? This was her fundraiser? Why didn't she tell me she was going to a coral regeneration gala?

The only mercy I see in this whole situation is the fact that I'm wearing a fish suit, so my identity is partially cloaked. But, my mother, as proficient a seamstress as she is, can't create a costume that rivals a theater production. So, the buck teeth of the humphead parrotfish fall just over my forehead. My face is visible through the gaping mouth of this pisces.

I'm staring at Alana long enough that she senses me—and turns. When she turns, the man standing next to her, who happens to be Rex Fordham, also turns. And so does the older woman to her left, a woman who looks so much like an older version of Alana that she must be her mother.

And now all three of them are staring at me. Directly at me. At me, in my fishy suit.

Rex bends toward Alana and says something into her ear. She pivots toward him and answers him. Her mother must have the ears of a fox, because her brows raise, and then the three of them are walking in my direction while the rest of the room stares at me like I'm a floating turd in their silver punchbowl.

I consider turning tail and swimming for safety, but I know they saw me. And, I'm here for the cause. So I stay, awaiting my fate. This isn't exactly the "meet the parents" moment I had imagined when I dared think about meeting Alana's parents, but sometimes life picks for you and you just have to flow with the current.

"Stevens?" Alana says to me.

"Yes. Hi."

"I thought you must know one another the way you were staring at her," Rex says.

He's tall and imposing, but not in an overly egotistical way, just in a way that says he's so successful he doesn't have to even try to make an impression. Whereas my presence says something more like, I need to retreat behind a kelp bed and reconsider all my life choices.

"So, how do you two know one another, exactly?" Alana's mother asks.

"I'm ... her ... well, I ..."

I don't know what to say. I don't know what Alana wants me to say.

Despite looking every bit the movie star she is, Alana stutters. "We ... uh ... actually ... Stevens is, um ... my yoga instructor! Yes. He's my yoga instructor."

Her mother sizes me up, and while she's doing that, Alana looks straight through the mouth of the fish costume, past the buck teeth, into my eyes, and mouths, "Sorry," to me.

I get it. She's trying to protect me. We hadn't planned for me to be publicly known as her boyfriend yet. And certainly not dressed as a coral chewing, sand spewing fish with a bulbous forehead and protruding dental formation.

"*This* is the yoga instructor?" Her mother sizes me up. "The one I heard over the phone?"

Ah. Yes. That is what Alana told her mom when I showed up with tacos. If only she could have met me then.

"Yes. Yep. This is him." Alana nods a little too emphatically.

"Hi," I say to Alana's mother. "I'm Stevens the ... uh ... yoga instructor."

I then make the mistake of trying to bend my knees and extend two finned hands into warrior one pose. There's the distinct sound of ripping fabric right up my backside. It appears I've split a tail fin.

"Well," I say, looking from the horrified face of Alana's mother to the pitying faces of Alana and Rex. "I think that's my cue to practice catch and release."

Practice catch and release? Ugh.

I back away from them and continue to walk backward until I'm at the double doors leading from the ballroom into the bar/foyer area. Then I turn and head out of the event venue as fast as a man in a fish suit can go.

~

I wake in my bed after chartering a private boat home and doing the golf cart drive of shame to my house, garment bag in tow. I want to burn that costume. The first thing I did when I got in the house was to check the invitation I had hung on my fridge.

I was right. The gala had been a costume party. At least it started out that way. The invitation I had posted in my home was one sent out four months ago. I checked my email after double checking my fridge, and sure enough, I found two emails in my spam folder stating that due to the high-profile celebrities they had arranged to invite, the event had been changed from costumes to formal wear two months ago, and confirmed as such a month later.

I went to bed trying to shake off the memories of the evening, but I had dreams that I was officiating an underwater wedding between Alana and Rex. I was a fish. The o-fish-iant. I chuckle. It's come to this: private, unspoken dad jokes.

My head swims with thoughts of Alana and how perfect she looked standing next to Rex while I struck a pose and ripped a seam in my fish costume. If Atlantis were habitable, I'd consider relocating. I'm not jealous. But I am shaken, and not only a little. After about an hour alone with my thoughts, I've had enough. I head out the door and over to Kai's home. He's still living on this side of the island until he and Mila get married.

I knock on his door and he pulls it open with a cup of coffee in his hand and a casual smile on his face.

THIRTY-TWO

Stevens

You're not perfect, sport.
And let me save you the suspense.
This girl you've met, she isn't perfect either.
But the question is whether or not
you're perfect for each other.
~ Good Will Hunting

"Stevens, hey. What brings you here so early in the morning?"

"I'm up in my head about Alana. I need a sounding board."

"Come on in. Coffee?"

"Better not. I'm amped up as it is."

"Surf?"

"Maybe yeah. After we talk."

"Have a seat." Kai waves at his couches.

I sit on the edge of one, resting my elbows on my knees and cupping my head in my hands.

"Did something happen, or are you just freaking out that she's an internationally famous movie star?"

"Thanks for that reminder. No. Yeah. Something happened."

I fill Stevens in on the whole parrothead debacle. He laughs at times. Which helps, in a weird way. We're both laughing by the time I get to the part where I struck an impromptu yoga pose.

"Man. That is not what I expected when you said you were up in your head."

"I know, right?"

"So where's your head at now, besides feeling appropriately mortified?"

"I guess after all was said and done, it wasn't just the fish suit that set me apart."

"Though, it did set you apart."

"For sure."

We both chuckle.

"I mean, usually I see her in this setting. Here on Marbella. In her house. The beach. Out on the water together. She's more ... normal ... here. But last night I saw her in that element. And she was at home—she just fit.

Kai nods. Then he sits back, obviously considering me and my situation.

After a few moments of Kai's silence, I say, "My parents used to have this St. Bernard. The dog was lethargic and sweet. But, honestly he spent a good portion of the day lying around panting, and on hot days it was worse. We took him with us to my uncle's cabin in Mammoth one winter. He came to life. It was such a lesson in creatures and their habitats."

"That would be the lesson you took out of that."

"Is there another lesson?" I ask.

"Maybe adaptability. That dog had a good life. Sure, he was more lethargic at times here, but he was loved by a family. He could make a life in both climates. He adapted."

"Well, seeing Alana in that ballroom in that dress ..." I shake my head, remembering what she looked like. "That's her habitat."

"Are you sure? Because I've seen her here—and the other

275

night, on the beach with you? She looked so at home. I don't think I've ever seen her smile like that."

"Rex," I mutter.

"What's that?"

"Rex. He's her species. I'm not. She's out of my league. I honestly never saw so acutely the reality of how much they are made for one another until last night. And now I can't shake it. Up until now she was just Alana, my SaturdayIslandGirl, the one who also acts for a living. But last night—last night she was Alana Graves and I was a guy who has feelings for her, standing there in a fish suit doing yoga."

Kai studies me. "You think Alana's out of your league? Does that make you unique? As if Mila's not out of mine?"

He stares at me.

"You're an ex pro surfer," I remind Kai.

His answer is swift. "She's a better person than me."

"That's not the same. And, as awesome as Mila is, I don't think she's a better person than you. You two are well matched."

"What about Ben and Summer?" Kai suggests.

"Ben with anyone." I laugh and Kai does too.

In reality, Ben is a great guy. I'd tell that joke in front of him and he'd jab back in good fun.

"Summer was just starting out as an actress when they first dated," I point out. "Alana ... she's Alana Graves. It's not the same. If we had met when we were younger, before she skyrocketed, maybe. But she's always been destined for this life of superstardom. Her parents are in the business. They predetermined and groomed her for it."

"She's not Alana Graves when she's with you," Kai points out. "She's just Alana. And I have a hunch there aren't a lot of places in the world where that woman gets to be just Alana. You've given her something she needed."

"I think I'm falling for her."

I haven't even said those words to myself yet, but they tumble out without a filter. And it's the truth. I'm falling for Alana, not Alana Graves.

"I want the smallest things with her. Just to take out her trash or cook her a meal. To watch her face light up when she laughs. I want to walk holding her hand. To see the way the sunlight plays across her hair when she's sitting on the porch looking out at the ocean. I want to see her every chance I get—not just occasionally. My days are measured by the number between the last time I saw her and the next time I'll be able to. Cheesy, huh?"

"I know that feeling. Man, do I."

"And? What do I do?"

"You hang on for the wild ride. When it boils down to it, love is never easy. But it's worth it. And really, we have no choice. Once we fall, we're gone. It's too late to course correct. We just make the best of our circumstances and enjoy the sweetness of having found a woman who wrecks us daily with simply a smile or a toss of her hair. Not everyone gets to have that kind of love. So, if you find it, you hang on with both hands. Don't let the fact that she's a superstar factor in. You're just like the rest of us—two people who fell in love. It happens every day. Somewhere, right now, someone is falling in love, or they're about to. But when it's your day? It feels like your whole life led up to this. Nothing else matters but her and making a life with her."

I nod. And, *this*. This is why I came knocking right after the sun came up. My head is right again by the time I walk back to my house. I'm falling for Alana. Her career is secondary. What we feel for one another takes precedence over everything. So her mom met me in a fish costume? That was yesterday. It's a new day.

Kai and I meet up with Ben and Bodhi for some surfing. I take two tours out later in the day. By nighttime, I haven't heard from Alana, but I'm sure she's occupied with photo shoots or interviews, or more events like the one last night. None of that matters. She has a life and a job. I have to keep that in perspective. Acting is her job. I can give her a life—if she'll let me.

And, I don't care what Kai says, she's way out of my league.

She would be even if she weren't a movie star. I'm going to treat my relationship with her like Charlie and his golden ticket. I'm going into Wonka's factory with a grateful smile on my face, knowing all along I don't belong there, so I'll never take this opportunity for granted.

I'm sitting down to dinner when my cell pings with a text notification.

I smile when I see her name.

Alana: *Hey. It's been a hectic twenty-four hours. I'm just now able to text. My mom's still here, but she's about to leave.*

Stevens: *Text me when you're alone. We need to talk.*

Alana: *That's a horrible line, merman. If you were writing a script, that would be the line before the leading man tells the leading lady he's moving on without her.*

Stevens: *That's not what it means here. I'm not in the catch and release program after all.*

Alana: *Good, because I'm not about to let you off the hook.*

Stevens: *Good one. Just text me when you can freely chat. Or better yet, call.*

Alana: *I will.*

About fifteen minutes later, my cell rings.

"Hey."

Alana's voice is soft. I can hear the exhaustion beneath her words. And instantly, I'm back into a place where nothing matters but what we share. The world around us can judge, shine a spotlight, or attempt to drive us apart. She might be better suited for a match with Rex on paper, but in reality, I know she's mine.

"Hey. You sound wiped out. Would it be better to talk in the morning?"

"No. I miss you. Waiting until the morning would only mean I wouldn't sleep well. You didn't stop running out the ballroom door when I called after you last night. I couldn't chase you down with so many eyes on me. I couldn't even raise my voice. But I wanted you to stop so we could talk. Are you okay?"

"I am, actually. I had to process some things. But I'm good."

"I'm so glad. I worried about you the whole day. I kept trying to find a minute to text you, but I literally had no opportunity. My mother was even at the door of the restroom whenever I went in there. I finally texted you from my balcony and then I had to stash my phone so she wouldn't try to see what I had texted."

"Sorry about how she met me. I didn't know you'd be at that event."

"My mother sprung it on me as a 'fundraiser.' I had no idea the cause or I would have mentioned it."

"It gave you more exposure with Rex." I grimace after the sentence leaves my mouth.

"Exactly. My mother has her methods."

I explain the costume mix-up and she and I have a good laugh about it. We talk a little longer. I listen as she tells me about an interview she did, and an appearance with members of the cast. I'd listen to her tell me about anything. It's just good to hear her voice—to be the person she calls at the end of a long day.

She yawns and then she asks, "Can you play for a while?"

"I'll stay up past my bedtime to play with you."

"Mmm. Good answer," she practically coos into the phone. "You're too far away."

"Agreed. But I'll see you when you're back."

"Tomorrow. I'll be back tomorrow."

"Then I'll see you tomorrow."

"Don't hang up, okay?" She sounds so sweet, her voice low and drowsy.

"Okay."

I pull up the game. She already initiated a match.

And her first word stares me in the face: APOLOGY.

"No need," I say. "I understand."

"It was unexpected, but I should have introduced you."

279

"No. I'm pretty sure you shouldn't have. I don't want to be in a fish costume when I first meet your parents."

I look at my tiles. And, unbelievably, I'm able to play ACCEPT. "I don't have an E or a D, but your apology is accepted."

"I'm so sorry, Stevens. I wanted to protect you from all this. My mother ... well, I'd rather you never meet her, to be honest. Fish costume or not, she's going to give you that same appraising look that broadcasts her disapproval. She's dead set on certain things which are honestly not her business."

"You can't protect me, Alana. Your mother is part of the whole package. The press, exposure to the public eye ... it's all part of the whole package."

Her voice is tentative when she asks, "Are you ready to request a return label and your full refund?"

"Not even close. I'm here. Now. Let's play."

We play nearly a full game while we talk about our days and eventually switch to a revealing game of would-you-rather where I learn a lot of idiosyncrasies and fun details about Alana. She keeps yawning, so I finally insist we set all games aside for the night.

"Don't hang up on me, okay?" she asks.

"You need sleep."

"I'm going to sleep. I just want you here with me. Leave your phone on, would you?"

"Okay."

She goes silent, and in a matter of minutes, I can faintly hear the sound of her breathing through the phone ... until I drift off too, connected to her across the miles and everything else that separates us.

THIRTY-THREE

Stevens

You had me at hello.
~ Jerry Maguire

I 'm dog sitting today. Kalaine went into labor a few hours ago and Kai went with them to the birthing center on the island. Shaka's curled up next to me on my couch. He goes everywhere I do. If I go into the kitchen, he follows—to the bedroom, he's there. Try to use the restroom? I've got a spectator. I can't imagine Shaka ever having been a stray. He's so attached to people. Maybe being homeless taught him to cling to us. It's hard to say.

There's a knock at my door. I'm not expecting anyone, and it's far too soon for Kai to be back here. Shaka barks a few times, then he stands staring at the door with his tail wagging. Definitely not a guard dog.

I open it and Alana's standing on my porch. She's not Hollywood Alana right now. She's my Alana—the Marbella Island version of herself. Her hair is down, curling around her face. Her makeup is barely there. And she's wearing jeans shorts and a white tank top with these heels that don't exactly match the casual vibe of the rest of her outfit.

"Um, hi." She smiles and bats her eyelashes at me and sticks one leg out toward me, pointing her toe. "I was wondering if you —or maybe any of your neighbors—happened to know a guy who is proficient at removing sandals."

"Hi." I stare into her eyes like I'm looking at a mirage. "I think I know a guy. And I'm pretty sure he wants to be the only man taking sandals off your feet. So please, come in and stop this door-to-door insanity."

"He wants to be the only one, huh?" She's playing, but I feel the need beneath her question.

"He's most definitely the only one. And he's not really interested in taking on any other sandal removal jobs at the time. He's pretty single-minded in his devotion to your sandals."

"Is that so?" She smiles.

I pull her toward me. Shaka runs through my legs, between us and then behind Alana, rubbing against us the whole time.

"You got a dog?"

Alana's still in my arms, but her head is pulled back so I can see her face. I bend down and kiss her. Then I brush the tip of my nose against the tip of hers and lean in so our foreheads are resting against one another.

"I did not get a dog. I'm dog sitting. Kalaine and Bodhi are in labor. Well, Kalaine is. Anyway, they're having their baby. And Kai is with them, so I'm temporarily caring for Shaka."

"Shaka, is it?" Alana releases me and squats low, rubbing Shaka behind the ears. "Aren't you a cutie? Yes, you are."

Shaka's tail wags furiously.

Alana looks up at me. "Actually, I came to ask you if you'd consider having dinner at my place."

"I'd love to, but ..."

"No. Yeah. I get it," she hedges.

"You get it?"

"After what happened at the gala, you might need to take some space."

"Alana, you apologized for that. I'm trying to put it behind us. I was going to say, 'I'm dog sitting.' He's a little clingy right now. I think he senses that Kalaine's in labor, and he's never been over here. He's a bit insecure right now. I don't want to leave him here alone."

"You could bring him."

"Are you sure?"

"Yes. I'm sure. I want to see you. And I want to make up for that horrible introduction to my mother and Rex."

"The scoreboard is wiped clean. We're good," I assure her. "That situation was as much my fault as yours. Actually, it wasn't really anyone's fault. Wires were crossed. We were blindsided. It's done."

"Okay." She nods as if she's accepting my explanation and is finally letting go. "I still want to have a meal with you. I may have a delivery arriving in an hour."

"A delivery?"

"Of tacos."

"Ahhhh ... Mitzi's?"

"Yes. I got your favorite. And chips and guacamole."

"Well, you drive a hard bargain, Graves. Let me get Shaka on a leash and we'll go have some tacos."

Alana had a driver drop her off when she came over. Apparently, she was that sure she was going to talk me into coming back with her. I'm glad she feels that confident in my commitment to her. After I text Kai to ask if Shaka can come with us to Alana's, we take my golf cart to her house, putting Shaka between us on the front bench.

The tacos arrive a half hour after we get to her home. Shaka finds a spot he likes in the front room, seeming even more comfortable here than he was at my place.

We dig into the bags and plate everything, and then we take our meals out on the porch. We're just finishing up our dinner when Shaka comes out the sliding porch doors onto the deck with something in his mouth.

"What do you have, buddy?" I ask, standing to take whatever it is from him.

It's a scrap of fabric, that much I can tell, but he's got it pretty wadded up and secured in his jaws.

"Shaka, drop it," I command in a firm voice like the one I've heard the Dog Whisperer use.

Alana starts laughing. She covers her mouth with her hands.

"Oh my gosh! Shaka!" she shouts through her laughter.

Alana stands up and approaches the dog. I try to corner him from behind. He darts away. Before I know it, we're chasing the dog through the house and he's running around couches and chairs, under coffee tables, into bedrooms and out again. When he returns to the deck, Alana and I head out after him. I shut the sliders and we corner him.

Alana approaches him with her pointer finger extended.

"Sit, Shaka."

Surprisingly, he sits.

"Drop it!" Her voice is firm and she has her hands on her hips like she means business.

Shaka's jaw pops open and a hot pink piece of fabric falls to the deck.

Alana scoops it up and holds it behind her back. "That was my ... um ... undergarments."

"Yeah. I saw the drawer open when I chased Shaka through there."

She looks at me and bursts out laughing. "The tabloids would have a heyday with this. I can see the headlines now! Alana Graves and A Mystery Man in Her Bedroom! Her Underwear Drawer Torn Open! It makes for some great clickbait."

We both chuckle, even though those headlines aren't so far-fetched.

"I like being your man of mystery," I confess.

"I love it a little too much, I'm afraid."

"No such thing," I assure her.

She disposes of Shaka's plunder and comes back out of her bedroom. I noticed a wall of framed photos while I was in pursuit of the dog, so I pause there to take them all in. It would be normal for Alana to have photos of herself in designer gowns, accepting awards, and attending red-carpet events. Instead, this wall is full of a very mundane, and obviously curated, selection of photos from her non-Hollywood life.

One photo catches my eye and I nearly swallow my tongue.

It's me.

But not me currently.

This photo was taken when I was eight or nine years old with a little girl I used to play with on the weekends in our favorite cove. I called her ... Oh. No. What? It can't be! I called her *Saturday girl*. She only came to that cove on Saturdays. And she stopped showing up the summer after I graduated from elementary school. I never saw her again. She disappeared without even saying goodbye. I think her family had a vacation home here. But most Saturdays she was at the same beach where my family went to spend a good portion of the day. Her name wasn't Alana, though. It was Genevieve. Then again, I was Ren.

I study the photo. It's definitely me. There's no doubt. And Alana has it because the little girl is *her*.

I'm about five seconds away from telling her when her phone rings.

"My mother," she mouths. And then my phone pings with a text.

Kai: *It's a boy! They named him Koa. And his middle name is Kai—after me. It means warrior and ocean. He's destined to be a strong surfer with that name—an ocean warrior.*

I smile.

Me: *Congratulations.*

Kai: *Can I meet you back at my place to get Shaka? He needs to eat and I'm going to leave Bodhi and Kala alone for a bit and then come back tonight to take a shift. Plus, I have to clean my house. My parents are flying into LAX tomorrow. They'll be staying with me.*

Me: *Sure. I'll leave Alana's in a minute and meet you there.*

I stare at the photo again. What are the odds? It was strange enough that Alana is my SaturdayIslandGirl on the game? She's liable to think I stalked her if I tell her about this uncanny overlap. After all we went through in LA, our relationship doesn't need another wallop.

Maybe I should tell her, though. She might be as pleasantly blown away as I am. I stare at the photo one more time. Then I take out my cell and snap a shot of it—two children, side by side on the sand, digging a ditch together, laughing. The brown haired boy is wearing blue swim trunks with a shark motif. The girl has impossibly curly blond hair and an orange one piece on with a sunflower adorning the top.

I follow the sound of Alana's voice into the kitchen. She's still on the phone.

"It's Brigitte now," she tells me.

"I have to get going. Kai needs me to bring Shaka back. Kalaine had her baby. A boy."

"Awww." She turns her attention back to Brigitte. "Hey, Bridge, let me call you right back. Stevens is leaving and I need to say goodbye."

She smiles and rolls her eyes. "No I will not. And I'm not saying that to him either." She chuckles. "I'll call you right back."

She clicks the phone off and sets it on the counter.

"What did she tell you to do?"

"That's confidential and irrelevant."

"Oh, really?"

I round the counter and gently poke that spot beneath her ribs, wiggling my fingertips just the slightest. She collapses into me in a fit of giggles.

"No fair!" she shouts. "Okay! Okay! She told me to give you a kiss you won't forget, and to tell you you're ten times hotter than Rex Fordham."

I can't help but grin. I'm not insecure, but the past forty-eight hours have been a blow to my usual confidence.

"And you refused her?" I ask.

"You got it out of me anyway."

"The confession, yes. That Brigitte thinks I'm attractive."

"I do. I think you're attractive. She doesn't matter." Alana loops her arms around my neck. "She's only encouraging me to tell you what I think."

"Well, then?" I'm taunting her. She knows it.

Alana looks directly into my eyes. "You, my merman, are ten times hotter than Rex Fordham. And that's a fact."

I can feel the prickle of self-consciousness climb up my neck and color my cheeks.

"Are you blushing?" Alana asks.

"Maybe."

She smiles and leans in to kiss me.

Then she walks me to the door. "Are you doing anything tomorrow?"

"I've got an early morning snorkel. Otherwise, I'm free. I've got a few tours here and there over the next few days. Then I have a job in Marin coming up."

"Let's get together after your snorkel."

"How about I make us a picnic lunch," I offer.

"I'd love that."

"I've got somewhere special I want to take you."

THIRTY-FOUR

Alana

I'm just a girl, standing in front of a boy,
asking him to love her.
~ Notting Hill

Stevens picks me up mid-morning and drives me down through established neighborhood streets on the North Shore. Beach bungalows sit next to larger homes, many with white picket fencing. It could be a location shoot for a movie set in a sleepy beach town.

Along the way, Stevens points to his childhood home.

"That's where I grew up. Also known as the current home to your second biggest fan."

"My second biggest?"

"My mom. We've already established that I'm your biggest fan."

"Of my movies?"

"Of you."

I can't help the ridiculous grin that splits my face.

"Consider yourself warned," his tone is light, teasing. "You need to steer clear until you're absolutely sure you want to meet my mother and endure all her exuberant fangirling—of which I can guarantee you there will be plenty."

"I'll keep that in mind. But I do want to meet your mom one day."

"I want you to. And my whole family."

The unspoken fact that I will do anything to keep Stevens a minimum of fifty miles from my family hangs in the air. I wish the situation were different.

Stevens parks near the edge of a cove only the locals on this side of the island know about. The entrance is through a path between two cliffs, so most people drive right by it, unless you know it's here.

He has no idea, but this cove means everything to me. It's the one I grew up going to as a kid when we'd come over to Marbella on the weekends. We didn't come every week. Sometimes I came with a nanny while my parents were filming. But I was here more often than not, and sometimes we'd come for a whole week or longer through the summer.

I often played with a boy named Ren. He was one of my safe people back then. Honestly, Stevens reminds me of him in a weird way—he's got that same quietly mischievous side. Not that Ren would ever intentionally break the rules. And Stevens obviously wouldn't either. Ren was a sweet boy. He always teased me in a friendly way. And he made me feel like all was right in the world. No matter what was going on, I looked forward to Saturdays on Marbella.

That's how I chose my gamer tag, SaturdayIslandGirl. Ren used to call me Saturday girl. Sometimes he'd just shout, "Saturday!" as if it were my actual name. Like, "Saturday, get some water in this bucket!" And I'd skip down to the shoreline and scoop a bucketful of saltwater and bring it back to him where he'd smile at me approvingly.

We walk between the two walls of cliffs and emerge on the beach. The sun is shining overhead with only a few clouds in the sky. There's a gentle breeze coming in off the ocean. A few families are further down the beach with chairs and umbrellas. Stevens lays out a picnic blanket in a spot set apart from the rest of the people who are here, and then he opens the basket he brought with him.

"I brought sandwiches and two kinds of salads."

"Impressive."

"Be very impressed ... with the Descanso Deli."

I laugh. "Okay. Well, it's still impressive. You planned and arranged all this."

We dig in, Stevens fills my plate and sits across from me. We talk about his brother's plans, his upcoming work in Marin, and I tell him about Brigitte's most recent dating disaster. She doesn't mind if I share with Stevens, and I'm glad because when I tell him the crazy highlights of her night, he laughs so hard he snorts. I've never seen him laugh that hard before.

The picnic seems to be restoring our homeostasis. As always, time together on Marbella makes everything else seem small and insignificant compared to my feelings for him and the deepening connection between us.

After we finish our lunch, I'm sitting between Stevens' legs, leaning back on him and he's got his arms propped behind him to hold us up. We're facing the ocean, watching the waves roll in.

"I used to come here as a boy," he says.

"To the North Shore?"

"To this cove. And ..." he pauses, kissing the top of my head. "There was a curly blond haired girl ..."

I pivot so I'm facing him. He looks me directly in the eyes.

"Her name was Gwendolyn."

It takes me a few beats. My ears feel like they're ringing with my childhood name and the ramifications of him saying it.

"Ren?" I feel my brow crease as I search his face for similarities between the man in front of me and the boy I knew.

He nods. "I'm Ren."

"But ... you're Stevens now?"

"And you're Alana."

"I changed my name for the business. I'll tell you the story later. But why would *you* change your name?"

"If you knew what Ren was short for, you'd have told me to change it."

"Oh, now I need to know."

"There are some things in life that are destined to remain a mystery."

"And your real name is not one of them. But we'll get back to that. How did you know I was Gwendolyn?"

"I saw the photo."

"In my hallway! The photo of me and Ren on the beach. My nanny took that."

"I couldn't believe it."

"Why didn't you say anything yesterday?"

"Your phone rang and then Kai needed me. And ... I didn't know if you'd think I had stalked you. I mean, what's the probability?"

"It's not as improbable as you might think," I tell him. "I loved this island. It's where some of my fondest childhood memories happened. So, when I started earning enough to afford multiple homes, I bought one here. Marbella became my refuge all over again. Just like it was when I was a child. You've never left. I came back. We have a pretty small population of locals. The probability is in our favor on this one."

"I love it when you talk all science-y," he teases, leaning in for a kiss.

I turn so I'm on my knees, facing him, with my legs folded beneath me, and I kiss him back. I'm not one to believe in luck or destiny. But I can't deny the way we feel meant to be ... from all those years ago, to finding one another on the game, to him being my water taxi driver, to now. Stevens is my person. I'm sure of it. And my heart has known it for longer than my head was willing to fully admit.

I cup his jaw with my hand and he cradles my cheek. Our kiss is soft, nearly reverent. Then I collapse back into him and we spend the rest of the afternoon lying on his blanket, running in and out of the water, and collecting shells.

∿

For the past few days I've been back in Los Angeles at my Hollywood condo.

Rex and I had a ComicCon appearance this weekend. We also had radio interviews on KROQ and KISS FM radio stations.

Brigitte is here with me and I've been unloading on her about my situation. I need to stop.

"I miss him. Is that weird?" I flop my head back onto the sofa in the living room of my condo.

"No." She mirrors my motion, but adds a little drama to the movement and I love her for it. "I miss him too. And I don't even know him." She giggles.

"Stop that." I loll my head in her direction and send her a playfully scolding glare.

"You know I'm just teasing you," she says. "But seriously. This is your life. You two are going to have to learn to work around all the things. You know what I mean. You film overseas. There's pre-release mania like we're in now. There's the two or three consuming months of filming any project, and then you have downtime that lasts so long you get squirrely. It's unconventional. He's going to have to adapt. Better sooner than later. And you're going to have to adapt to wanting to be with him constantly and having to juggle your insane life into the mix with your infatuation with this hot biologist. Which, may I add, should be a trope in romance. Hot biologist. It has a ring to it, doesn't it?"

"Brigitte."

"Yeah. Yeah. Okay. Anyway, that's me, straight talking to you. It's a get-over-it situation. And, also a get-creative sitch. That too."

"I know. And, thanks. You're right. I'll see him when I'm back on Marbella after he gets back from a job up north. It's just hard right now because being able to see one another face-to-face is so new. I'd be seeing him every day if things weren't so crazy."

"Awww. I love that. You really like him, huh?"

"I really, really do."

"Like ... more than like, like?"

"What are we, in seventh grade?"

"Do you love him, Alana?"

"I am definitely hovering somewhere near love. Maybe I'm actually there."

Am I? Do I love Stevens?

I definitely can't imagine life without him anymore.

Brigitte squeals. "That makes me so happy. You deserve this. And I'll do what I can to support you."

"You always do."

"I do, don't I?"

I laugh.

We spend the rest of the afternoon getting mani-pedis and massages at a private salon that is very discreet and serves a lot of Hollywood clientele.

We order Chinese to be delivered to my condo, and then Brigitte takes off to head home to the beach cities where she lives.

Before she goes, she says, "Oh! I ordered another delivery. Thank me later."

Then she shuts the door behind her and fully ignores me opening it and shouting after her, "What's the delivery Bridge? Tell me!" She doesn't respond to my inquisitive texts either. I guess I'll just have to wait. About a half hour later, she sends me a text.

Brigitte: *Almost forgot. Delivery guy has been given a pass-word so you can buzz him up. It's SEA OTTER. Got that?*
Me: *Yes. What's in the delivery?*

Brigitte: *Enjoy! Peace out. This is me saying goodnight, boss.*

I turn on the TV, something I rarely do. I scroll channels until I land on an old romcom. I'm sitting on my couch with my legs tucked under me and a cup of hot detox tea in my hand when there's a ring of the bell to let the delivery in.

"What's the password?" I ask into the intercom on my wall.

"Sea otter," a weird voice answers me. It's a man's voice, but he sounds high pitched, like he's forcing himself to sound more feminine.

Whatever. I wait by the door for the knock. I'm dying to see what Brigitte ordered. Usually it's good if she's being mysterious —which, she definitely is.

I peek through the keyhole. A man is standing there, wearing all brown. He has a ball cap on and he's looking down so I can't see his face. I open the door ...

And scream! "Stevens? What are you doing here?"

"Your assistant texted me that you were in need of something."

I double over at the waist, my hands to my face and squeal like a fangirl.

"Brigitte! I am going to give her such a Christmas bonus this year!"

"So, I take it you're happy to see me?"

"Get in here. Oh my gosh." Stevens steps inside my condo and I throw my arms around his neck and kiss his cheek. "You came to visit me?"

"Yeah. When Brigitte texted, I packed a bag."

"She texted you?" My arms are still around his neck and I'm grinning so big my whole face feels the glow of my happiness.

"She texted me," he repeats. "Wait. Give me a minute."

Stevens walks back out to the hall, grabs a duffel bag and a large brown paper bag and shuts the door behind him. Then he takes his phone out of his pocket and reads Brigitte's text.

"Stevens, I have a big, massive, monumental favor to ask you. As you know, among other things, my job is keeping Alana Graves happy. They say, 'happy wife, happy life,' I can't find a good rhyme for boss, but happy boss makes my life a whole lot easier. So, here goes. Can you manage a trip over to LA? She misses you. It's kind of all she's talking about. Let me know. We'll pay your fees for the ferry or whatever transportation costs you incur along with any other incidentals. P.S. Don't feed her too much. She's got to fit into her outfits for the next few days. But after the trip, get her a pizza. Mwah."

"She texted all that?"

"That was just the first text," he says with a chuckle.

I sit on the couch and pat the cushion next to me. Stevens joins me.

"She texted more?"

"When I texted back ..." He looks down at his phone. "Whatever Alana needs. I'm here to help. I miss her too."

He looks back up at me and I lean in and kiss his cheek again. Then I cup his face in my hands. "You were missing me too?"

"Of course."

"What did she say when you texted that?"

"More emojis than I even knew existed, and this word: squeeeee. And then 'You're the best! You're the best! Ohmygoodness, you're the best! And ... do you have a brother?'"

I chuckle. "I hope you didn't tell her about your brother."

"I didn't. He's moving. It wouldn't be fair if they hit it off, which they just might. They both seem to operate on the same frequency of zero-off-switch."

I chuckle that Stevens has Brigitte pegged after such a short time interacting with her.

"You're here!" I stare at Stevens and shake my head in disbelief.

"I am. It's really good to see you." Stevens loops his arm across the back of the couch and I lean into him, resting my head on his chest.

My phone rings on the coffee table. I groan. But I lift myself off Stevens and check it. The next few days are heavy and important for PR. I need to stay in the loop for any changes or updates.

"It's Brigitte."

Stevens smiles.

Before I even say hello, she says, "I know, I know. I'm awesome. Thank me later."

I laugh. "You are awesome, Bridge."

Stevens shouts into the phone, "You're awesome, Brigitte!"

"Okay, kids. You two have fun!"

She hangs up and I settle back into Stevens' embrace.

I kiss Stevens' cheek and then drop my head onto his chest. He holds me to himself, as if he doesn't want to let me go. The mood shifts between us—comfortable and settled. Like neither of us could really rest until we made our way back to one another. I don't lean on anyone, and yet I'm leaning on him—because I know I can.

"I used to have feelings about you," he murmurs into the top of my head. "... about Alana Graves, the movie star. But the more time we've spent together, the more I know that was infatuation, idolizing someone I thought I could know through the distant lens of a camera."

"You had feelings?"

"As evidenced by my stellar ability to act normal when we first met at the water taxi."

I chuckle.

"But now?" He tips my chin up so he can gaze in my eyes. "Now I have feelings for *you*—for Alana, my girlfriend, the one I know without a camera telling me what to think. Just you, unfiltered, unadulterated, you."

"Girlfriend?"

"Whatever you want to call yourself."

He backs off so easily, probably assuming I'm not ready for a label. Always considering me.

"Girlfriend works. I actually love that. I want to call myself your girlfriend. I'd pretty much get those words tattooed somewhere."

"Because that wouldn't bring the news outlets running from every corner of LA and beyond. And where, exactly, would this tattoo go? And what would it say?"

My body hums with the electricity between us. He always surprises me when his intelligence and thoughtfulness give way to this incredibly flirty side of him.

"Would it be here?" He taps my bicep softly and then gives it a gentle squeeze. I feel my eyelids flutter. "Or here?" He lifts my leg and runs his fingers along the top of my foot, and I shiver. I actually shiver. "Or here?" He flips my arm over gently so my hand is facing upward, and then he drags his pointer slowly along my wrist.

"Mm hmm."

"Mm hmm? All the places?" He chuckles.

"All the places. I'll just get multiple tattoos that say, *Stevens' girlfriend*. Or maybe just *Ren*."

"You can call me that. My mom still does half the time. I figure she earned the right."

"Your mom sounds awesome. I barely remember her."

"I want you to meet her, officially. We'll just have to borrow some sports padding from the high school for when she tackles you."

I giggle. "I'm tough. I think I can handle it."

"I think you can handle anything." His eyes are so sincere that I almost actually believe him.

"You've been so amazing about all of this," I tell him. "... hiding our relationship ... coming here. I hate that it has to be this way."

I sigh, frustrated with myself for shifting the mood in the room, for wasting precious time together bringing up the challenges my fame imposes on our relationship, for the fact that we have so many hurdles when we should be able to enjoy these early months of dating.

"I've been thinking so much about you—us," I tell Stevens. "And you should have everything. Of all the people in the world, you deserve all the normal things a man gets when he dates someone he really likes. You should have a girlfriend who can go to the movies with you, or ride on your boat without people swarming her for autographs at the dock, someone sweet, and kind, and beautiful. You should have someone who doesn't mess things up by being complicated."

I don't even look in his eyes because I'm tearing up a little now that the words are out of my head and lingering in the space between us.

Stevens brushes my hair back, and I ache from the contact. There's a visceral tug to give in, to take what I want without thinking of him and how my life messes his up.

My voice feels quiet and meek when I look up into his eyes. "I wish I could give you all of that and more."

"Give me what, exactly?" His tone is soft, compassionate.

"A beautiful version of normal."

He chuckles, as if the fact that my life doesn't allow for the kind of romance he deserves isn't the worst news ever. Maybe it's not, to him.

He runs his hand along my jaw, tilting my head so my eyes can't avoid his. In the silence between us, he studies my face and stares softly into my eyes, Then he leans in and places a gentle, comforting kiss to my forehead. When he pulls away, he says, "Alana, sweetheart. It's okay."

"It's not okay. This is so abnormal. How can it be okay?" I sound like a pouty prima donna.

He holds my chin between his pointer finger and his thumb. "I'm here. I came here of my own free will. Brigitte didn't drug me or bribe me. She called, and I wanted to come. I wouldn't want to be anywhere else with anyone else. This isn't perfect, but it's us. You and me. I knew you were a star when I pursued you. Navigating the public and the paparazzi and your mother's expectations for you is part of your life. And if I want to be a part of your life, I need to adapt. And because it's you, that's not even a hardship."

He runs his hand down my cheek and holds my gaze. "I want to. I want to do whatever it takes for us to have a chance at this."

"Why?"

"Because I'd rather have pieces of you than nothing at all."

He smiles broadly, as if remembering the pieces of me that are his is more than enough for him. "Because now that you're mine, I'm not giving you up. I already had a life without you. And, if I have anything to say about it, I'll never have life without you again. Ever."

THIRTY-FIVE

Alana

People became more interested
in my love life than in me,
and that has a certain effect.
You start to feel very empty
and worth nothing, you start to become a piece
in a board game you never wanted to play.
~ Anna Friel

S tevens stayed in my guest room last night, though he barely slept there. We were up far past any hour that either Brigitte or my mom would approve of. When I came out of the bathroom from getting ready for the night, Stevens was in his pajama bottoms and a T-shirt, curled up with his book, wearing those glasses that drive me to a level of madness I can't explain.

I had on loungewear. We sat on the couch together, reading our books, or trying to, but then he'd tap my toes with his. I'd let my foot rest against his leg. Eventually, we gave up trying to pretend we were going to read and pay attention to our books, and we set them aside.

I had tipped my head toward him and said, "Better than the fantasy." He answered me by asking, "What was that?" I could tell he knew exactly what I had said, so I told him, "You heard me." Then that adorable, late-night half-smile crept across his face and he said, "I did. I just want to hear it again." So I tickled him, and he tackled me. And that's how we ended up kissing on my couch.

But then we talked and talked. I made us tea. And we talked some more. About acting, about his job and his passion project, about our dreams for our futures. I can never thank Brigitte enough for this gift of undivided time with Stevens here, in LA.

We have to sneak Stevens out the back entrance of the condo this morning. Brigitte thought she saw some paps lingering out front through the cameras we have trained on the entrance. She can access the feed through her phone, and she texted me this morning. The thought that someone might catch a photo of Stevens leaving with me makes my skin crawl. They'd make this into something tawdry, defaming the sweetness and purity of what we've found in one another.

Miguel is waiting in the black Town Car when we come out the back door into the alley. Tank exits the front passenger door. "Miss Alana. Mister Stevens."

Four words? Okay, then.

Stevens extends his hand to Tank. "Nice to finally officially meet you, Ken."

Tank gives Stevens a firm handshake, if the look on Stevens' face is any indication. The men eye one another in some weird show of testosterone I'd never expect from Stevens. Whatever is happening, it ends with Tank nodding once, as if they've come to an understanding.

Stevens and I get into the back seat. When I grab his hand, he winces.

"Did he hurt you?" I whisper.

"Of course not. I'm just making a show of it for your benefit."

"You know, you could join me in this industry. I know people."

"That's what Ben and my mom would call a hard pass."

I giggle. Then I catch Tank's eyes in the rearview mirror and I'd swear he had been smiling. Of course the smile is gone by the time I look up, but I saw traces of it retreating, and I feel like that's a bigger win than if my mom were to give me her stamp of approval.

Miguel turns onto the freeway and navigates LA traffic as we make our way to the docks in Ventura. At some point along the drive my head tilts onto Stevens' shoulder. Our hands are intertwined on his thigh. I drift to sleep and wake to Stevens' voice telling me we're here. Tank already has the car door open.

Joel is sitting in the boat when we walk down the dock. It's obvious Stevens and I are a couple. I don't know what Brigitte has told Joel, but his wide eyes tell me she hasn't told him a thing. He's got an NDA on file. He won't disclose our relationship to anyone. Knowing Brigitte, she withheld information on purpose so she could hear about Joel's reaction later. I can't blame her. It is pretty priceless.

"So ...?" Joel points between me and Stevens.

Stevens boards the boat, drops his duffel and extends his hand to me. I take it and board the boat.

"He's my boyfriend," I say with a smile I can't suppress and wouldn't want to.

"He's your ...?" Joel's mouth pops open. "Man. If I knew that was on the table, I would have shot my shot, Alana."

Joel winks at me playfully.

Stevens wraps a possessive arm around my waist. "It wasn't on the table."

"I'm joking, man. I have no interest in Alana. But this? What happened? I leave for one week for Wisconsin and you two hook up?"

I look at Stevens, curious as to how he'll answer.

He smiles down at me. "Exactly. That's just what happened." Then he places a chaste kiss on my forehead.

Joel shakes his head, but he leaves us to find our place at the stern while he walks to the helm.

"You're not going to tell him?" I ask Stevens.

"Later. I'll give him a little while longer to marvel at the fact that a woman like you fell for a guy like me."

I chuckle. "It's not that far-fetched."

"Did you hit your head? It's totally far-fetched. But you're mine now, and we're not practicing catch and release. Remember?"

"I do remember. I'm yours." I kiss the side of his scruffy face. He didn't bother to shave this morning, and I love him like this.

"Thank you," I say, looking up at Stevens.

"For what?"

"For coming to LA. I'll never forget the past two days."

"I'll always come for you. Don't ever doubt that."

∾

I'm home in Marbella, unwinding from the days in LA. Stevens has been up north on a job. He'll be back today.

My phone rings. It's my mother.

"Hello, darling."

"Mother. You sound winded."

"I'm just ..." She takes a deep breath and exhales it slowly. "Doing damage control."

"Damage control?"

"A photo leaked to the press of a man entering your property. One headline says. 'Who Is This Man Entering Alana Graves' Condo?' The article goes on to say that he went in but was not seen leaving. Another article says, 'Is There Trouble So Soon in Paradise?' and it goes on to describe you cheating on Rex with a mystery man."

Crud.

"What's going on, Alana? Did you have a gentleman in your condo?"

As if women all around LA aren't having their boyfriends over. Why does this have to be newsworthy? We ate a meal, talked, read books together, talked some more. Slept in separate rooms. This is not news. And yet, it is.

I sigh. "You know how the press is."

"Is there something I should know?"

I hedge. "Not that I know of."

There's a knock at the door. It's Stevens. He called to ask if he could bring me lunch before his afternoon tour.

"Mom, I've got to go."

"Is it that yoga instructor?"

I open the door and look Stevens right in the eyes. "Yes. It's my yoga instructor."

He strikes a pose on my porch. Then another. I try to hold in my laugh. He strikes another pose and I can't.

"What's funny, dear?"

"Nothing, Mom. I was just thinking of his costume."

"That was not funny, darling. That was mortifying."

"Not for you. You weren't the one dressed like a fish among a bunch of people in tuxes and formal gowns." I stare him in the eyes and smile. "I think he handled himself beautifully, considering."

He bows.

"Well, I think grown men should act like grown men. But you always did have a softer heart than I do. And I love that about you, dear."

"Thank you, Mother. I'll talk with you later."

"Call Caroline!" she shouts as I click the end call button.

Stevens holds out one of the two paper bags in his hand. "I brought salad—to please the diet police in your life."

He bends down toward my porch and grabs something just outside the doorway.

"But Brigitte did tell me to get you pizza. And I need to stay in her good graces, soooo ..."

He presents the pizza box to me. "It has vegetables, if that helps."

"It totally helps."

"And there are cookies in here." He holds up the other paper bag. "... which I'll gladly take back to the watersports shack if they go against whatever strict code you follow to make sure you remain gown-ready."

I giggle. He's so adorable.

"I'm having a cookie," I declare. "Just try and stop me."

"I won't stop you from doing anything. Have you not noticed that about me yet?"

"I have. It's one of my favorite qualities about you."

I step aside so he can pass by me. He grabs the pizza away from me and leads his way into my kitchen. I try not to think about my mother's call. There's nothing I can do about it now.

I'm not telling Stevens about the rumors. There's no need. We can't do a thing about them. They'll blow over. He was disguised as a delivery man. It's just another day in the life.

I'm on my second slice of pizza when my phone rings. It's Caroline, my publicist.

THIRTY-SIX

Alana

Listen to me, mister.
You're my knight in shining armor.
Don't you forget it.
~ On Golden Pond

I look at Stevens, "I'm going to take this."

I step out onto the deck to take Caroline's call.

"Hey, Caroline."

"Alana. I know your mother spoke with you. I need you to check a post on the StarNews feed on Instagram. I'm sending the link in a text right now. You know I try to shield you from a lot of this kind of thing and handle it myself, but I need you to be up to date so we can stay ahead of this. I'm assuming you had a man up to your condo. I'm not even going to ask you to confirm or deny that, because, at this point, the truth doesn't matter. All we need to focus on now is what we do with what's being said."

I don't bother to volunteer the truth since Caroline doesn't want it anyway, and she's right. In this case, the truth won't help. If only I weren't pretending to date Rex right now, this wouldn't be a feeding frenzy for the media. I could come clean. Or maybe, not. This kind of fiasco, the one looming on the horizon, is exactly what I'm trying to protect Stevens from.

"Is that it? Just check the Instagram link?"

"For now, yes. But, if I'm shooting straight, no. This is pre-release. You need the press of you with Rex—the happy couple reuniting before the film launches. The tabloids are buzzing about this mystery man and how he went into your place and never came out. It looks bad, Alana. You having a secret relationship when you were just trying to reconcile with Rex does not give the spine we hoped for."

I let out a sigh. "They're assuming the man was my guest. There are four tenants in my building."

"That doesn't matter. No one's interested in an Asian mogul of finance, an elderly couple, or a hairstylist to the stars. They are not the reason a *delivery man* would enter and not leave. And even if they were, you know the media is hungry for news about you. This is a crumb." She shifts gears so quickly, my head spins. "Okay. Read the post. We'll talk."

There's the telltale click and the line is dead.

I tap the link. There's nothing really significant beyond what my mother told me. A fuzzy photo of Stevens entering the building. Another one of him pushing three on the elevator panel. *How did they get that? Or did they manufacture it?* And then speculation as to why a man would be coming into my condo and not leaving. A portion of the post raises the question as to whether I'm cheating on Rex so soon into our attempt to reconcile. There are thousands of comments already. I don't read any of those. That's a doom spiral I usually ask Brigitte to take on my behalf.

I drop the hand holding my cell to my side and stare out over the treetops. I look in through the sliding glass doors at Stevens. He's waiting in my kitchen.

When I walk back inside, he takes one look at my face and asks. "What was that all about?"

I set my phone on the counter and pick up my slice of pizza, answering him before I take another bite.

"Apparently you were photographed going into my condo."

"Did they get my good side?" Stevens is all smiles.

"Thankfully, no. The photo is blurry."

Stevens glances at my face, studying me and obviously sizing up my concern. Then he stands and brushes my hair back, gently bracing his hands on my biceps.

"Hey. It's going to be okay." He's that man playing violin on the deck of the Titanic. "Let's play Scrabble."

Yep. Titanic. Stevens is the guy lulling everyone into a state of calm when an iceberg is about to hit the ship. But I can't help but dance to his tune. He's just that soothing, that grounding. He makes me forget all about the outside world and the damage they could do.

We walk into the living room to grab the Scrabble board, and like the brilliant, caring man he is, Stevens starts his attempt at distracting me from our reality.

"Ask me what my favorite marine animal is."

"The sea hare."

I make a futile effort at resisting his charm.

One foot is here with him, the other is in Hollywood, feeling the avalanche about to fall all around us. He has no idea. He can be cavalier because he hasn't tried to survive an unnatural disaster of public attack and media smears. It starts with the smallest snowball innocently rolling downhill, and somehow that leads to a cataclysmic release of all the snow on the mountain. You could find yourself buried in the devastation in a matter of minutes. That's how fast gossip and rumors grow and spread. I want him to take shelter, and he's grabbing a sled and asking me to hop on for a joy ride.

"Not the sea hare," he smiles calmly. "Guess again, or just ask me."

I look over at him, he's grinning boyishly. Okay. Okay. One last sled ride before the hill collapses.

"Okay. Tell me." I pull the Scrabble board out of the cabinet and stand.

Rain starts to fall outside. A summer squall.

"Looks like we're playing inside," I say.

Stevens grabs the board and walks into the kitchen. He sets the game up on the island and takes a stool.

"Would you rather talk about something more interesting?" he asks.

"Nope. Now that you brought it up, I want to know."

"It's the sea cucumber."

"Seriously?"

"Yes. They are scavengers that feed on small food items in the benthic zone. That's the seafloor to you non-science-y people." He winks. "They also eat plankton, algae, aquatic invertebrates, and waste particles in the water column. They eat with tube feet that surround their mouths. And they can range in size from less than an inch to over six feet."

"Six feet! That's quite a cucumber."

"It's the giant red." He smiles at me like it's an inside joke we're sharing.

As much as I want to resist him, I feel my resolve crack. He's soothing the sting of Caroline's call with his presence and the ease between us.

"Of course it is." I chuckle.

"I find it fascinating how they eat with their feet and breathe by dilating their anal sphincter to suck water into their rectum, where specialized structures called respiratory trees, or butt lungs, extract oxygen."

"So, they basically breathe through their butt?" I cover my mouth and look away, but I can't control the laugh that bubbles up.

Stevens looks at me seriously for a beat and then he starts laughing. "There she is."

"Why are you so hot right now?" He purposely picked that

animal to talk about so I would laugh in the face of the media avalanche, and I love him for it.

"You think I'm hot, while I'm telling you about an animal who breathes through his hindquarters?" He gives me a purposely smoldering look.

This whole tactic is working very well. It's the best sled ride of my life and I never want to get off.

"You are." I place my hand over his. "Very. I'm pretty sure you could read me something from a high school biology textbook and I'd find you irresistible."

"Is that right? I'll have to dig up one of my old textbooks for our next date."

I walk around the corner of the island and cup his face. "Thank you for making me laugh."

He kisses me gently. It's a sweet kiss, one meant to comfort and assure me—and it works.

My phone rings and I pick it up. I notice I never shut the Instagram app, so I swipe that out before I answer the call

Caroline.

And just like that, the slope gives way and everything is sliding downhill in a swell of white.

"Alana!" Her voice is nearly a shout, definitely panicked. "You left your camera filming live on Instagram. Your whole conversation just now, and the kiss you shared with that dark-haired, definitely-not-Rex man went through to all your followers."

I fall backward onto a barstool. Stevens' face is etched with concern.

I did this. It was bound to happen, but I was the trigger.

"Stay put. Don't do a thing. Hang up your phone. Stay off social media. Only take calls from me and your mother and Brigitte. I'll be in touch." Caroline pauses. "And breathe."

I stare across the kitchen, numbly trying to make sense of where we go from here. I've got nothing. The thought of packing everything essential and stealing Stevens away to Fiji or Lake Como flashes through my mind. I could manage to pull off an escape. We could be on a plane in a few hours. But then what? We'll have to face this someday. Like he said before. It's part of the whole package.

Brigitte calls next.

"What is going on? Your mom isn't answering my calls yet. They go straight to voicemail. I'll be hearing from her, though. You can be sure I will. All I know is my feed is blowing up with posts that have links to the major gossip sites. We've got headlines like: 'Alana Graves: Cucumber Fanatic,' and 'Sea Cucumbers. Who knew?' There's one, 'Doing a Deep Dive on Alana's New Love Interest.' I thought that was a clever play on words, actually. And then we've got the question I've been asking for weeks summed up in this title, 'Do Biologists Have More Fun?' Talk to me, Alana. What happened?"

I fill Brigitte in on what I know from the Instagram post about Stevens coming up to my apartment to the huge mess I created by accidentally bumping the live video option on my phone and leaving it on while Stevens tried to cheer me up.

My other line rings through. Stevens is sitting next to me. I haven't even had a chance to directly tell him all that's going on, but he heard my explanation to Brigitte, so he knows. His hand is over mine on the countertop and his face is as placid as ever. He's naive, unscathed for now. But that's all about to change.

"Bridge, my other line is ringing. It's Caroline. I'll call you back."

"Whatever you need, I'm here. You'll get through this. No. We'll get through this. You're never alone in these disasters. And they do blow over. Hang in there, babe."

I hang up with Brigitte and take Caroline's call, holding eye contact with Stevens the whole time. If I were Rose, I'd make space on my driftwood for Jack. No. I'd give Jack my driftwood. Someone's got to drown here. I won't let it be him.

"Hey, Caroline."

"Okay, give me the whole story. Who is this man? Obviously you're seeing someone. I need everything. You should have kept me in the loop. You don't start a relationship and not let me know. I can spin this. I can't get ahead of it. But we can turn it around, I hope. You are in a relationship, yes? This isn't a fling or some weekend of fun with a biologist, am I right?"

"He's my boyfriend." I stare at Stevens as I say the words and he smiles a broad, reassuring smile.

He quietly mouths the words, "I've got you."

I smile back at him. He's got me. I know he does. And I'll never be able to thank him enough for his willingness to walk through fire for me.

Sometimes love means going the distance for another person. But sometimes it means taking the bullet. Stevens may think he can weather the upcoming storm, but he's never been through anything like what's about to come our way. And it won't be merely a passing storm. Once he enters the public eye, he will never have the option of exiting it again.

I care too much about him to let him endure this for me.

If it were just one wave of paparazzi and all the ensuing rumors, I'd possibly take him up on his incredible offer. But this is only the tip of the iceberg. We'll hit massive impact time and again until what we have no longer resembles the simple, pure relationship we started to build. The media will have their way. They'll come at us relentlessly from now on once they know about him. I can't ask him to endure all that for me. Even if he thinks he's willing. If he knew the magnitude of what he's offering, he might not be so quick to step up and declare his loyalty.

Caroline's still talking. "I need to get Rex on board. And we have to act quickly. We're going to do a photoshoot with the two of you. And then some shots with the two men. They're friends. Rex loves this guy for you. That's the angle. You and Rex tried, but you realized you only have a strong friendship. Rex met your biologist and he saw the chemistry. Hey! That's not bad. Biology. Chemistry. I like it. Okay. That's the spin."

Rex actually does like Stevens for me. That's not publicity. It's reality.

"I don't want to drag Stevens further into this mess."

Stevens shakes his head at the same time Caroline says, "Alana, baby. You don't have a choice. It's either that or you make a bigger show of being together with Rex. You need to embrace this relationship or reject it. You can't stand still. That's never an option. The old sayings, 'It will pass,' and 'The public will lose interest,' are myths. The public may move on, but they never forget.

"And a mystery only provides everyone a blank canvas. The media and your fans—and your haters—will all go wild filling in the blanks unless we fill them in for them. So, take your time."

She pauses. "And by *take your time*, I mean you have two hours to decide. One is better. Yes. One hour. It's Rex or this biologist. We're either saying the biologist was hired to run lines for a script you're considering. He's an employee providing a service, and the script reading accidentally was filmed when you bumped your phone. Then you declare that you are madly in love with Rex and still pursuing a reunification with him. The other option is to film a publicity shoot in the next twenty-four hours—preferably tomorrow—during which you disclose your secret boyfriend to the world. Take your time. One hour."

Click.

The line goes dead.

I look at the clock.

One hour.

I've got one hour.

THIRTY-SEVEN

Alana

I'll get you, my pretty, and your little dog, too!
~ The Wizard of Oz

S tevens has a tour scheduled. He needs to leave shortly. I have an hour to decide what to do about this mess.

"I can cancel my tour," he offers.

He's still sitting at the kitchen island with me, his hand over mine on the counter, his face etched in concern.

"No. Don't. It's probably better if I have a little time to process everything."

"I'll call you when I'm finished."

"Okay. And I'm sorry." I smile weakly at him.

"For what? You weren't the one discussing echinodermata sphincters on social media. I'm pretty sure I owe you an apology."

"What did you just say?" I laugh despite the weight hanging over my head.

"Echinodermata sphincters. And trust me. That's the last time I'm saying it."

I snort laugh. "I bet I could get you to say it again."

"I bet you could get me to do anything." He walks around the island, leans down and kisses my forehead. "We'll get through this. Please don't worry about me or what this will do to me. I'll be fine. Remember. I survived a whole era of sea hare fame. I've got this."

I lean in and hug Stevens. He wraps me in his arms, absorbing everything. I don't know how he does it, but for a moment, I believe him.

He's not out the door five minutes when my mother calls.

"Alana! What is this Caroline is telling me? I saw the video of your conversation with this man. Is he the yoga instructor? The man in the fish suit?"

"One and the same."

"You're dating a yoga instructor who somehow has a penchant for strange sea creatures? You're too young for a midlife crisis, Alana. This has to stop. Your father and I have a plan. We've spoken to Rex. He's on board. We'll be sending a driver to pick you up this afternoon."

"Mother …" I try to interrupt her, but she's driving forward, intentionally giving me no openings.

"We have close to a month until your premier, darling. You and Rex promised me you would continue your relationship at least until then. Have you even given that man a chance? Rex was nominated for an Oscar. He's a kind man. You two are well suited for one another. I'm not one to step into your personal life. You know that. After all, I allow you to live on that island in your hut on the hill, but the antics must stop, Alana."

She sighs heavily, but then continues. "You may as well be taking cans of red and white paint and donning a target on your chest. Do you realize the heyday the press is having with this? They're calling you a cheater. They're speculating that you're carrying this man's child. It's getting out of hand and the story is not even a few hours old. Couple this with the blurry photo outside your LA apartment and they think he may be a UPS driver! Alana. A *U.P.S. DRIVER*! How is this even happening?

Your father and I are trying to set you up to inherit the production company. And you are undermining yourself at every turn."

My mother takes a deep breath. There's the sound of her swallowing water. "I'm going to have to schedule a deprivation tank session after this is settled."

She sighs.

Oddly, I feel for her.

"Mother?" I wait to see if I'll actually get a turn this time.

"Yes?"

"I love him."

"Oh, Alana. Please. Don't start in with that. Love is something that comes and goes. It's a trite emotion driven by so many variables. I mean, I love my manicurist. And Jobert. Goodness knows I love Jobert. And your father, of course. He's been good to me. And I love you, darling. But that's different. You're my child. But honestly, this romantic notion of having one soulmate who sets your stomach swirling and your nerve endings dancing and your heart rate spiking. The one? The one you wake thinking of, who invades your thoughts throughout the day? The one you'd sacrifice everything to have a life with? That's an emotion, Alana. And emotions come. Emotions go. They are more fickle than the weather. You do not build a life on love. You build it on hard work and strategy. Alliances? Yes. Love? Hardly."

I don't even know what to say—not in response to my mother's cynical view of life. I knew that's what she thought. Of course, I did. Hearing her spell it out makes it all so real.

Mother blows out an exasperated breath.

"Alana. I love your heart. You always had such a soft heart. And I'm glad you found someone who makes you feel all that. Unfortunately, he can't be anything but a fond memory and a sweet distraction. He was that. And you can always remember the fact that a fan got close enough to you to show you affection in person. But that's all this can be. You simply cannot afford the fallout of a relationship with some Gilligan boat captain who goes around in fish costumes at galas and talks about slimy sea creatures breathing through their ... My word. It's over dear. That's all you need to know. Your father and I have to step in on this one for your sake. And we are."

"I need to go. I'll handle everything. I don't want you and Dad getting involved."

She won't see what she won't see. At least her call did me one favor. It clarified my decision. I know what I'm going to do.

"We'll be sending a car and arranging a boat taxi for you, Alana."

"Don't bother."

"Alana. Be reasonable."

"I've been reasonable. I think I've practiced being reasonable since I started taking ballet, tap and jazz at three years old ... and studying Spanish that same year. I'm pretty sure I've done my time being reasonable."

"Alana!"

My mother is saying more, but I interrupt her, despite the fact that I never override her in anything. It's high time I interrupted my mother.

"Goodbye, Mother. I'll be in touch. I have a call to make to *my* publicist. Caroline does work for me, after all."

I hang up.

I. Just. Hung. Up. On. My. Mother.

I have the urge to call Brigitte so she can do a happy dance. Later. I'll do that later. Besides, Brigitte will try to change my mind. She'll tell me there are ways around things. Her hope springs eternal. She may be close to my life, but she does not live it. Only I know the real impact going public will be to Stevens. And I love him too much to make him go through that for me.

My phone pings with a text.

Stevens: *The paparazzi were all around the boat when my tour arrived. I didn't say anything. Waiting on your instructions. I'm on the water now. Just me and the guests on my tour. Also, I'm thinking I need to tell my mother and* *the rest of my family about our relationship since news is spreading. I want them to hear about us from me, not some skewed article or post.*

I'm about to answer when another text comes in.

Stevens: *Please don't worry about me. I'm fine. Do what you have to do. Just let me know what you need from me.*

All I can think is, it's my mother's loss not getting to know this man.

Me: *You're amazing. I hope you know that. I'll get back to you with details.*
Stevens: *Anything for you, Graves.*
Alana: *Thank you. I'll keep you posted.*

I almost reflexively type, *I love you.* Those are three words I've never said to a man. I've said them to my mother, my father, and Brigitte. I've jokingly said them to Tank to make him squirm. I may never tell Stevens my true feelings for him, but my actions will convey my devotion.

I'd rather lose him than harm him.

That's real love.

I always thought love would be enough. I think my parents have a degree of love for one another. They definitely share a mutual respect and a deep commitment to each other. I never wanted what they had. I wanted a love that woke me up, settled me down, and made me reorganize my life for another person. And now, I've found it. Only, I can't ask Stevens to do what he thinks he wants to do for me. I need to take the bullet.

I call Caroline as I'm walking out the door. There's one person I need to see as soon as possible—the woman who understands me, Hollywood, and Marbella Island. I'm on my way down the hill to her house as I call my publicist.

Caroline answers on the first ring. "Alana, tell me. What's your decision?"

"Hi, Caroline. I'm ready to do the shoot."

"Good news. So, what's our angle?"

I fill Caroline in on my thoughts and what I've decided. She responds to me with the neutrality that makes her one of the most consummate professionals in her line of work in our industry. While Caroline outlines point by point what we'll be doing and the part I'll play, I shift gears into actress mode. I can pull off any role. Once I know my motivation and have a feel for what's needed, I'll deliver a performance. And this one will be my greatest and most necessary performance to date. I have no choice. It's plain. Either I throw Stevens to the sharks, or I pass him the driftwood I've been clinging to and help him avoid drowning. He can survive the aftermath of the wreckage—but only if I make a way for him to float through it to safety.

"We have a complication," I tell Caroline.

"Your mother?"

"How'd you guess?"

"I just got off a call with her."

"That quickly? I just hung up with her less than five minutes ago."

"That woman moves quickly. She didn't get where she is by lying down in the face of things going against her will. She's a fighter. She's earned her place in Hollywood because of her fight, her talent, and her beauty. I'd never underestimate your mother, that's for certain."

"Well, it sounds like she and my father have a plan to try to show the world I'm still with Rex. And, according to her, they have Rex in their back pocket, or on their leash ... whatever you want to call it. She told me he agreed to whatever it is they're planning."

"To announce your engagement to him?"

"To ... what???"

"She planned to have Rex and you on camera with them. Rex

was going to bend the knee. I think your father may have sweetened the deal with some film opportunities, but don't quote me on that."

I'm speechless.

"Anyway, I wouldn't worry about it." Caroline's voice is breezy, dismissive even.

"You wouldn't worry? Why not? My parents are bribing a man to fake a proposal to me so I can escape a scandal that doesn't even exist. The only thing I've done wrong is falling for a marine biologist. And since when was that a high crime?"

"When I say don't worry, I mean don't worry." Caroline's confidence calms my nerves. "Rex had already agreed to the shoot with you. For all we know, he's under the impression from your parents that you want to pull off this fake engagement ... which, I'm not sure was meant to be fake, actually, but that's irrelevant."

Irrelevant? My parents are treating me like I'm living in the Middle Ages or a country where they still practice arranged marriages.

"And, Alana, it's irrelevant because I'm quite sure when I talk to Rex again he'll understand your decision and want to support you in it."

"And if he doesn't?"

"May I remind you that you pay me to manage your image. I will do my job."

"Sorry. I know you will. And, thank you, Caroline. I truly appreciate you. I hope you don't experience any fallout from choosing to do things my way on this one."

"Your mother did use the words, 'I'll ruin you. You won't work in this town again after this.'"

I roll my eyes. "She's grasping at straws. If you pull off salvaging my image ..."

"*When* ... When I pull off salvaging your image. It's not if I do it, but when."

"Okay. When. When you salvage my image, people will be banging down your door to have you rep them."

"I don't have room for more clients, Alana. I'm good. Besides, your mother won't be too put out by your choice. It's enough of a concession on your part that she will be pacified."

I can only hope—for Stevens' sake.

I'm standing outside Phyllis' home, finishing my phone call. When I pocket my cell, I walk through the gate and up the porch stairs. Phyllis swings the door open before I knock.

"I thought you might pop by."

"You heard?"

"Dear, I'm retired, not dead. I keep my ear to the ground about Hollywood gossip. Most of the time it serves to keep me grateful I got out when I did."

"Do you miss it, though? The good parts?"

"Of course." She walks out onto the porch. "Let's sit."

Phyllis takes one of two comfortable seats set around a bistro table on her porch. I take the other.

"So, in answer to your question, yes. I miss memorizing scripts, bonding with my fellow actors, the well-stocked tables of food during filming, though we weren't supposed to eat most of it. I miss acting. And I miss the fans. But I don't miss all this—the invasion of privacy, the need to please the press, the fact that you don't really fully belong to yourself."

"Fame is like this living thing," Phyllis says, looking me in the eyes as if to emphasize how important her words are. "You have to feed it, and then it grows. And you think it's fun and harmless, alluring and desirable, until it turns on you. You thought you had the leash, but one day you wake up wearing the collar with fame yanking the chain. So, to answer your question, yes. I love acting. I'm not sure I love being famous. But I didn't hate everything about being famous, even though my star never rose to the heights yours has."

"I don't hate everything about it either. I love being an actress, the variety of roles, being known. The best part is when I get to make a fan's day by posing for a photo or signing something. I love so much about it. But this part? Not so much."

"Of course not. And you wear it well. But you have become accustomed to being holed up in that house of yours. You can't even go out to buy your own loaf of bread without being mobbed. It's a price you pay. I hope it's worth it."

"Most days it is."

"So, about Stevens," Phyllis says. "I know him. Did you know that?"

"Do you? What do you think?"

"He's remarkable. Such a bright boy. And kind."

I chuckle at the thought of Stevens being a boy. Though, I knew him then too.

"We played together at Locals' Cove as children. Isn't that wild?"

"It's not so far-fetched. The island is small. You both were here on weekends. What a thing—finding one another after all these years."

"It's been the most amazing surprise. My parents *hate* me being with him."

"I can only imagine. He's not exactly boyfriend-to-a-star material. Not on the surface. I'd venture to say he's been very good for you. You've been reclusive, even lonely. And now you have that glow to you lately. It's the glow of a woman who knows she's loved."

Loved?

"I'm not sure if he loves me."

"Well, from what I hear, he's being awfully loyal for a man who's merely in like."

"I desperately want to protect him from the paparazzi machine. I'd do anything to keep him from facing all that brutality and invasion into his private life. He's just so ... good. He's a truly good man. He's my Marbella. My safe place."

"Yes. I see that," Phyllis says. "And your parents are your Hollywood. I've been hoping this for you—that you would find friendships, even a romance, where you don't feel like a pawn in someone else's game.

"I held them off as long as I could: my parents, the paparazzi, the public eye. But now I messed up and he's about to be in the thick of it if I don't do something to pull the attention away from him."

"And what do you have in mind?"

"I need to make the press believe he's not what he is to me—that he was just running lines from a script, a stand-in to help me get a feel for the production. He can't be seen as my boyfriend. The press will eat him alive—and not just this once. It won't end for him. They'll be persistent like a terminal disease, even in remission it looms on the horizon with the threat of a relapse. I can't put him through that."

Phyllis clucks her tongue. "I'm not going to tell you that you need to decide what you really want, but ... you need to decide what you really want. Not for him—for you. You've already sacrificed so much for your career. Do you really want to sacrifice him too?

"Stevens is a catch. And I'm wagering that he loves you. Your life is what it is. You can't protect him from your life and the blessings and curses that come with it. Either you are going to claim him and take this hit from the press. And, it will be a hit. No one wants to see a star dating a common man. You need to at least date a supermodel or a mogul or a billionaire—you know, no pressure." Phyllis laughs.

"You'll either claim Stevens publicly, or you're going to have to publicly disown him. And that may cost you your relationship. Take it from one who knows the cost of losing a relationship that mattered. I believe you're strong enough to take a stand for yourself and him, if that's what you truly want."

"Then again ..." Phyllis winks knowingly at me. "You can always cave one more time, and let the media and your fans, and most of all, your parents, drive your private life." She stares at me with her head tilted so she's looking through her lashes. "It's up to you."

"I've already made my decision. And it's the one I know I have to make for his highest good. This isn't about me. It's about him. I love him too much to drag him through the mud for the rest of his life."

Phyllis' lips thin. She spears me with a look that says she disagrees. For a moment, I almost second guess myself. And then I remember the reality: this will never be over for him once it starts. And I'm the only one with the power to stop the media before the neverending frenzy unleashes into Stevens' life.

Phyllis says, "I've found, over the years, that what benefits one person, benefits both, as long as the decision is made in love. I hope you choose well."

"Sometimes neither choice is a good one," I quip quietly, almost under my breath.

"Yes. But there's always the choice that leads forward—the one that might be harder, but has the greatest benefit despite the pain. That's the one you have to make."

THIRTY-EIGHT

Stevens

I'm not a smart man. But I know what love is.
~ Forrest Gump

As soon as my tour pulls into the slip, the men and women with cameras and microphones swarm the dock. I ask them to make way for my guests to get through, and they oblige. They aren't as willing to let me pass. I keep saying, "No comment. No comment." It's what I've seen in movies and in TV shows. It eventually works. I'm able to pass through the mass of reporters. But some are relentless and follow me, not even trying to hide their invasion of my privacy.

I walk over to the Alicante and find Ben's friend Cam. He works in customer service on the main resort property. I spot him at the guest services desk in the center of the expansive lobby.

"Can you help me?" I ask Cam.

I look over my shoulder. A few stragglers from the press have entered the resort behind me. Persistent, I'll give them that.

"Sure, Stevens. What can I do for you?"

"I've got a situation. Some members of the press are here

trying to get me to talk about my relationship with Alana. I need to ditch them."

"Okay. I've got you. Follow me."

Cam says something to his co-worker who is with him behind the desk and then he walks out and heads toward the bank of elevators. I follow him, trying to discreetly check over my shoulder to see if we're being trailed. The reporters are eyeing me. But none are being so bold as to follow us.

Cam pushes the elevator button for UP. Once we're inside he pushes five, six, seven.

"We'll throw them off that way. We'll get off at six."

"Huh. Good thinking."

We exit at the sixth floor and I follow Cam along hallways to the stairwell.

"Stay behind me."

"Have you done this before?" It seems like he has a method and plan.

"A few times for celebrities or dignitaries."

We take the stairs down six flights, Cam in front, keeping a pretty good pace.

"It always adds a little adventure to my day. Okay. Here we are. Lobby. This door will let you out in a service hallway. You can follow the hall down to an exit door that leads out to the side of the building. Walk out that side walkway, look around and make a break for it."

Cam peeks out the stairway door, gives me the all clear and we part ways. I ditch the reporters, and head to my home, where, thankfully no paparazzi are hanging out. Not yet, they aren't. I won't be surprised if they do end up coming here sometime in the near future. I smile. Not because I want reporters swarming my home, but because Alana's worth it. She's so worth it. I only hope she decides to give us a chance.

I change out of my tour clothes and hop onto my bicycle. On a bike, I can maneuver the back roads between my house and the North Shore more easily instead of taking the streets closer to the beach. I make my way to my childhood home, hoping my mother hasn't heard the news about me and Alana before I have the chance to tell her.

I walk in the open front door. "Mom? Are you home?"

My mom walks around the corner through the living room toward the entryway of our home.

"Ren! What a sweet surprise. Come in. I'm having an exciting day purging my Tupperware."

I follow my mom through the house to the kitchen where nearly every surface is covered in plastic storage containers of all sizes and shapes.

"Where were you hiding all this?"

"You'd be surprised. They stack. And apparently multiply like rabbits in those cupboards. I'm giving most of these away. Your dad and I don't need to keep all this. It's just the two of us now."

"Mom?"

She looks up from sorting piles of containers. "What is it, Ren? Are you okay?"

"I am. I ... uh ... I have a girlfriend."

She claps her hands together and squeals. "Well, isn't that the shizzle!"

I chuckle.

"Ren. A girlfriend. This is wonderful. Who is she? Where did you meet? How long have you been dating? Here. Here. Come sit."

She clears a space in front of a chair at the kitchen table. It's a round table where I ate breakfasts and many lunches growing up. Chairs are tucked in on one side of the table and a bench against the bay window sits on the other side. The view looks out over rooftops toward the beaches on the North Shore, including the beach where I played with Alana on so many Saturdays.

"Do you want iced tea? Lemonade? Arnold Palmer? Tell me everything."

Mom's giddy and she doesn't even know the biggest piece of my news.

"Tea's fine. I can get it. You keep cleaning."

"Oh, I couldn't clean right now. Not when you come bearing news like this. Can you bring her to family supper? Or is it too soon? I promise to behave."

"I want to bring her to supper. We met online."

"Ooooh. Really. Have you met in person? Where in the world is she? I'm very open minded, you know. Lots of people say you still shouldn't talk to strangers on the net. I agree if you're under eighteen. But you're thirty. I say cast that net far and wide. So, where is she?"

At this rate, I'll never get to say.

"She and I played a word game for about six months or so. Then we discovered we're both here on Marbella."

"Well, would you look at that? What are the odds? Of course you could probably figure those odds out to the decimal. But I know they're slim. She's here? On the island?"

"Yes. She lives here part time. She actually was someone I knew years ago." I pause and look at my mom, willing her to maintain her sanity. "Saturday girl."

"Oh! Gwendolyn. I loved that girl. It was so sad when she left. I think she was taking a crack at show business. She always had some sort of lesson going on—singing, dancing, acrobatics, what have you. That girl was like a trick pony."

"Do you remember the day you took me to paint in the cove?" Maybe if I ease her into this she won't have an actual heart attack.

"Of course, but let's talk about that later. I want to hear all about this girlfriend first. Is she Gwendolyn?"

"She is, actually."

"Well, my word. That's the bomb dot com. Who would imagine. All these years later."

"Mom, you'd better sit down."

"Why? Stevens? What is going on?"

"Just sit. Trust me. I think sitting is better for this next bit of news."

"Okaaayyy." She clears another spot on the table.

"Gwendolyn. Well, you see ... she did leave to take a crack at show business. And it went pretty well for her, I'd say."

"Well, that's just wonderful."

"It is. Mostly. Anyway, she had to change her name for reasons in the business. And her name ... well, she was sitting behind us in Harry's paint class."

"Oh, Stevens. After that weekend I thought about it, and I'm almost positive the woman behind us was ..."

Mom's eyes go wide as saucers. Her mouth pops open. Her face passes through a series of expressions as the reality of what I'm not saying settles deeper into her awareness.

"She's Alana Graves? You are dating *Alana Graves*? Are you sure? Alana Graves? Do you know what you're saying here? This is Alana Graves. She's Alana Graves. Was it my words at paint class? Did she seek you out after that? Oh! Stevens! Alana Graves! Wait. She's coming *here*? For dinner? I have to clean. And cook. And ... oh, my. Alana Graves is coming for dinner!"

I sit back, crossing my arms, waiting for this wave of shock to wash over like a squall at sea.

"Alana Graves," Mom mutters with a tone of awe in her voice.

I'm pretty sure she is trying to break the world record for saying Alana's name the most times in one minute.

"Alana Graves. Of all the things. My son is dating Alana Graves." Mom looks at me. "I'll act so normal. Don't worry. I'll be like the poster child for normal moms. I'll even hide her movies. Should I? Or would she like to see them out? What do you think?"

I smile at my mom. She's coming down slowly. A few more minutes and she'll be able to hold a conversation.

"Alana Graves. Stevens. What in the world? Here I thought you were going to be married to the sea like that old man in that famous poem. And you're dating Alana Graves. *The* Alana Graves."

She looks at me, smiling wide.

When she's quiet for about fifteen seconds straight, I finally take my shot at telling her everything else.

"She's not Alana Graves to me, Mom. She's just Alana. And I think I'm falling for her—not the movie star, the woman. She's bright and witty. She has a dry sense of humor and she's very protective of me. It's sweet."

"Protective? Why would she need to be protective?"

I fill my mom in on all the mess with the media. Then I backtrack and explain how I substituted as Alana's water taxi driver and how we set up our first date. I tell her Alana loves Mitzi's tacos. When I finish, we've been sitting at the table for nearly an hour.

"Well, she doesn't need to protect you, Stevens. You're strong enough to face anything. She'll see."

"I hope she will. It may come your way too, you know. Sometimes the media spreads their claws far and wide. They may come snooping through my life to discover all they can about me."

"You think you love her?" My mom skips over everything I just said about the press possibly prying into her life and hones in on the most intriguing fact to her—my feelings for this amazing woman.

"I think I might."

"Oh, son. I'm so happy for you. And for her. Do you think she loves you too?"

"I don't know. She definitely cares about me."

"Alana Graves."

One more time for the people in the back.

"Mom. You have to do me a favor."

"Anything."

"I need you to think of her as this woman named Alana who has a job acting. She's not Alana Graves to me. It's just better if we can all treat her like a normal person."

"Stevens. Have a little faith. And besides, she's not a normal person. You do realize that, don't you?"

"I do. But when she's with me, she is."

I spend a few hours at Mom's between the conversation and helping her load boxes with enough Tupperware to store leftovers for the whole neighborhood for weeks, maybe months.

As I'm leaving, Mom reminds me to ask Alana to dinner Sunday. I will do that. I want to.

I want everything with Alana.

The choice is up to her as to what she wants with me.

THIRTY-NINE

Stevens

Love isn't easy; that's why they call it love.
~ The Big Sick

I'm up early, but not early enough. As soon as I woke, I ran to Joel's boat to try to head Alana off at the pass. Joel's boat was already gone, which means, Alana's on her way to LA—without me.

Last night Alana and I were up, strolling on Locals' Cove beach with the stars in the sky and our hands intertwined late into the night. Alana had called to ask me to meet her there. She told me about her conversation with her mother. And then she broke the news to me.

She said, "This madness with the press won't end. We might make it through this particular round without too much fallout —and that's highly doubtful. You're already being hounded and chased at work. You don't know the media and the public like I do. This is a portal. And once it's opened, you can never go back. Your life will cease to be your own."

There weren't enough words or promises in the world to

convince her I wanted to walk that gauntlet with her. I literally said, "I don't care what I have to endure if it means us staying together and building on what we've started to find in one another."

She turned to me with a sadness in her eyes I had never seen before and hope I never have to see again. And then she kissed me. It was a kiss laced with regret and hopelessness. A kiss goodbye. We both knew it.

I questioned everything when I returned home, fighting the urge to call her, and then spiraling when I remembered who she is and what she does. Outside of my initial reaction to her, and the time I was blindsided at Ben and Summer's barbecue, she's been Alana, my SaturdayIslandGirl. Last night I was slammed with the fact that she's *Alana Graves*. I'm just a marine biologist on a small island off the coast of California. Who am I to fight for her?

I've been up since four, out of bed and dressed. I tossed and turned all night when I finally went to bed. Sometime within the last hour, my conversation with Kai hit me like a pep talk in a locker room. It doesn't matter what Alana does for a living. What matters is how we feel about one another. The more I thought about our childhood connection and our bantering on *Play on Words*, the more this relentless momentum built up in me. I couldn't get to the private docks fast enough. I need to stop her before she publicly denies our relationship and commits herself to a farce that will force us to stay separated forever.

I grabbed my wallet and left my house, hoping to beat Alana and Joel to the boat before she left for her impromptu interview with Rex in Los Angeles—the one where she's going to solidify the illusion that the two of them are a couple and I'm just some guy who ran lines with her for an upcoming movie.

I don't know if I have an actual plan. I had thought I would go with her. We would face this—anything and everything— together. It's obvious she's never had someone who bears the load with her—someone who wants to absorb some of the backlash of her fame for her. Alana doesn't believe I can withstand what she lives with daily. Stepping into the public eye may not be ideal, but losing her is not an option.

Last night, Alana explained to me that she was making this decision for me. She said, "Stevens, you may not see it now, but I'm choosing you. By letting you go, I'm choosing you." She shed a few tears. I could tell she was doing everything in her power to hold herself together. I nearly shed tears of my own.

I suggested a clandestine relationship, staying together, but keeping things under the radar the way we had been doing all along. She stiffened, shoring herself up against the option. Then she said it would only be a matter of time until a hidden relationship blew up in our faces. And the outcome would be worse the second time the media got a whiff of me. So much worse.

She said she's choosing me. And I believe she thinks she is. But she's not the only one with a choice in this situation. I might have a plan—it's forming as I stand here staring at the slip where Joel's boat should be parked.

She chose me.

I'm going to show her that I'll choose her every day from here forward if she'll let me.

I pull out my cell phone and dial the one person I believe has the power, influence, and access to help me get through to Alana.

"Hello, Brigitte here. What took you so long, Stevens?"

"Long? The sun is barely up."

"I figured you'd call me yesterday."

"Alana only dropped the news on me last night. I tried to beat her to the water taxi this morning. I missed her. I should have slept on the dock."

"That's the spirit! Don't worry. I've got you. What's the plan?"

"That's what I was hoping you could help me with. I need to get to Alana."

"Oh. I've got that covered. I figured you'd need to get to Alana. I've got a car scheduled to meet you at the docks in Ventura harbor. How soon can you be there?"

"A little over an hour? I have to get to my boat and I'll drive it to Ventura."

"Great. Do you have any thoughts as to what you'll do once you reach her?"

"A few."

"Well, get to your boat and fill me in on what you're thinking. I've already given your information to the guard at the studio gate. You're cleared to get in."

"Thanks, Brigitte. You're the best."

"You know it. I live for this kind of thing. Grand gestures are my jam. And, to top it off, Cruella de Vil will lose her ever living mind over this."

"Cruella de Vil?"

"Alana's mom."

I chuckle.

While I walk to my boat, I fill Brigitte in on the details of the plan that's forming in my mind. She approves most of it, but has a few modifications and additions. By the time I'm parking my boat in a slip in Ventura, we've hung up and she's set all the balls in motion. I walk down the dock toward the spot where Ken usually stands waiting to greet Alana.

As soon as I'm in the parking lot, Brigitte hops out of a Town Car.

"Heyyyy! It's time to show those paps where it's at!"

I climb in the back seat next to her. No security detail is in the car. Miguel isn't our driver.

"We're picking Rex up at his home," Brigitte says. "Wait til you see this place, Stevens. It's massive. Like, why does one guy need six bedrooms and three bathrooms? But you do you, boo. You know? Anyway, we're picking him up and then we're meeting Caroline at the studio."

Brigitte's so unaffected by the fame she's surrounded by daily. It makes sense why she works so well with Alana. To Brigitte, these are all just people.

Brigitte runs through the plan we formed together. "You'll be at the interview Alana and Caroline arranged on the Sharla Gibson show. After the interview, select media reps hand picked by Caroline will be allowed in for an exclusive." Brigette looks over at me. "Sorry about all of this. She was miserable this morning, if that helps."

"I don't want her to be miserable. I understand why she made the choice she did. She explained it all last night. She thinks she's protecting me."

"Alana's heart's in the right place, even if she's dead wrong." Brigitte smiles. "She's trying her utmost to keep you out of the insanity that is the public eye. She's sacrificing her potential happiness to shield you. But she's being dumb. I said just as much straight to her face two and a half hours ago when she arrived on the dock. We're not stars, but we're not wimps. What you're about to do is one hundred percent awesome."

I smile at Brigitte.

"Caroline got a hold of Rex," Brigitte explains. "He knows what you and I are up to. Alana doesn't know a thing. As far as she's concerned, you're still in Marbella today, tucked safely away from the media, her parents, and her fans. But, no! We're turning what they were treating like trash into a five course meal at a three star Michelin restaurant on opening night. Invite only, baby. You want a piece of this? See the chef!"

I chuckle. Brigitte's optimism is contagious.

We drive from Ventura to Beverly Hills. Rex's home is up some winding streets and behind a sliding iron gate. The driver punches in a code and we pull up until we're at the circle driveway right in front of the mansion. Rex comes walking down the front stairs looking like he's playing a billionaire in a movie.

The driver steps out of the car, opens the front passenger door for Rex and Rex slides into the seat.

"Morning, lovely people." He extends his hand back through the center console toward me. "Good to see you again, Stevens."

"Thank you for doing this," I tell him, trying to ignore the memory of our first meeting when I was dressed as a parrotfish.

"Anything for Alana," Rex says. "She's been my co-star in three films. And she covered for me and my girlfriend last year. I sort of owe her one, don't you think?"

We drive to the studio and are met there by Caroline. Alana is expecting Rex. She is definitely not expecting me. Caroline leads us into the backstage area of the studio. A monitor near the entrance to the actual soundstage shows Alana sitting alone on a couch facing an empty loveseat. Rex walks past me, patting me on the back as he strides out onto the stage toward the couch where Alana is sitting.

I'm hidden from her sight for now.

Next, Sharla Gibson, the host of the talk show, appears from the opposite entryway. She walks on stage and takes her seat across from Alana and Rex.

I think I'm numb. I'm standing offstage, two world-famous stars and one of America's favorite talk show hosts less than forty feet away from me. I'm just a simple marine biologist who fell in love playing *Play on Words*. Yet, here I am. This is now my life. And I'm going to fight for it—fight for her, the woman I love.

Brigitte steps up next to me. "You know when to walk out, right?"

"Yes. When Sharla says, 'special surprise guest.'"

"Exactamundo. You've got this."

"Thanks."

On the set, Sharla says something to Alana and Rex. I can't tell what because her mic isn't on yet.

Brigitte squeezes my shoulder.

The cameraman gives a countdown and the show goes live.

"Well, America!" Sharla says in a very cheerful talk-show-host voice. "I have such a surprise for you today. Although, looking at the couch across from me, I'm guessing my surprise is mostly out of the bag. Today, it is my distinct pleasure to be hosting two of America's hottest stars. With me are Alana Graves and Rex Fordham, the co-stars of the upcoming soon-to-be box-office smash, *Blasted*. And we're all counting the days til that releases. But Rex and Alana are not here to talk about the movie today.

"No. Today we're going to take an exclusive peek behind the very private and usually well-guarded doors of Alana's love life." Sharla turns from the camera, toward the couch across from her. "Alana, Rex, welcome."

Alana is the embodiment of poise and confidence. "Thank you, Sharla. It's a pleasure to be here."

Rex smiles broadly at Sharla. "I wouldn't miss this interview for anything."

Alana gives Rex a barely perceptible questioning glance over her shoulder.

"Well, before we get into things, I have another surprise for everyone," Sharla says with a wide smile. "A very special surprise guest!"

I glance quickly toward Brigitte. She gives me a thumbs up and I walk onto the soundstage.

Alana's face morphs from confusion to concern. Our eyes lock and her mouth pops open for a beat, then she regains her stage presence and schools her features into a mask of neutrality, but her eyes never leave mine.

"Come join us, Stevens!" Sharla nearly shouts.

Rex scoots over so the spot on the couch between him and Alana is open to me.

Sharla turns toward the cameras and talks to the television audience who are watching live. "Alana had no idea Stevens was coming here today, so let's give her a moment to get over the shock. Meanwhile, I'm going to introduce you to the man who many of you may have heard discussing sea cucumbers with Alana just yesterday. America, get ready to fall for a marine biologist! This is Stevens."

"My fifteen minutes of fame," I joke. "And I spent it discussing the finer points of the sea cucumber."

Rex chuckles to my right. Alana is still quiet, looking at me with an expression that isn't quite as extreme as when I first walked out. I smile a reassuring smile at her.

"So, Stevens, do you mind if I give a little backstory here?" Sharla asks.

"Be my guest."

I lift my arm and drape it behind Alana. She reflexively leans into me.

But then she turns and mumbles under her breath, "What are you doing here?"

I lean into her so that my mouth is near her ear and my lips can't be read by anyone watching the show. "I'm making what Brigitte calls a grand gesture."

Alana shakes her head in disbelief. A soft smile spreads across her face.

I lean in toward her again and tell her, "I want this life—or any life—with you. And I don't want a future without you, so I'm here to step into the whirlwind. We'll face the public criticism, the paparazzi, and your parents, together from now on."

Alana puts her hand on my knee and smiles up at me.

"Oh! I love you two already," Sharla says. Then she turns toward the cameras. "I got a call asking me if I would host Rex and Alana. And you know I snatched that opportunity up like a housewife grabbing the last remaining toaster at a Black Friday sale. But then, this morning, I got another call from Alana's publicist. And she told me Stevens wanted to be here to set the record straight with America. I know you've all been dying to hear the story behind the viral social media post. So, of course, I invited Stevens here."

Sharla turns to Rex, "So, I take it you and Alana are definitely not dating."

Rex smiles and chuckles softly. "No. We are not. Alana's a good friend. She's an amazing and talented actress, someone I deeply respect. Working together fosters the kinds of relationships that can lead to romance. For us, though, we've realized we make better friends than anything else. We were not dating when she and Stevens got involved with one another." Rex turns toward the cameras. "And, to the guy who wrote the piece for the Hollywood Star Journal, she's also not carrying anyone's alien baby."

Sharla laughs. "Tabloids, am I right?"

Then she asks Rex, "So, you give Alana and Stevens your official stamp of approval?"

"Not that they need it, but I definitely approve of how he makes her smile. They're obviously good for one another."

Sharla turns to me and Alana. "Well, that clears up a whole lot of speculation."

Alana relaxes into me.

Sharla asks me, "Stevens, tell us how you came to know Alana."

"We met through mutual friends. Though it feels like I've known her forever."

"Awww." Sharla smiles at me and then Alana.

"Any details you want to add to that, Alana?"

Alana looks up at me. I smile down at her. We're here, together. And nothing has imploded or exploded yet. Maybe it will. And when it does, I'm going to scoop her up and block her from as much shrapnel as I can. And then we'll dust off and move on.

I have no idea what Alana will tell Sharla. Will she admit we met building sandcastles on a private beach when we were kids? Or will she share that we were friendly competitors on *Play on Words*? I doubt she'll disclose that I happened to fill in as her water taxi driver. Maybe she'll go with the least invasive disclosure, that we bumped into one another at a friend's barbecue.

Alana surprises me by turning toward the camera and saying, "Actually, Stevens and I just discovered that we've known one another since childhood. But, as he said, we recently connected through mutual friends, among other things."

Sharla lets out a little squeal. "So, you're telling me you two just reconnected after knowing each other as children?"

"That's right," I say.

"That's so romantic." Sharla says, beaming at us and then the cameras.

When Sharla turns back to us, she asks, "What's the thing about Alana that drew you to her—besides the obvious fact that she's Alana Graves? I mean, how does a marine biologist end up dating a movie star?"

I laugh. "I really don't know the answer to how this happened. Some things in life are just mysteries." I wink at Alana and she smiles up at me. "But I wasn't really attracted to her because of her stardom. If anything, that mostly intimidated me whenever I thought too deeply about it. I'm drawn to her despite her life as an actress. She's got a kind heart, a bright mind, and those captivating eyes." I look over at Alana and smile. "And her laugh." I tell Alana, "I love her laugh."

She's beaming at me now, obviously adjusting to my insistence that I'm not backing away at the first sign of trouble.

"And Alana, I'm taking it by the way you're leaning into Stevens that you have feelings for him too?"

"I do. He's an amazing man. He's smart, thoughtful, funny, and he's got this quiet confidence that always makes me feel safe. He's really good at flirting too."

I glance from Alana to Sharla. "I'm really not. She's seen my awkward side on more than one occasion." I look back at Alana. "I think you just bring that out in me."

Alana smiles at me and then she tells Sharla, "Stevens is actually ..." Alana turns her head so she's looking straight into my eyes. "... my boyfriend."

"Your boyfriend!" Sharla exclaims, putting both hands to her cheeks. Then she turns toward the camera. "You heard it first here, America. Alana Graves has a boyfriend. Stevens Reed, a marine biologist. And for those of you who need glasses, I'll confirm, he's gorgeous, and you can already tell he's got personality to spare."

I feel the blush rise up my neck.

Sharla looks at me with a smile. "What America really wants

to know is if you were a fan of Alana's movies before you started seeing her romantically."

"I do enjoy her work—especially the trilogy with Rex. My mom is a huge fan."

"And have you met his mom yet?" Sharla asks Alana.

"Not yet."

"Okay, well, we have some viewer questions coming in. Are you three open to answering some spontaneous questions from your fans?"

"Sure," Alana says, placing her hand on my knee.

I cover her hand with mine.

"I just have to say," Sharla says, "You two are too cute together. I think America is going to love you, Stevens. This is sort of a reverse Cinderella story, isn't it?"

Alana answers before I can. "Not exactly. Stevens wasn't sweeping chimneys for his evil stepmother. If anything, he's my Prince Charming."

"Awww. A real life Prince Charming. I love that." Sharla turns to the teleprompter and reads the viewer's question. "Julie in Kettering, Ohio wants to know if you're single, Rex."

"I am single." Rex smiles at Sharla and then the camera.

Sharla makes a show of fanning herself and then she says, "You heard that ladies! Rex is officially single."

Sharla looks back at the teleprompter. "Okay. Dana from Rochester, New York wants to know if you have any brothers as handsome as you, Stevens."

"I do have a brother, and a sister."

"And ... ?" Sharla raises her eyebrows.

"I guess my brother and I look a bit alike."

"Good to know!"

"Susan from Scottsdale, Arizona wants to know if you have plans for the future, Alana and Stevens."

Alana looks at me, and then she says, "Just spending as much time together as we can. We both have unconventional work schedules, so we're going to have to figure out how to make room for one another between all the shoots and his trips up and down the coast. But we'll make it work."

We'll make it work. That's all I needed to hear from her. I squeeze her hand gently and she smiles over at me.

Sharla continues taking questions from the teleprompter and then we wrap up the show. I'm ready for a long nap, and more importantly, time alone with Alana, but a group of reporters enters the room and once we've had a chance to drink some water and take a short break, we return to the couch so the press can ask us a barrage of questions.

When it's all over, Alana and I have our first moment where we're almost alone. Rex is on his phone to our left, but he's barely aware of us or anything right now. Alana and I are holding hands and I'm about to say something to her when Caroline approaches us.

"You did great! I think that should do it. We've set the tone, rewritten the narrative. The story is out there now from the mouths of the three people involved. I think America is going to eat this up. Rex, I think your car is here. You're free to go."

Rex hugs Alana and shakes my hand. We thank him for showing up, and then he's out the door.

Caroline looks at me after Rex leaves. "Be prepared. There will be haters. But, I'm guessing you'll have ten to one in your favor. America is going to love you. Just be careful on your social media, Stevens."

"He doesn't have social media and he's not a follower of gossip sites," Alana says.

"You're kidding me. Wow. What a Renaissance man."

The way she says it, I can't tell if it's a compliment or not.

"Well, as I was saying, there will be haters. But we can't help that. Overall, I think we accomplished what we set out to do. Now we'll just take some photos."

Alana and I pose for the photographers who stayed around just to get pictures of us. I guess those will be published somewhere.

When the reporters and photographers have cleared out, I'm standing with Alana in a spot offstage, waiting for Ken to come escort us to our car.

"I can't believe you came." Alana says, looking up at me.

"I meant it when I said I'll always come for you."

She stands on tiptoe and kisses me and I pull her in and hold her to me.

FORTY

Alana

*I came here tonight because when you realize
you want to spend the rest of
your life with somebody,
you want the rest of your life
to start as soon as possible.*
~ When Harry Met Sally

W e're walking up to Stevens' childhood home. The news
of our relationship spread like wildfire across America
and international magazines, websites and television syndicates
have picked up the story. My parents have gone radio silent for the
time being. I'm not making the first move for once. They can
come to their senses in their own time. I've got more important
things to focus on tonight, like meeting Stevens' family.

Stevens' brother, Dustin, throws open the door when we
walk up.

"Alana!" He shouts my name as if we're old friends.

Stevens wasn't kidding. They do look alike, but Dustin must

eat tree trunks for breakfast and bench used cars for exercise. He's not as massive as Tank. But then again, who is?

"Come in, come in. We've got your favorite."

"My favorite?"

"Mitzi's tacos!" Dustin's all smiles.

I turn to Stevens. "You told them about my secret obsession with your sister's tacos."

He just smiles down at me.

"You know, Alana, I've been told I'm the far cuter brother ..." Dustin winks at me and then glances at Stevens, obviously waiting for his reaction.

Stevens reaches over, and in a totally unexpected move, pulls Dustin into a headlock and gives him a noogie on the head.

"Okay! Okay! Kidding!" Dustin says through his laughter.

I'm already in love with this family.

"What's all the ruckus?" A woman in her later fifties or early sixties walks through the living room. Oh! Yes. She's the woman from paint class. I forgot. I have met Stevens' mom recently. I barely remember her from the times I saw her as a child. She looks a lot different now.

"Oh! Alana! You're here. And you're Alana. Graves. The Alana Graves. And you're here. Oh. My ..."

"Mom ..." Stevens warns.

"Right. Right. Normal. I promise I'm normal, Alana. After all, we met at paint day. And I wasn't weird then. Was I? Oh, I hope I wasn't. Someone please help me stop talking."

A tall man who looks like Stevens and Dustin but with distinguished salt and pepper hair walks up behind Stevens' mom and wraps an arm around her waist.

"Give her a minute, will you, Alana? She'll be much better once she gets over the initial rush. Boys. Go help your sister with the food."

To my surprise, both Stevens and Dustin say, "Yes, sir," and walk through the living room.

"I'd love to help too," I offer.

Stevens' mom blanches. "Oh, no. No, dear. We can't have you helping. You're Alana ..."

She's obviously about to reiterate the fact of who I am to the world. I don't mind. I'm used to this sort of initial reaction. But Stevens' dad interrupts gently. "Alana, we'd be glad to have you help. Go straight through to the kitchen and they'll put you to work. I'll just be giving my wife an oxygen treatment and we'll meet you momentarily unless we have to resort to smelling salts. That might take a few minutes longer."

"Dennis! Really?" Stevens' mom says to her husband.

I hear Mr. Reed's next words as I make my way through the house toward the kitchen.

"I'm just taking precautions, dear. You are practically hyperventilating. Remember what Stevens said. She's just Alana here. Let's let her be the first girl he brought home since prom, okay?"

The three Reed siblings are taking food out of bags and scooping it onto platters and into bowls when I enter the kitchen. It's like a sitcom come to life. Stevens catches my eye and smiles over at me.

"Mitzi, this is my girlfriend, Alana. Alana, this is my sister, Mitzi, the owner of your favorite taco place."

"I love your tacos," I tell her.

She walks over and gives me a hug. It's not awkward or fangirlish at all. Just welcoming. "It's so good to meet you. I love your movies."

"Thanks. Stevens told me your mom is a fan."

Dustin laughs. "A fan? She's rabid. Like shrine-level ..."

Stevens nudges his brother with an elbow and makes an exaggerated slicing motion across his throat.

"Did I say shrine? I meant to say, fine. Fine appreciation. She has a fine appreciation for your work." Dustin laughs and then we all laugh.

Stevens' parents walk into the kitchen.

"What's left to do?" Mr. Reed asks.

"Nothing, Dad. We've got it," Mitzi says. "Mom, are you over whatever that was out there?"

"One hundred percent. I'm golden. I'm not freaking out anymore. I'm not. I'm cool. Chillin' like a villain."

"And, that's our mom," Dustin says with an affectionate wink at his mother.

Mrs. Reed looks at me. "Sorry about that, Alana. I told myself all day you coming here was going to be no big deal. I even practiced in the mirror—the yeah-this-is-no-big-deal face. It was working for me then. But when I saw you? Well, it was a bit much."

"Ya think?" Mitzi says, and then she blows an air kiss at her mom.

"I understand," I say. "I was the exact same way when I met Katharine Hepburn."

"Oh my lands! You met Katharine Hepburn?"

"I did. She was nearly ninety when I met her. It was one of the greatest honors of my life. I may have stuttered and then completely lost my train of thought. She was full of grace for me, though. She even said she was a fan. I think she was just being polite."

"I think I would have fainted," Stevens' mom says. "No offense. It's not like I didn't almost faint for you. You are definitely worth fainting for."

"Mahhhm," Mitzi says with a smile. "Not an improvement."

I chuckle. "No offense taken. And I fully agree. Katharine was one of the greats."

We move into the dining room and set the platters of tacos on the table along with a bowl of chips, salsa and guacamole, and Spanish rice.

Once we're all seated, Stevens' dad says, "Well, Alana, we are glad you could join us for dinner. We try to do this once a week, but it gets more challenging as the kids age. Sometimes Stevens is away on a job, or Mitzi is needed at the restaurant, or Dustin is out fighting a fire or singing a gig. So, anytime we get to have all our kids around the table, Judith and I consider ourselves fortunate. And to have you here with Stevens makes this night extra special."

"Dad, the tacos are getting cold. Could we wrap up the Academy Awards acceptance speech?" Mitzi says.

"Right. Right. Well, let's dig in."

Platters are passed and the conversation picks up about Dustin's plans to move to Tennessee, some employee situations at Mitzi's restaurant, and then our appearance on Sharla's show this week.

We laugh a lot. People listen to one another. Dustin cracks the occasional good-natured joke. Mitzi flashes a smile when she glances over at me. It's hard to put words to the feeling I have as Stevens' hand finds mine under the table and he gives it a gentle squeeze. This is what a family feels like. It's warm and messy, silly and forthright, and there's this sense of shared history that makes for an unshakable bedrock. It's the solid center I've always sensed inside Stevens. This table—this house—these people are what formed that firm foundation. And he carries it with him wherever he goes.

After the meal, I insist on helping clear the table.

Dustin asks Stevens, "Hey, can I grab you for a minute?" Then he leans in and kisses his mom's cheek. "Ma, you and Mitzi just set all the dishes on the counters. Stevens and I will wash everything after I pull him for a quick chat."

"Sweet boy," Mrs. Reed coos.

"Kiss up," Mitzi shouts playfully after her brother as he leads Stevens outside onto the back porch.

Mitzi and I are gathering plates in the dining room. The windows are open. We can hear the conversation between Dustin and Stevens.

"I can hear every word they're saying," Mitzi whispers to me.

"I know."

"Shhh. Let's listen. If it becomes obvious we're not supposed to hear them, we can move into the kitchen." She

349

smiles a conspiratorial smile that makes me want to go along with her.

Mrs. Reed walks into the dining room. "Hey, Mitzi, can you ..."

"Shhhh, Mom. We're trying to eavesdrop here."

I start to back away, but Mrs. Reed joins us and tugs me closer to the window while giving me a delightfully mischievous smile. "We won't keep listening if it gets too personal, but I carried both those boys in this body and I put up with all manner of craziness when they were growing up. I earned the right." She points at Mitzi. "And this one. She's the only girl. She earned it too."

"Shhh, Mom. We're missing the good stuff." Mitzi puts a finger up to her lips.

All three of us go quiet just in time to hear Dustin say, "Man, you and Alana Graves."

"It's crazy on paper," Stevens says. "But, in reality, she's perfect for me."

"Pretty sure she's perfect for half the male population." Dustin chuckles.

Stevens doesn't say anything, but then Dustin says, "Sorry, sorry. You know I'm joking. I see it. It's good between the two of you. I'm so happy for you. And I saw that interview. I just wanted to tell you to hang in there."

"Oh, I'm hanging in. As long as Alana lets me."

Stevens' mom smiles over at me. Her pride in her son is written across her face.

"She has this idea that I'm fragile," Stevens says. "She kept trying to protect me from what she lives with daily. Why should she take these hits alone?"

Mitzi nudges me. "Exactly. You're not alone. Don't face that craziness alone. You've got us now."

I nearly tear up.

"That's awesome, bro," Dustin says. "You're right, too. Dad didn't raise any slouches. We're not about to let a woman face challenges without us by their side."

Mrs. Reed whispers, "Dad raised them? What about me?"

"He means both of you, Mom. Now shush so we can hear."

Stevens is laughing. "Says the guy who is still woefully single."

"You never know. Maybe I'll meet someone in Tennessee. I'm not opposed to the idea. I'm just waiting for the right one."

"If you find her in Tennessee, you'll break Mom's heart for good."

Mrs. Reed whispers, "He will. It's true."

Dustin says, "She'll live."

"No I won't," Mrs. Reed says in that same raspy, hushed voice, but she's smiling.

Dustin says, "After all, you secured favorite son status for the rest of our days. You're already one point ahead for sticking around Marbella. Now you're dating her favorite actress?"

"That did get him some points," Mrs. Reed says quietly, nodding her head.

I smile. I'm feeling guilty for spying even though this seems to be par for the course, but I also feel ... included. I try to imagine my mom, hunkered down with me trying to overhear a harmless conversation. It would never happen.

But maybe I shouldn't say never. People can change given the right amount of motivation. Maybe one day she'll come around. I hope she does. She may own a production company and her name may be known around the world, but she's missing out on this. And connections like the Reed family have are worth more than all of that put together.

Stevens and Dustin come through the door from the screen porch into the house.

Stevens is saying, "You'll always be her baby boy."

Dustin says, "Got that right."

The three of us are suddenly scrambling to look busy, but we're all laughing too hard to pull it off.

"Oh, so that's how it is?" Stevens says, crossing his arms and looking at the three of us with a huge, comfortable smile on his face.

"I should have known," Dustin says. "You two are shameless." He points to his mother and sister. "And corrupting Alana on her first night in the family. Pitiful, I tell you."

Stevens walks over to me and places his arm around my back. He pulls me in toward himself and kisses my temple.

"Can I take a raincheck on dishes? I'll do double next week." He doesn't take his eyes off mine.

"Oh, sure. Get a girlfriend and shirk responsibilities," Dustin teases.

"Yes. Of course," Stevens' mom says. "You two have had quite an ordeal this past week. Get your girl home safely."

Dustin mutters, "Favorite son status."

Stevens answers him. "Mom's baby boy."

Mrs. Reed ignores her sons and walks over to me. Stevens drops his arm so his mom can pull me into a hug.

"Alana, it was delightful to have you here. I'm so glad you and Stevens found one another. You're welcome here anytime."

"Thank you so much for having me."

"You know where to find me," Mitzi says.

"I sure do. And I'll have you up to the house one day soon. We can just hang out, the two of us."

"I'd love that."

FORTY-ONE

Stevens

I vow to fiercely love you in all your forms,
now and forever.
~ The Vow

W e're heading toward the door when my mom shouts out, "Next time, I'll have Stevens' baby books out for you, Alana."

"Okay!" I shout back. "We're going now."

Alana stops mid-stride. "I'd love to see Stevens' baby pics next time. And you know what I'd love even more?"

My mom steps out onto the porch. "What's that, dear?"

"I'd love to know his first name. We called him Ren as a boy. What is that short for?"

Dustin steps out next to our mom and says, "Ooh! Ooh! I know!"

I put my hand on the small of Alana's back. "Okay see you later. Love you, family. Bye."

Dustin calls out, "Clarence! Like the angel in *It's A Wonderful Life*!"

I playfully cup my hands over Alana's ears so she won't hear him, but she already heard.

"Clarence?" Alana's laughing.

I look back at the porch. My mom has her hand over Dustin's mouth and he's acting like he can't wriggle free.

"You think that's funny, huh?" I ask Alana as I open the gate and lead her onto the sidewalk.

"It's hilarious! I love your family."

"They're a handful. You've got the paparazzi. I've got these crazies."

"I like your crazies." She smiles up at me.

"I'll keep them." I smile down at her. "I'm pretty sure they're in love with you already. And not Alana Graves. Just you."

"So soon?"

"Yeah. They're like that. My mom basically adopted Ben when she found out his family lives all the way in the Midwest."

"Wow. My mom might not even claim me after this fiasco." A note of wistfulness creeps into Alana's tone.

"I'm guessing she'll get over it in time," I assure her. "Once she sees I'm not going anywhere."

She doesn't answer that. I hope I'm right. Family needs to stick together. I understand her family functions differently than mine, but they're still family.

"You can borrow my family while you're waiting for your parents to come around."

"I think I'd like that." Alana laughs. "So, Ben is basically your adopted brother."

"Tell me about it. I already had Dustin. Now I have Ben too. You'd think Mom could have adopted someone more chill like Kai."

"So ... Clarence." She smiles up at me.

"Yeah. Ren comes from Clarence. It's a family name. Lucky me. I couldn't have been born into a family where the hand-me-down name was something like Alex or Conan."

"Conan? Like the barbarian?" Alana giggles.

"You don't think it fits?"

"Conan the merman. It has a certain ring."

We laugh and I reach for her hand. She slips her fingers between mine. Our palms nestle together. And then we walk in the silence that settles between us until we're at her front porch.

"Thank you," I say, tugging her in toward me.

Alana looks up at me and brushes her fingers through my hair. "For what? For dragging you into a life where you're under the magnifying glass? Where you have to sneak through a resort to escape the paparazzi, and you can't run your tour business without being swarmed by reporters?"

"No." I smooth a hand down her arm. "I chose this life. You didn't even have the luxury of choosing it because you were raised to walk right into your role. But I am choosing it—choosing you. I mean, thank you for allowing me in. For giving me a chance to actually know you. For letting me love you."

Alana stands on tiptoes and brushes a kiss across my jaw.

"Love me?"

"Yes. I love you. I'm hoping that's obvious, but in case you were wondering, now you have no doubt. I'm seriously in love with you. You were not what I expected, and it's beyond what I can wrap my head around how we found one another. All that only adds to the fact that I'm yours. My heart belongs to you. "

"I'm so grateful for you," she whispers. "There really aren't words."

"There are words. We'll always find words. After all, words are how I found you."

She smiles softly at me. She doesn't have to say she loves me. I know it. Declaring it is extra. She showed me her love by being willing to give us up just to ensure I didn't have to endure public scrutiny and intrusion into my private life.

"Stevens?"

"Yes?"

She brushes her hand along my cheek and runs her fingers through my hair.

"I love you too." She stares up at me. "I've never said those words to another man. I guess I've been saving them for you."

Here we are, two of the most unlikely people to find one another, and yet life kept weaving our stories together. We both seem caught up in this moment full of something just shy of magic. I don't know who kisses who first, but our lips brush so tentatively—a soft touch of skin to skin, feather light, testing the waters.

Alana lifts her hands and grips onto me. Then she gently leans away from me, but she doesn't release her hold on my shoulders. Her eyes sparkle in the moonlight. I run the back of my hand down the side of her cheek and under her jaw. I hold her chin and study her beautiful face. Neither of us says a word. We stare into one another's eyes, a feeling of awe permeating the space between us.

I've watched Alana kiss on the big screen. She's played the part of a woman in love and I've studied her image, twenty times larger than life as she gave herself to whomever her leading man was at the time. Her kisses on film always appear real, passionate, engaged, believable.

I lean in and capture her mouth again. I linger there, our lips soft and gentle. This kiss between us isn't anything like the ones I've watched her give her co-star in a movie.

She's tentative, careful—not hesitant, but somehow unexpectedly fragile.

This kiss is real. She's choosing me, taking a walk out over the Grand Canyon on the glass cantilever bridge. She's on a free dive, leaving all gear on the sand and going deep into the salty water with nothing but her own lungs to sustain her. *This.* This is trust. She's trusting me.

Alana's hands gently squeeze my shoulders, as if she's afraid I'll stop or leave, or maybe she just needs something to hold on to while waves of emotion ripple and swell between us. My hands hold her to me in answering assurance. I'm here. This is worth the risk. We are worth the risk.

I feel the moment she releases whatever held her back. The war inside her ends and she surrenders to the pull between us. She smiles against my mouth and I kiss her through the smile. Our connection deepens and I lose track of myself, time, and thought. Everything is her, and she is everything. I only know how she feels in my arms, the tug of my hair in her soft fist, the delicious scrape of her nails down the back of my neck.

She tilts her chin up and I take the unspoken invitation, running my mouth along the column of her neck, peppering kisses along her jaw, lingering on the soft curve at her hairline, and lightly nipping her earlobe before kissing my way back to her mouth.

I am moving at the speed of a barracuda now, and I need to reel myself in before I take things too far. I place one last kiss on her lips, and then I tug her toward me, burying my face in her hair. She smells of the expensive perfume she always wears, and that now-familiar scent that's all her.

Home. She's becoming my home.

I thought I might lose her when everything blew up with her mother and the press. But now I know. Alana's everything to me. Each of us might not be able to fend off the paparazzi or the public on our own, but together we're strong enough to endure whatever comes at us.

We hold one another. I smooth my hand down her back.

I'm overwhelmed with hope and thoughts of a future with Alana—a future we'll build together.

"I love you, Graves," I say the words into her hair, following them with a kiss to the top of her head.

"I love you, too, my merman."

~ *THE END* ~

Epilogue

L O V E

*I'd be crazy not to turn my life
upside down and marry her.*
~ *You've Got Mail*

"I have everything, Mother. I'll see you and Dad at the premier."

I pace my apartment, while Brigitte watches me like she's at Wimbledon. Her head swivels to the left. I turn. Her head pivots toward the right. I walk the length of the couch and spin to walk the other way. Brigitte's gaze follows me, back and forth, back and forth.

Brigitte stands and snatches the phone away from me. "Angelique, hi! It's me, Brigitte."

I'm stunned, but also amused.

I don't hear my mother's answer, but then Brigitte says, "Right. Right. Yes. Of course. I've got her and all the things she needs." She pauses. Rolls her eyes. "Angelique, have I ever let you down?" Brigitte smiles at me and waves her hand, shooing me toward my kitchen where I set my glass of water.

"That's right," Brigitte says. "And I will never let Alana down. Now go get pampered so you can look your best tonight. We've got everything covered on our end."

I take one more sip of water and then I walk back over to Brigitte, stick my hand out and stand with my other hand on my hip so she knows I mean business. I appreciate her trying to smooth the waters with my mother and shield me from any additional stress with my premier for *Only the Remnant* only hours away. Still, if I've learned anything over the past year, it's that I need to stand up to my mother, especially when it comes to my personal life.

A month after the talk show appearance with Sharla Gibson where Stevens showed up unexpectedly to take his place in the public eye as my boyfriend, my mother finally caved and called me. Stevens and I continued to date, while the media eventually tired of following us and commenting on our every move.

Of course, Mother and I saw one another at the premier for *Blasted*. I brought Stevens and he walked the red carpet by my side. Bringing him made a statement—to my mother, the press, my fans, and most of all, to Stevens. My mother was civil, but we still hadn't spoken outside of our public appearances together.

She went radio silent for a week after the premier while the press publicized photos of me and Stevens on every tabloid, celebrity news outlet, and gossip site. Some stories were extremely positive and some were smears. I tried to avoid most of them and let Brigitte act as my filter.

When my mother finally called, she brought up an event she wanted me to attend. She dove right into her agenda as if nothing had been amiss, not Sharla's show, not Stevens attending the premier, and certainly not the fact that I was falling deeply in love with a marine biologist who had no desire to share the spotlight except if he could soften the blow for me and stand by my side to celebrate my work.

"Mother?"

"Oh. Alana. You're back. Brigitte didn't even say goodbye."

"Right. Sorry. She's handling something for me. I just wanted to see if there was anything else you needed before we hung up."

"Nothing big. I just wanted to tell you Rex will be at your

premier as your father's and my guest. He's coming alone—to support you."

"Mother."

"Alana, dear. I know you've had your fun with this fisherman. It's definitely run its course. You've made your point."

I pinch the bridge of my nose, look over at Brigitte and let out a long sigh. "I must not have made the actual point I intended to make."

"What point is that, darling?"

"I'm choosing him, Mother. I choose Stevens. He's an amazing man—a marine biologist, actually, not a fisherman or whatever else you've called him. Not that there would be anything wrong with him being a fisherman. He has multiple degrees. He's brilliant. But beyond all that, he's kind and thoughtful, and he'd do anything for me. And I love him.

"Do you remember when you said love was nothing to build a life on?"

She's silent, so I keep talking. "I feel all those things you described—for Stevens. And my feelings for him aren't going to diminish or go away. They've actually grown over the past year. I can't imagine a day my face won't break into a smile at the sight of him. For the first time in my life I found someone I can fully trust and be my whole self with.

"He would die before he'd let anything horrible happen to me. And if something sneaks by him and tries to level me, he'll be there, walking through the shrapnel with me. He stood by me before he even knew I would be his. And this whole year that you've kept your distance outside our shared public appearances, he's been with me, right next to me, or cheering me on from his place in the shadows.

"I will never throw the man I love under the bus. I'm not going to a premier with Rex, even if he's my co-star again in the future. I'll do the requisite photo shoots and appearances, but I'll make it clear Stevens is my boyfriend through it all. And if it comes down to sparing Stevens any pain or embarrassment, I'll sacrifice a movie or any other fame or position in this world to support and protect him. Because that's what love does."

I take a breath, and come to my senses. I was on a roll. Brigitte is standing at my kitchen bar, beaming.

My mother is still silent, so I finish out what I have to say. It's what I've wanted to say all this time, only she never gave me the opening. Today's not the ideal time to have this conversation when we're hours away from my big night, but I'm taking the chance while I have it.

"I really wish you would get to know him—this man that I love. But it's definitely your loss if you don't. Stevens is not a passing fancy or a diversion. He's my boyfriend. And he's the only man I hope I spend the rest of my life with."

I'm done. There's nothing more to say.

My mother is silent for a longer stretch than usual. I give her the respect of waiting for her to process my declaration.

She finally says, "Very well."

I wait for more.

She doesn't say anything else.

"He'll be there with me tonight, walking down the red carpet, answering reporters' questions if they ask him anything, sitting next to me, and leaving with me for the afterparty. If you are so inclined to be respectful toward him, I'd love to officially introduce you and Dad to him."

It goes without saying my mother won't be welcome to meet Stevens if she can't show him common decency.

"Knock, knock," Stevens steps into my condo.

He has a key, and promised to be here as soon as he was able to wrap up a tour this morning, catch the ferry, and meet my driver at the docks.

My heart rate levels out at the sight of him. But then it picks back up because this man in a tux might just be my undoing. And then he smiles that smile that always gets to me—the one where his mouth tips up on one side and those two dimples pop just right.

"I've got to go, Mother. I'll see you at the premiere."

"Alana?"

"Yes?"

"I'll ... Let's find a time for you to introduce your friend to me and your father tonight."

"My boyfriend."

"Yes. Yes. That."

I chuckle. Would it kill her to say the word? Maybe. At least she's stepping forward to make an effort. I'll gladly meet her halfway. Last year, I wouldn't have. But now, I know. Stevens and I are strong. What we have can weather attacks from the press, the reaction of my fans, and even the blatant meddling and rejection of my own mother.

If she wants to make an attempt at neutrality and acceptance, I will pave the way and make it easy on her. What she and Stevens will have won't ever come close to what I've gained with Stevens' family. They've treated me like one of their own ever since that first night I officially met all of them. I don't expect miracles. I'll take an imperfect gesture and a cordial welcome over the stone wall we've been living with for the past twelve months.

"See you tonight, Mother."

"Yes, dear. We'll see you tonight. I can't wait to watch you shine yet again in a film your father and I had the privilege of producing."

I don't respond to her last comment. Instead I say goodbye and we hang up.

"You look amazing," I tell Stevens.

He walks toward me. "Not as amazing as you." He kisses my cheek, obviously being respectful of Brigitte's presence.

"And you, Brigitte," Stevens says, looping his arm around my waist and looking into the kitchen where Brigitte has her head stuck deep in my refrigerator.

"Yeah. Yeah," she says. "You don't have to say that, merman. I'll still like you even without the gratuitous compliments. Alana! Why don't you have any decent snacks? Where's the chocolate or yogurt that isn't straight out of a cow? I'm not eating whatever that is in there."

"Do you need food?" I ask her.

"Food. Yes. This macrobiotic, nutritionally sound, bland, science experiment stuff? No."

"We'll feed you, Bridge," I promise.

I whisper, "She gets hangry," to Stevens.

He chuckles.

"I heard that. I don't get hangry." She pauses, shoots me a look, and adds, "Much. Not much."

"Let's leave early and drive through some place to get you tacos," Stevens suggests to Brigitte.

"You hear that, Alana? Count your lucky stars. You found yourself a man whose love language is the giving of tacos."

I laugh, remembering the first time Stevens sent me tacos instead of flowers. And he's been doing that ever since.

Brigitte tells Stevens. "You should have seen your girl here. She just talked you up to her mother, and she didn't hold back."

Stevens turns to me. "You did, did you?"

"Maybe."

He kisses the top of my head.

"Don't you two worry," Brigitte says to me. "Queen Grimhilde won't rock the boat because America is already capti-vated by the two of you. Half the women I know wonder if there are more hot, eligible marine biologists on the market. I'm just waiting for men to start putting 'lonely marine biologist' on their dating profiles. You know? With photos of them holding what-ever creature Stevens mentioned all over their socials. That ocean pickle."

"Queen Grimhilde?" I ask, even though I probably should just go along with Brigitte's ramblings whenever she's hungry.

"The stepmom of Snow White? You don't know Queen Grimhilde? And you call yourself an actress. Sometimes I don't know what to do with you, Alana. Stevens, tell me you know who Queen Grimhilde is."

He nods. Smart man.

I change the subject while I walk toward the sofa to grab my purse. "It was a sea cucumber, by the way. Stevens was talking about the sea cucumber. And," I chuckle. "As long as those women don't come for *my* marine biologist, I'm fine with starting a trend."

A whole year later and Brigitte can't help but bring up that momentous fail that became the unplanned way I broadcast my relationship with Stevens to the world.

"We'd better go," Stevens says, calmly.

"Tacos, here I come!" Brigitte says, waving her hands in the air overhead like she's rooting for her winning team.

We pile into the limo parked behind my condo, and as promised, the first stop is a local taco place to get Brigitte food.

"You're in your reclaiming era," Brigitte says to me around a bite of tacos. "That talk with your mom. That's you taking back territory you had surrendered to her for far too long. Yes, ma'am. You're reclaiming your voice and your power. It's your time to shine."

She's coming back to herself already after only a few bites of taco. I smile warmly at her.

"Did you eat enough today?"

"I did. This morning I had a green drink, followed by a Caramel Ribbon Crunch from the 'Bucks. Gotta keep the diet balanced, you know." She wipes the back of her hand across her mouth.

I chuckle. "You are priceless, Bridge."

Brigitte affects a deferential tone with a slight British accent. "All for you, Miss Alana."

I make eye contact with Tank in the rearview. I could swear I heard him chuckle. But when I look up front at him, his face is a mask of stone.

"Stevens, you chose well," Brigitte says. "Who's your mama? That's right! Alana."

I bust out laughing. Tank cracks a smile. It's only about a

millimeter change in his expression, but it happened. I know I saw it. All these years I wanted to be the one to draw that out of him. Of course, it's Brigitte who finally achieves it, and she doesn't even notice.

Brigitte gobbles down two tacos and an iced tea on the way to the theater. We drop her off at the back entrance and then the limo drives around front where a throng of fans and reporters waits behind the ropes on both sides of the red carpet leading to the front doors.

Stevens steps out and the crowd cheers. Some even shout his name. But his focus is fully devoted to me. He extends me his hand and smiles down at me. I step out and people cheer and shout, "Alana!" "Alana!" "Over here!" "We love you!"

Stevens extends me his hand and we walk the red carpet together, pausing to have our photo taken or to answer brief questions along the way.

We make our way inside the theater and are escorted to the front row. This is my film—the one where I played Ember, one of the few survivors of an apocalypse. I had to use my martial arts training, hone my skills at sword fighting, and do a few technically challenging stunts. My parents did produce the movie, and I'm grateful for their support. I only hope they can extend that same level of support to my private life someday.

The theater fills with more cast members and crew along with other invited guests. My co-star Bensen Stiles is sitting next to me and Stevens with his date for the evening. My parents are also in the front row with Rex, about ten seats down from us. I don't focus on them. I hold Stevens' hand and take in the movie, watching myself as if I'm someone else on screen.

When the show ends, the lights go up. Stevens stands prematurely. I'm about to discreetly tell him to sit back down when he walks toward the stage. Our director, Abraham, walks up the opposite set of stairs and meets Stevens halfway at center stage.

What is going on?

"Thank you for coming out," Abraham says in that naturally

commanding and charismatic voice of his. "Alana has no idea we've planned this, but as a special treat I'd like to invite her up here to demonstrate a few sword handling moves. Of course, we won't ask her to show off her proficiency for the martial arts in that stunning Monique Lhuillier gown she's wearing. Wouldn't want her to pop a pearl!"

The audience laughs.

"Come up here, Alana!" Abraham says with a flourish of his hand.

I point to myself, even though I know I'm the only Alana who can wield a sword in this crowd. At least, I think I am.

"Yes. Yes. Alana, dear, come up here for a moment."

I stand from my seat and walk toward the stage to the cheers of my cast mates, other actors and prominent people in the industry.

I give Stevens a questioning look and he softly winks at me. I don't know how he does it, but that simple gesture puts me at ease. Whatever this is, he's in on it.

A stagehand walks out and hands me a sheathed sword.

Abraham thanks him and then says, "Oh. Wait. I forgot something. I have a clip I want to show first. Come stand over here, to the side of the stage with me, Alana."

I'm even more confused. Maybe they're reshowing one of the scenes where I engaged in a sword fight.

I follow Abraham. We're not a quarter of the way across the stage when the house lights dim and the screen comes to life. But it's not a clip from *Only the Remnant*. Taylor Swift's *Invisible String* plays through the sound system while a slide show of me and Stevens fills the big screen. There we are on his boat, me laughing when he said something funny, us at a bonfire with friends, him holding me in his hammock and taking a selfie of the two of us, there's a shot of us on Sharla's couch at the interview, us in my kitchen, a snorkeling clip from the GoPro he brought on a dive. We're underwater, making goofy faces with our goggles on. There's a series of photos of us with his family at Christmas, a bunch from our trip to Hawaii, us at Kai and Mila's wedding. The slideshow ends, appropriately, with a shot of us on my deck playing scrabble as the sun sets over the water in the distance.

The house lights come up, and Stevens is still standing center stage, staring at the fading image of us on my deck. I was so caught up in the slideshow I lost sight of what might be happening. What did that montage of me and Stevens have to do with me demonstrating sword skills?

Abraham leans in toward me and quietly says, "Maybe you ought to hand me that sword. We don't want anyone getting hurt. After all, my insurance for this production only covers so much."

I look at him with an obvious expression of confusion. I feel my brow draw in.

"What's going on, Abraham?"

He simply extends his hand and I place the sword in it.

Stevens starts to calmly stride toward me and Abraham.

I notice he's got a telltale earpiece in his ear. He's mic'd up.

Before I can make sense of this bizarre string of events, Stevens drops to one knee.

All the seemingly unrelated pieces from the past fifteen minutes fall into place in an instant. Stevens ... the slideshow ... that song.

Stevens looks up at me. "Alana, I've known you for most of our lives, and I found you in the most unconventional way. We've talked about this before—how serendipitous our repeated connections were. And, at every turn, it's been you. You're my best friend, the one I wake thinking of and the one I dream about. You've shown me sides of myself I didn't know existed. And you've shared with me parts of your heart that belong to no one else. I'm the most privileged man on earth—not because I love Alana Graves, but because I love you, my Saturday Island Girl. I've got a question I want to ask you."

He stands and points out into the audience.

I thought he was proposing. But now, he's standing, and there's no ring in sight. This night keeps getting weirder.

I follow the line of vision to where Stevens is pointing. The doors at the back of the theater open, and people enter, walking down the aisle until they're lined up on stage holding up Scrabble tiles. A few people have two tiles, most only hold one. The image of this group is shown on the screen so everyone in the theater can see.

And these aren't just random people. It's Stevens' family and our friends: Mitzi, Stevens' parents, Cam and Riley, Kai and Mila, Ben and Summer, Kalaine and Bodhi. The letters they are holding spell W I L L Y O U M A R R Y. The last two tiles are missing.

Brigitte comes running onto stage, "Me! Me! Sorry! Here I am!" She holds up her tiles, at first they say, EM. Bodhi gives her a nudge. She looks down. Shakes her head and changes the order so the tiles she's holding spell M E.

Stevens drops down to his knee again. "Alana Graves, my Saturday Girl, will you marry me?"

I look down at this man, this humble, beautiful, kind man, the one whom I've known since we were children. The one who found his way back to me through an online game, who ferried me across the ocean, tried to teach me to drive a boat, always believed in me and never saw me as just some movie star. A tear tracks down my cheek. I never knew I could have someone like him. And here he is, despite all that he's had to do to hang on to our relationship, bending the knee to ask me for my forever.

"Yes," I say softly. "I would be honored to marry you."

Our friends and Stevens' family start cheering and the people in the audience applaud and shout.

Abraham cups his hands around his mouth and announces, "She said, yes!"

Stevens stands and pulls the ring from his pocket. He slips it on my finger, pulls me into his embrace, and leans in to kiss me.

Mitzi comes running up with her phone on. "Dustin wants to say congratulations!"

We hover around the phone and I show Dustin my ring. He

hoots and shouts from his spot in the firestation. A group of firemen behind him start whooping and yelling.

When we hang up, our friends gather around us with hugs and congratulations. The crowd in the theater starts to disperse. Some make their way towards us, others file out to the after-parties.

My parents walk up the steps. I sense their presence despite the fact that I'm staring at Stevens. His arm is around me and Brigitte is chatting on about how hard it has been on her to keep this particular secret, and how romantic Stevens is, and how cute his brother, the fireman, is.

"Alana," my mother's voice cuts through the other conversations.

I turn toward her, ready to defend Stevens, or even to run out the back door of the theater if I have to, tugging him behind me. I'll withstand her criticism, but I won't ever make him endure it. He's far too good for me, and I'll never let someone pretend that's not the case.

"Yes?" I answer my mother.

"You wanted to make an introduction?"

Stevens steps forward, extending his hand to my dad. "Mr. Graves. It's a pleasure. Ideally, I would have asked your blessing. I didn't have any legitimate way to contact you without blowing the surprise. I hope you understand. I love your daughter. And I intend to spend my life protecting her and supporting her."

"Good to meet you, Stevens, is it?" My father's commanding voice doesn't seem to faze Stevens in the least.

"Yes, sir. Stevens. I'm glad we're finally officially meeting."

My dad nods. He's not smiling, but it's not exactly a grimace.

Stevens turns toward my mother. "Mrs. Graves. I'm sorry our first encounter was under such unusual circumstances. I had been told that the gala was a costume party. If I had checked my email more consistently I would have known it was a black tie affair. I'm glad we're finally meeting when I'm not in a fish costume."

My mother's smile isn't genuine, but it's not forced. It's the smile of a well-trained socialite. I'll take it. She's not being cruel, so that's progress.

"We're a bit shocked by your proposal," she says to Stevens.

"Yes. I'm sure. Alana and I have been dating for over a year now, as you know. She's everything I want in a woman. We make one another happy."

Mother smiles again—that constipated grin that makes me wish I had Jobert on speed dial.

"Well, happiness is not exactly a life-foundation. But I am glad for you. Alana seems set on marrying you, so we'll accept both of your decisions."

Another man might be insulted or put off. Not Stevens. He just smiles this broad, sexy, irresistible smile as if my mother just told him they were thrilled about our engagement.

"Thank you, Mrs. Graves."

"We should get going to the afterparty," I tell my parents.

"Yes. Of course." Mother smiles at me and leans in for a light hug and a cheek kiss.

She whispers into my ear, "I hope you know what you're doing."

"I've never been more certain of anything in my life," I answer her at full volume.

"Well, we'll have pre-nuptials drawn up," she says under her breath.

"I won't sign them," I whisper back to her. "I don't need them."

I turn to Stevens, eager to get back to celebrating our engagement.

"Let's get to the car. My fans and the reporters are still out front. We can share the news on our way to the limo."

Stevens smiles at me and loops his arm behind my back. I lean into him—like I always can.

We say our goodbyes to my parents, our friends and Stevens'

family, then we walk out to the burst of camera flashes and the sound of adoring fans and eager reporters.

I turn toward the crowd and hold my hand in the air so everyone can see the ring on my finger.

Aiming myself at the nearest microphone, I say, "Tonight, the man of my dreams proposed to me!"

The crowd goes wild with squeals and screaming. Cellphones are raised in our direction, everyone eager to capture this moment and spread the fact that they were a small part of it.

I turn toward Stevens and look up into his eyes.

He smiles down at me. Then he scans the crowd and shouts, "And she said yes!"

Then he pulls me in for a kiss that ends up in every major newspaper the following morning.

～

Thank you for reading!

There's more Marbella Island sweetness ...

Can't get enough of Ben? Read how he wins Summer's heart in *A Fish Out of Water.*

Want to read the story that started it all? Check out Cam, Riley and Ben's road trip down Route 66 in *Are We There Yet.*

Do you love older brother's best friend romance? Catch all the feels in Kalaine and Bodhi's second-chance romance *Catch a Wave.*

If you love sweet, heartfelt fake-dating stories, Pick up Kai and Mila's friends-to-lovers romcom in *Resorting to Romance.*

～

Savannah loves writing books that make you laugh with characters and settings that draw you in and make you feel like a part of a community.

If you loved *Reel Love*, hop over to Amazon, BookBub or Goodreads and leave a short review telling other readers how much you enjoyed Alana and Stevens' story.

More from Savannah Scott

If you love laugh-out-loud, small-town, closed-door romcoms, come on over to Bordeaux, Ohio (pronounced Bored-Ox) **The Getting Shipped Series** is Savannah's well-loved stories set in rural Ohio with found family friendships, meddling townspeople, and book boyfriends so hot they could pop a whole row of corn.

You can fall in love with a Frenchman in Savannah's ***Sweater Weather*** story from the famous multi-author series: *A Not So Fictional Fall*.

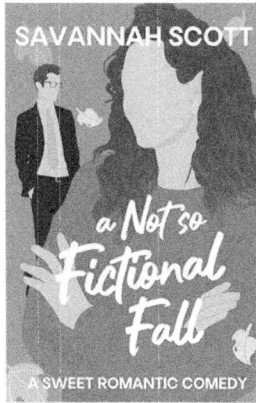

And then, if you still need to hear another man call a woman "Cher," pick up *He's So Not My Valentine*, a single mom romcom with heart.

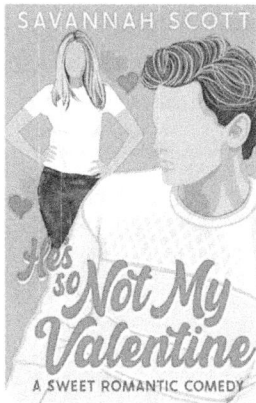

Connect with Savannah Scott

Be one of the readers who hears about new releases first, gets to participate in special giveaways, and sees sneak peeks into Savannah's writing ... join her weekly newsletter for all this and more.

Looking for a sweet group of readers who share life and books together? Join Savannah's Sweet Readers Facebook Group.

Or Follow Savannah on Instagram
And follow Savannah on Amazon for automatic notifications of new releases directly in your inbox.

All the Thanks ...

First of all, thank you to **Paul and Jon**, you make room in our home and our lives for me to live this dream of being an indie author. I'm so grateful to the two of you.

I want to thank **Gila Santos,** my copy editor. You are truly gifted. The way you squeal over a well-written portion of story makes my day. Most of all, thank you for constantly challenging me to grow and to be the best writer I can be. I thank God for you.

Tricia Anson. I can't express the gratitude I have for you. I never imagined what was in store for us when I asked you to be my PA. You are truly the keeper of my sanity, and such a gift in my life. And, a special thanks to the original Ben for always making me laugh.

Jessica Gobble, the sister of my heart. You prayed me here. You believed when others didn't see where I was heading. You taught me how to see my worth as an author. I love you, bestie.

To my **Awesome "Shippers" and especially the CORE Team and the Chatty IG Girls** who love me and my books so thoroughly, and to the **AMAZING Bookstagram Community**. I am so thankful for the way you support each book I write. I never knew what a gift I'd receive when I started sharing my author life with you. I love you to the moon and back.

Thank you to **Mary Goad,** my sister and my friend**,** for this cover. It's your best yet. You just keep getting better and better. You are so, so very talented. I love you.

Most of all, I want to thank **God** for calling me to be a story-teller and for giving me the ability to make others smile, laugh, and feel all the feels.

Happy Reading!

379

Savannah

Made in the USA
Las Vegas, NV
24 August 2024

94377290R00225